# NEW CENTURY BIBLE COMMENTARY

*General Editors*

RONALD E. CLEMENTS
(Old Testament)

MATTHEW BLACK
(New Testament)

# Haggai, Zechariah and Malachi

# THE NEW CENTURY BIBLE COMMENTARIES

EXODUS (J. P. Hyatt)
DEUTERONOMY (A. D. H. Mayes)
JOSHUA, JUDGES, RUTH (John Gray)
1 AND 2 KINGS, Volumes 1 and 2 (Gwilym H. Jones)
1 AND 2 CHRONICLES (H. G. Williamson)
EZRA, NEHEMIAH, AND ESTHER (D. J. Clines)
JOB (H. H. Rowley)
PSALMS Volumes 1 and 2 (A. A. Anderson)
PROVERBS (R. N. Whybray)
ECCLESIASTES (R. N. Whybray)
THE SONG OF SONGS (John G. Snaith)
ISAIAH 1–39 (R. E. Clements)
ISAIAH 40–66 (R. N. Whybray)
JEREMIAH (Douglas Rawlinson Jones)
LAMENTATIONS (Iain Provan)
EZEKIEL (John W. Wevers)
HOSEA (G. I. Davies)
THE GOSPEL OF MATTHEW (David Hill)
THE GOSPEL OF MARK (Hugh Anderson)
THE GOSPEL OF LUKE (E. Earle Ellis)
THE GOSPEL OF JOHN (Barnabas Lindars)
THE ACTS OF THE APOSTLES (William Neil)
ROMANS, Second Edition (Matthew Black)
1 AND 2 CORINTHIANS (F. F. Bruce)
GALATIANS (Donald Guthrie)
EPHESIANS (C. Leslie Mitton)
PHILIPPIANS (Ralph P. Martin)
COLOSSIANS AND PHILEMON (Ralph P. Martin)
1 AND 2 THESSALONIANS (I. Howard Marshall)
PASTORAL EPISTLES (A. T. Hanson)
HEBREWS (R. McL. Wilson)
1 PETER (Ernest Best)
JAMES, JUDE, AND 2 PETER (E. M. Sidebottom)
JOHANNINE EPISTLES (K. Grayson)
THE BOOK OF REVELATION (G. R. Beasley-Murray)

*Other titles are in preparation*

# NEW CENTURY BIBLE COMMENTARY

*Based on the Revised Standard Version*

# HAGGAI, ZECHARIAH AND MALACHI

## PAUL L. REDDITT

**Marshall Pickering**
*An Imprint of* HarperCollins*Publishers*

WILLIAM B. EERDMANS PUBLISHING COMPANY
GRAND RAPIDS

Marshall Pickering is an Imprint of
HarperCollins*Religious*
Part of HarperCollins*Publishers*
77–85 Fulham Palace Road, London W6 8JB

First published 1995 in Great Britain by Marshall Pickering
and in the United States by Wm. B. Eerdmans Publishing Co.,
225 Jefferson Ave., S.E., Grand Rapids, Michigan 49503.

Printed in the United States of America
for Marshall Pickering and Wm. B. Eerdmans

1  3  5  7  9  10  8  6  4  2

A catalogue record for this book is
available from the British Library

Marshall Pickering ISBN   0-551-02832-7
Eerdmans ISBN   0-8028-0748-8

# CONTENTS

PREFACE                                                          vii
LIST OF ABBREVIATIONS                                            viii
BIBLIOGRAPHY                                                      xi
INTRODUCTION                                                     xxvii

INTRODUCTION TO HAGGAI                                             I

A. Historical Background                                           4
B. Authorship                                                    10
C. Literary History and Structure                                11
D. Message                                                       12
E. Contents                                                      13

COMMENTARY ON HAGGAI                                             15

1:1–15a    Haggai Calls the People to Work on the Temple         17
1:15b–2:9  The New Temple Versus the Old                         23
2:10–19    The Founding of the New Temple as the Turning Point   25
2:20–23    Zerubbabel as God's Signet Ring                       31
           Summary                                               33

INTRODUCTION TO ZECHARIAH 1–8                                    35

A. Authorship                                                    38
B. Literary History and Structure                                38
C. Message                                                       43
D. Contents                                                      45

COMMENTARY ON ZECHARIAH 1–8                                      47

1:1–6      Do Not Be Like Your Fathers                           49
1:7–17     Vision of the Horsemen: God's Return to Jerusalem     51
1:18–21    Vision of the Horns and the Smiths: the End of Foreign
           Control                                               56
2:1–5      Vision of a Man Measuring Jerusalem: the Return of
           Prosperity                                            58
2:6–13     Exhortation to the Exiles: Return Home                59
3:1–10     Vision of the Cleansing of Joshua                     62
4:1–14     Vision of the Lampstand and Olive Trees: God's Presence  67
5:1–4      Vision of the Flying Scroll: the Cleansing of Jerusalem  72

5:5–11    Vision of a Woman in a Basket: Wickedness Sent to Babylon 73
6:1–8     Vision of the Four Chariots: God at rest                  74
6:9–15    Exhortation to Returned Exiles: Make Crowns as a
          Memorial                                                 76
7:1–14    The Question about Fasting                               79
8:1–23    Ten Words about the Future                               84
          Summary                                                  88

INTRODUCTION TO ZECHARIAH 9–14                                     91

A. Authorship, Date and Historical Background                      94
B. Literary History and Structure                                  102
C. Message                                                         103
D. Contents                                                        105

COMMENTARY ON ZECHARIAH 9–14                                       107

9:1–17       The Davidic Empire Restored                           109
10:1–12      The Reunion of the Homeland                           118
11:1–17      The Treachery of the Shepherds                        122
12:1–9       The War against Jerusalem, Version I                  128
12:10–13:9   The Cleansing of Jerusalem                            132
14:1–21      The War against Jerusalem, Version II                 137
             Summary                                               144

INTRODUCTION TO MALACHI                                            147

A. Date and Historical Background                                  149
B. Authorship                                                      151
C. Literary History and Structure                                  152
D. Message                                                         155
E. Contents                                                        157

COMMENTARY ON MALACHI                                              159

1:1–5      God's Love for Israel                                   161
1:6–2:9    Pollution by the Priesthood                             163
2:10–16    Unfaithfulness within the Community                     169
2:17–3:5   Cleansing of the Community                              175
3:6–12     Paying for Cultic Worship                               178
3:13–4:3   Hope for the Community                                  181
4:4–6      Living in the Community                                 185
           Summary                                                 186

CONCLUSION                                                         188
INDEX OF AUTHORS                                                   193
INDEX OF SUBJECTS                                                  194

# PREFACE

In the Fall of 1967, I enrolled in a Hebrew class at Vanderbilt University taught by Dr Herbert May. During the semester the class translated the book of Haggai, and Dr May shared a paper he had prepared: "'This People' and 'This Nation' in Haggai," published by *Vetus Testamentum* 18 (1968) 190–97. Dr May was originally asked to prepare a volume on Nahum to Malachi in this series, but he was unable to begin the assignment before his death. It is gratifying to me as one of his former students that I have been allowed to undertake the last half of his task.

My indebtedness to Dr May and a number of other scholars will be apparent in the pages that follow. Several people, however, deserve special mention. Dr Joe Lewis, formerly the Vice President for Academic Affairs at Georgetown College, not only encouraged me but also read the Hebrew text with me and offered suggestions on early drafts of several chapters. (Indeed, I am grateful to Georgetown College itself for supporting my work in various ways, including granting me a sabbatical leave for the Fall, 1992 semester.) The editors of *The Catholic Biblical Quarterly* have served as my sounding board as they have pushed my thinking and agreed to publish a series of articles growing out of this commentary. Further, I would like to thank Dr Ronald Clements, Old Testament editor of the series, for his confidence in me in allowing me to prepare this volume. Finally, I would like to thank my wife, Bonnie, who not only encouraged my work, but also proofread the entire manuscript, some parts more than once.

Paul L. Redditt
Georgetown, Kentucky
March 10, 1993

# ABBREVIATIONS

## BIBLICAL

OLD TESTAMENT (OT)

| | | | | | | |
|---|---|---|---|---|---|---|
| Gen. | Jg. | 1 Chr. | Ps. | Lam. | Ob. | Hag. |
| Exod. | Ru. | 2 Chr. | Prov. | Ezek. | Jon. | Zech. |
| Lev. | 1 Sam. | Ezr. | Ec. | Dan. | Mic. | Mal. |
| Num. | 2 Sam. | Neh. | Ca. | Hos. | Nah. | |
| Deut. | 1 Kg. | Est. | Isa. | Jl | Hab. | |
| Jos. | 2 Kg. | Job | Jer. | Am. | Zeph. | |

NEW TESTAMENT (NT)

| | | | | | | |
|---|---|---|---|---|---|---|
| Mt. | Ac. | Gal. | 1 Th. | Tit. | 1 Pet. | 3 Jn |
| Mk | Rom. | Eph. | 2 Th. | Phm. | 2 Pet. | Jude |
| Lk. | 1 C. | Phil. | 1 Tim. | Heb. | 1 Jn | Rev. |
| Jn | 2 C. | Col. | 2 Tim. | Jas. | 2 Jn | |

## GENERAL

*ABR* — *Australian Biblical Review*

*AJSL* — *American Journal of Semitic Languages and Literature*

*ANEP* — *The Ancient Near East in Pictures Relating to the Old Testament*, ed. J. Pritchard, Princeton, 1954

*ANET* — *Ancient Near Eastern Texts Relating to the Old Testament*, ed. J. B. Pritchard, 3rd edn, Princeton, 1955

*ATR* — *Anglican Theological Review*

*AV* — *Authorized Version* (King James Version) (1611)

Baldwin — Baldwin, Joyce A. *Haggai, Zechariah, Malachi*

*BARev* — *Biblical Archaeology Review*

*BDB* — F. Brown, S. R. Driver and C. A. Briggs, *Hebrew and English Lexicon of the Old Testament*

*BHS* — *Biblia Hebraica Stuttgartensia*, edited by K. Elliger and W. Rudolph, 1967/77

*BHK* — *Biblia Hebraica*, ed. R. Kittel, 1929/37

*Bib.* — *Biblica*

*BibLeb* — *Bibel und Leben*

*BN* — *Biblische Notizen*

*BR* — *Biblical Research*

| | |
|---|---|
| BSac | *Bibliotheca Sacra* |
| BT | *The Bible Translator* |
| BTB | *Biblical Theology Bulletin* |
| BWANT | *Beiträge zur Wissenschaft vom Alten und Neuen Testament* |
| BZ | *Biblische Zeitschrift* |
| BZAW | Beihefte zur *ZAW* |
| CBQ | *Catholic Biblical Quarterly* |
| CURTM | *Currents in Theology and Mission* |
| D | The Deuteronomic Source of the Pentateuch |
| EgliseTh | *Église et Théologie* |
| EI | *Eretz Israel* |
| Elliger | Elliger, Karl. *Das Buch der zwölf kleinen Propheten*, ATD |
| ETL | *Ephemerides theologicae lovanienses* |
| ETR | *Études théologiques et religieuses* |
| EvT | *Evangelische Theologie* |
| ExpTim | *Expository Times* |
| G-K | *Gesenius's Hebrew Grammar as edited and enlarged E. Kautzsch, revised by A. E. Cowley*, 2nd edn, London, 1910 |
| HAR | *Hebrew Annual Review* |
| Heb. | Hebrew |
| Horst | Horst, F. *Die zwölf kleinen Propheten: Nahum bis Maleachi.* HAT |
| HUCA | *Hebrew Union College Annual* |
| IB | *The Interpreter's Bible* |
| IEJ | *Israel Exploration Journal* |
| Int. | *Interpretation* |
| IR | *Iliff Review* |
| ISBE | *International Standard Bible Encyclopedia*, rev. edn, Edited by G. W. Bromiley |
| JB | *Jerusalem Bible* |
| JBL | *Journal of Biblical Literature* |
| JETS | *Journal of the Evangelical Theological Society* |
| JJS | *Journal of Jewish Studies* |
| JNES | *Journal of Near Eastern Studies* |
| JNSL | *Journal of Northwest Semitic Languages* |
| JSOT | *Journal for the Study of the Old Testament* |
| JTS | *Journal of Theological Studies* |
| Jud. | *Judaica: Beiträge zum Verständnis des jüdischen Schicksals in Vergangenheit und Gegenwart* |
| Kodell | Kodell, Jerome. *Haggai, Zechariah, Second Zechariah, Malachi, Obadiah, Jonah, Baruch.* Old Testament Message |
| LXX | Greek Septuagint Version |
| Mason | Mason, Rex. *The Books of Haggai, Zechariah, and Malachi* |

| | |
|---|---|
| Meyers | Meyers, Carol L. and Meyers, Eric M. *Haggai, Zechariah 1–8*. AB |
| MS, MSS | manuscript(s) |
| MT | Masoretic Text of the Old Testament |
| *NAB* | *New American Bible* |
| *NEB* | *New English Bible* |
| *NRSV* | *New Revised Standard Version* (1991) |
| *OTS* | *Oudtestamentische Studien* |
| P | Priestly Source of the Pentateuch |
| *PEO* | *Palestine Exploration Quarterly* |
| Pesh. | Syriac Peshitta Version |
| Petersen | Petersen, David L. *Haggai and Zechariah 1–8*. OTL |
| *RB* | *Revue Biblique* |
| *RevExp* | *Review and Expositor* |
| *RTR* | *Reformed Theological Review* |
| Rudolph | Rudolph, Wilhelm. Haggai–Sacharja 1–8–Sacharja 9–14–Maleachi. KAT |
| Sellin | Sellin, Ernst. *Das Zwölfprophetenbuch übersetzt und erklärt.* KAT |
| Smith | Smith, Ralph L. *Micah–Malachi.* |
| *ST* | *Studia Theologica* |
| Targ. | Aramaic Targum Version |
| *TBT* | *The Bible Today* |
| *TDOT* | *Theological Dictionary of the Old Testament*, eds. G. Johannes Botterweck and Helmer Ringgren |
| *TLZ* | *Theologische Literaturzeitung* |
| *TZ* | *Theologische Zeitschrift* |
| *VT* | *Vetus Testamentum* |
| *VT Suppl.* | Supplements to *Vetus Testamentum* |
| Vulg. | Latin Vulgate Version |
| *ZAW* | *Zeitschrift für die Alttestamentliche Wissenschaft* |
| *ZTK* | *Zeitschrift für Theologie und Kirche* |

# BIBLIOGRAPHY

## COMMENTARIES

Baldwin, Joyce G., *Haggai Zechariah, Malachi*, Tyndale Old Testament Commentaries, Leicester, Intervarsity, 1972.

Bič, Milos, *Das Buch Sacharja*, Berlin, Evangelische Verlagsanstalt, 1962.

Coggins, R. J., *Haggai, Zechariah, Malachi*, Old Testament Guides Sheffield, *JSOT* 1989.

Cohen, A., *The Twelve Prophets*, Soncino Books of the Bible, London, Soncino, 1948.

Dentan, R. C., "The Book of Zechariah, Chapters 9–14"; "The Book of Malachi", *The Interpreter's Bible* 6, New York, Nashville, Abingdon, 1956.

Elliger, Karl, *Das Buch der zwölf kleinen Propheten*, Das Alte Testament Deutsch, 25, Göttingen, Vandenhoeck and Ruprecht, 1982.

Horst, F., *Die zwölf kleinen Propheten: Nahum bis Maleachi*, Handkommentar zum Alten Testament, 14, Tübingen, Mohr, 1964.

Jones, Douglas Rawlinson, *Haggai, Zechariah and Malachi*, Torch Bible Commentaries, London, SCM, 1962.

Kodell, Jerome, *Lamentations, Haggai, Zechariah, Second Zechariah, Malachi, Obadiah, Jonah, Baruch*, Old Testament Message, Wilmington, Del, Michael Glazier, 1982.

Mason, Rex, *The Books of Haggai, Zechariah, and Malachi*, The Cambridge Bible Commentary on the New English Bible, Cambridge, Cambridge University Press, 1977.

Meyers, Carol L. and Meyers, Eric M., *Haggai, Zechariah 1–8* Anchor Bible, 25B, Garden City, NY, Doubleday, 1987.

Mitchell, H. G.; Smith, J. M. P.; Bewer, J. A., *Haggai, Zechariah, Malachi and Jonah*, The International Critical Commentary, Edinburgh, Clark, 1912.

Nowack, W., *Die Kleinen Propheten*. III:4, Göttinger Handkommentar zum Alten Testament, Göttingen, Vandenhoeck & Ruprecht, 1922.

Petersen, David L., *Haggai and Zechariah 1–8*, Old Testament Library, Philadelphia, Westminster, 1984.

Rudolph, Wilhelm, *Haggai–Sacharja 1–8–Sacharja 9–14 – Maleachi* Kommentar zum Alten Testament, XIII. 4, Gutersloh, Gerd Mohn, 1976.

Sellin, Ernst, *Das Zwölfprophetenbuch übersetzt und erklärt*, Komentar zum Alten Testament, XII, 2nd–3rd edn, Leipzig, Scholl, 1930.

Smith, George Adam, *The Book of the Twelve Prophets*, 2 vols, Rev. edn, New York and London, Harper and Brothers, 1928.

Smith, Ralph L., *Micah–Malachi*, Word Biblical Commentary 32, Waco, Texas, Word, 1984.

Thomas, D. W., "The Book of Haggai"; "The Book of Zechariah, Chapters 1–8", *The Interpreter's Bible*, Vol. 6, New York, Nashville, Abingdon, 1956.

Verhoef, Pieter A., *The Books of Haggai and Malachi*, The New International Commentary on the Old Testament, Grand Rapids, Eerdmans, 1989.

Wolff, Hans Walter, *Haggai*, Minneapolis, Augsburg and Philadelphia, Fortress, 1988.

## MONOGRAPHS

Ackroyd, P. R., *Exile and Restoration*, Old Testament Library, Philadelphia, Westminster, 1968.

——, *Israel Under Babylon and Persia*, Oxford, Oxford, 1970.

Beuken, W. A. M., *Haggai–Sacharja 1–8, Studien zur Überlieferungs der frühnachexilischen Prophetie*, Studia Semitica Nederlandica, 10, Assen, Van Gorcum, 1967.

Beyse, K.-M., *Serubbabel und die Königserwartungen der Propheten Haggai und Sacharja, Eine historische und traditionsgeschichtliche*

*Untersuchung*, Arbeiten zur Theologie 48, Stuttgart, Calwer, 1972.

Bič, M., *Die Nachtgesichte des Sacharja*, Biblische Studien, 42, Neukirchen-Vluyn, Neukirchener Verlag, 1964.

Carroll, Robert P., *When Prophecy Failed*, London, SCM, 1979.

Glazier-McDonald, Beth, *Malachi: The Divine Messenger*, Society of Biblical Literature Dissertation Series, 98, Atlanta, Ga, Scholars, 1987.

Hanson, Paul D., *The Dawn of Apocalyptic*, Philadelphia, Fortress, 1975.

Jeremias, Christian, *Die Nachtgesichte des Sacharja*, Forschungen zur Religion des Alten und Neuen Testament, 117, Göttingen, Vandenhoeck and Ruprecht, 1976.

Kippenberg, Hans G., *Religion und Klassenbildung im antiken Judaea, Eine religions-soziologische Studie zum Verhältnis von Tradition und gesellschafter Entwicklung*, Studien zum Umwelt des Neuen Testaments, 14, Göttingen, Vandenhoeck & Ruprecht, 1978.

Kreissig, Heinz, *Die Sozialökonomische Situation in Juda zur Archämenidenzeit*, Schriften zur Geschichte und Kultur des Alten Orients, 7, Berlin, Akademie der Wissenschaften der DDR Zentralinstitut für alte Geschichte und Archäologie, 1973.

Lutz, Hanns-Martin, *Jahwe, Jerusalem und die Völker, Zur Vorgesicht um Sach 12:1–8 und 14:1–5*, Wissenschaftliche Monographien zum Alten und Neuen Testament, 27, Neukirchen-Vluyn, Neukirchener Verlag, 1968.

Myers, J. M., *The World of the Restoration*, Englewood Cliffs, NJ, Prentice-Hall, 1968.

O'Brien, Julia M., *Priest and Levite in Malachi*, Society of Biblical Literature Dissertation Series 121, Atlanta, Scholars Press, 1990.

Otzen, Benedikt, *Studien über Deutero-Sacharja*, Copenhagen, Munksgaard, 1964.

Petitjean, A., *Les oracles du Proto-Zacharie, Un programme de restauration pour la communauté juive après l'exile*, Paris, Gabalda, Louvain, Orientaliste, 1969.

Plöger, Otto, *Theocracy and Eschatology*, Richmond, John Knox, 1968.

Rignell, Lars G., *Die Nachtgesichte des Sacharja*, Lund, Gleerup, 1950.

Saebø, Magne, *Sacharja 9–14*, Wissenschaftliche Monographien zum Alten und Neuen Testament, 34, Neukirchen-Vluyn, Neukirchener Verlag, 1969.

Seybold, K., *Bilder zum Templebau: Die Visionen des Propheten Sacharja*, Stuttgarter Bibelstudien, 70, Stuttgart, KBW, 1974.

Utzschneider, Helmut, *Künder oder Schreiber? Eine These zum Problem der "Schriftprohetie" auf Grund von Maleachi 1:6–2:9*, Beiträge zur Erforschung des Alten Testaments und des antiken Judentums 19, Frankfurt, et al., Peter Lang, 1989.

Willi-Plein, Ina, *Prophetie am Ende, Untersuchungen zu Sacharja 9–14*, Bonner Biblische Beitrage, 42, Cologne, Hanstein, 1974.

Wiener, Aharon, *The Prophet Elijah in the Development of Judaism; a Depth-Psychological Study*, London, Henley, Boston, Routledge and Kegan Paul, 1978.

# ARTICLES

*General*

Ackroyd, Peter R. "The Book of Haggai and Zechariah I–VIII", *JJS* 3(1952) 151–6.

——, "Two Old Testament Historical Problems of the Early Persian Period", *JJS* 17 (1958) 13–27.

Andrew, M. E. "Post-Exilic Prophets and the Ministry of Creating Community", *ExpTim* 93 (1981) 42–6.

Broshi, M. "Estimating the Population of Ancient Jerusalem", *BARev* 4 (1978) 10–15.

Budde, K., "Zum Text der drier letzen Propheten", *ZAW* 26 (1906) 1–28.

Carroll, Robert P. "Ancient Israelite Prophecy and Cognitive Dissonance Theory", *Numen* 24 (1977) 135–51.

——, "Prophecy and Dissonance: A Theoretical Approach

to the Prophetic Tradition", *ZAW* 92 (1980) 108–19.

——, "Twilight of Prophecy or Dawn of Apocalyptic?" *JSOT* 14 (1979) 3–35.

Childs, Brevard S., "The Canonical Shape of the Prophetic Literature", *Int.* 32 (1978) 46–55.

Clark, David J., "Sex-Related Imagery in the Prophets", *BT* 33 (1982) 409–13.

Cook, S. A., "The Age of Zerubbabel", *Studies in Old Testament Prophecy Presented to T. H. Robinson*, ed. H. H. Rowley, Edinburgh, T. & T. Clark, 1950, p. 19–36.

Cresson, Bruce C. "The Condemnation of Edom in Post-exilic Judaism", *The Use of the Old Testament in the New and Other Studies: Studies in Honor of William Franklin Stinespring*, Durham, N.C., Duke University Press, 1972, pp. 125–48.

Cross, Frank Moore, "A Reconstruction of the Judaean Restoration", *JBL* 94 (1975) 4–18.

Dumbrell, W. J., "Kingship and Temple in the Post-exilic Period", *RTR* 37 (1978) 33–42.

Galling, Kurt, "Serubbabel und der Wiederaufbau des Tempels in Jerusalem", *Verbannung und Heimkehr, Wilhelm Rudolph zum 70. Geburstag*, Tübingen, Mohr, 1961, pp. 67–96.

Gelston, A, "The Foundation of the Second Temple", *VT* 16 (1966) 232–5.

Jagersma, H., "The Tithes in the Old Testament", *Remembering All the Way . . . OTS* 22, ed. B. Albrektson, et al., Leiden, Brill, 1981, pp. 116–28.

Japhet, Sara, "Sheshbazzar and Zerubbabel – Against the Background of the Historical and Religious Tendencies of Ezra–Nehemiah", *ZAW* 94 (1982) 66–98.

Laberge, Leo, "Ministres et esprit dans les communautés postexiliques", *EgliseTh* 9 (1978) 379–411.

Long, Burke O., "Two Question and Answer Schemata in the Prophets", *JBL* 90 (1971) 129–39.

Mason, Rex A., "Prophets of the Restoration", in *Israel's Prophetic Word*, eds. R. Coggins, A. Phillips, M. Knibb, Cambridge, Cambridge, 1982, pp. 162–88.

——, "The Relation of Zechariah 9–14 to Proto-Zechariah", *ZAW* 88 (1976) 227–39.

McEvenue, S. E., "The Political Structure in Judah from Cyrus to Nehemiah", *CBQ* 43 (1981) 353–64.

Miller, John H., "Haggai–Zechariah: Prophets of the Now and Future", *CurTM* 6 (1979) 99–104.

Newsome, James D., "Toward a New Understanding of the Chronicler and His Purposes", *JBL* 94 (1975) 201–17.

Overholt, Thomas W. "The End of Prophecy: No Players without a Programme", *JSOT* 42 (1988) 103–15.

Pierce, Ronald W., "Literary Connectors and a Haggai–Zechariah–Malachi Corpus", *JETS* 27 (1984) 277–89.

——, "A Thematic Development of the Haggai–Zechariah–Malachi Corpus," *JETS* 27 (1984) 401–11.

Porteous, N. W., "Jerusalem-Zion: The Growth of a Symbol", *Living the Mystery, Collected Essays*, Oxford, B. H. Blackwell, 1967, pp. 93–112.

Portney, Stephen L. and Petersen, David L., "Biblical Texts and Statistical Analysis: Zechariah and Beyond", *JBL* 103 (1984) 11–21.

Radday, Yehuda T. and Wickman, Dieter, "Unity of Zechariah Examined in Light of Statistical Analysis", *ZAW* 87 (1975) 30–55.

Radday, Yehuda T. and Pollatschek, Moshe A., "Vocabulary Richness in Post-exilic Prophetic Books", *ZAW* 92 (1980) 333–46.

Sauer, Georg, "Serubbabel in der Sicht Haggais und Sacharjas", in *Das ferne und nähe Wort. Festschrift für Leonhard Rost*, ed. F. Maass, BZAW 105, Berlin, Töpelmann, 1967, pp. 199–207.

Seybold, K., "Die Königserwartung bei den Propheten Haggai und Zechariah", *Jud.* 27–8 (1971–2) 69–78.

Siebeneck, Robert T., "Messianism of Aggeus and Proto-Zacharias", *CBQ* 19 (1957) 312–28.

Wanke, Gunther, "Prophecy and Psalms in the Persian Period", in *The Cambridge History of Judaism*, eds. W. Davies and Louis Finkelstein, Cambridge, Cambridge, 1984, pp. 162–88.

Waterman, Leroy, "The Camouflaged Purge of Three Messianic Conspirators", *JNES* 13 (1954) 73–8.

Wilson, Robert R., "Prophecy and Ecstasy: A Reexamination", *JBL* 98 (1979) 321–37.

*On Haggai*

Ackroyd, P. R., "Studies in the Book of Haggai", *JJS* 2 (1950–51) 163–76, 3 (1952) 1–13.

——, "Some Interpretive Glosses in the Book of Haggai", *JJS* 7 (1956) 163–7.

——, "Two Old Testament Historical Problems of the Early Persian Period", *JNES* 17 (1958) 13–27.

Andersen, F. I., "Who Built the Second Temple?" *ABR* 6 (1958) 1–35.

Bloomhardt, P. F., "The Poems of Haggai", *HUCA* 5 (1928) 153–95.

Carroll, Robert P., "Eschatological Delay in the Prophetic Tradition", *ZAW* 94 (1982) 47–58.

Clark, David J., "Problems in Haggai 2:15–19," *BT* 34 (1983) 432–9.

Koch, Klaus, "Haggais unreines Volk", *ZAW* 79 (1967) 52–66.

Mason, Rex A., "The Purpose of the 'Editorial Framework' of the Book of Haggai", *VT* 27 (1977) 413–21.

May, H. G., "'This People' and 'This Nation' in Haggai", *VT* 18 (1968) 190–97.

North, Francis S., "Critical Analysis of the Book of Haggai," *ZAW* 68 (1956) 25–46.

Peter, Friedrich, "Zu Haggai 1:9", *TZ* 7 (1951) 150–51.

Petersen, David L., "The Prophetic Process Reconsidered", *IR* 41 (1984) 13–19.

Pfeil, Rüdiger, "When is a goy a 'goy': the Interpretation of Haggai 2:10–19", *A Tribute to Gleason Archer*, eds. Walter C. Kaiser, Jr and Ronald F. Youngblood, Chicago, Moody, 1986, pp. 261–78.

Steck, O. H., "Zu Haggai 1:2–11", *ZAW* 83 (1971) 355–79.

Townsend, T. N., "Additional Comments on Haggai 2:10–19", *VT* 18 (1968) 559.

Verhoef, P. A., "Notes on the Dates in the Book of Haggai", *Text and Context: Old Testament and Semitic Studies for F. C. Fensham*, ed. W. Claassen, *JSOT Suppl. 48*, Sheffield, *JSOT*, 1988, pp. 259–67.

Whedbee, J. William, "A Question-Answer Schema in Haggai 1: The Form and Function of Haggai 1:9–11", *Biblical and Near Eastern Studies*, ed. G. A. Tuttle, Eerdmans, Grand Rapids, 1978, pp. 184–94.

Wolf, Herbert, "Desire of All Nations in Haggai 2:7: Messianic or Not?" *JETS* 19 (1976) 97–102.

## On Zechariah 1–8

Amsler, Samuel, "Zacharie et l'origine de l'apocalyptique", *Congress Volume, Uppsala, 1971*, eds. Henrick Samuel Nyberg, et al. *VT Suppl. 22*, Leiden, Brill, 1972, pp. 227–31.

Baldwin, J. G. "Ṣemaḥ as a Technical Term in the Prophets", *VT* 14 (1964) 93–7.

Blocher, Henri, "Zacharie 3: Josué et le Grand Jour des Expiations", *ETR* 54 (1979) 264–70.

Clark, David J., "The Case of the Vanishing Angel", *BT* 33 (1982) 213–18.

——, "Discourse Structure in Zechariah 7:1–8:23", *BT* 36 (1985) 328–35.

Davis, J. D., "The Reclothing and Coronation of Joshua, Zech. III and VI", *Princeton Theological Review* 18 (1920) 256–68.

Eichrodt, Walter, "Vom Symbol zum Typos: Ein Beitrag zur Sacharja-exegese", *TZ* 13 (1957) 509–22.

Galling, Kurt, "Die Exilswende in der Sicht des Propheten Sacharja", *VT* 2 (1952) 18–36.

Gese, Hartmut, "Anfang und Ende der Apokalyptik, dargestellt am Sacharjabuch", *ZTK* 70 (1973) 20–49.

Good, Robert M., "Zechariah's Second Night Vision", *Bib* 63 (1982) 56–9.

Halpern, Baruch, "The Ritual Background of Zechariah's Temple Song", *CBQ* 40 (1978) 167–90.

Harrelson, Walter, "The Trial of the High Priest Joshua: Zechariah 3", *EI* 16 (1982) 116–24.

Hyatt, J. Philip, "A Neo-Babylonian Parallel to Bethel-Sarezer, Zech 7:2", *JBL* 56 (1937) 387–94.

Kloos, Carola J. L., "Zech. 2:12: Really a Crux Interpretum?" *VT* 25 (1975) 729–36.

Le Bas, Edwin, "Zechariah's Climax to the Career of the Corner-Stone", *PEQ* 83 (1951) 139–55.

——, "Zechariah's Enigmatical Contribution to the Corner-stone", *PEQ* 82 (1950) 102–22.

Lipinski, E., "Recherches sur livre de Zacharie", *VT* 20 (1970) 25–55.

Long, Burke O., "Reports of Visions Among the Prophets", *JBL* 95 (1976) 357–63.

Mastin, Brian A., "Note on Zechariah 6:13", *VT* 26 (1976) 113–16.

May, H. G., "A Key to the Interpretation of Zechariah's Visions", *JBL* 57 (1938) 173–84.

Mason, Rex A., "Some Echoes of the Preaching in the Second Temple: Tradition Elements in Zechariah 1–8", *ZAW* 96 (1984) 221–35.

Marenof, S., "Note Concerning the Meaning of the Word Ephah, Zechariah 5:5–11", *AJSL* 48 (1931/2) 264–7.

McHardy, W. D., "The Horses in Zechariah", *ZAW* 103 (1968) 174–9.

Mittmann, Siegfried, "Die Einheit von Sacharja 8:1–8", *Text and Context: Old Testament and Semitic Studies for F. C. Fensham*, ed. W. Claassen, *JSOT Suppl. 48*; Sheffield: *JSOT*, 1988, pp. 269–82.

North, Francis S., "Aaron's Rise in Prestige", *ZAW* 66 (1954) 191–9.

North, Robert, "Prophecy to Apocalyptic via Zechariah", *Congress Volume, Uppsala, 1971*, ed. Henrick Samuel Nyberg, et al. *VT Suppl. 22*. Leiden, Brill, 1972, pp. 47–71.

——, "Zechariah's Seven-Spout Lampstand", *Bib.* 51 (1970) 183–206.

Orr, A., "The Seventy Years of Babylon", *VT* 6 (1956) 304–06.

Petersen, David L., "Zechariah's Visions: A Theological Perspective", *VT* 34 (1984) 195–206.

Petitjean, A., "La mission de Zorobabel et la reconstruction du temple; Zach., III:8–10," *ETL* 42 (1966) 40–71.

Press, R., "Das erste Nachtgesicht des Propheten Sacharja", *ZAW* 54 (1936) 43–8.

Redditt, Paul L., "Zerubbabel, Joshua, and the Night Visions of Zechariah", *CBQ* 54 (1992) 249–59.

Richter, Hans Friedrich, "Die Pferde in den Nachtgesichten des Sacharja", *ZAW* 98 (1986) 96–100.

Rost, Leonhard, "Bemerkungen zu Sacharja 4", *ZAW* 63 (1951) 216–21.

——, "Erwägungen zu Sacharjas 7. Nachtgesicht", *ZAW* 58 (1940–41) 223–8.

Rüthy, Albert E., "Seben Augen auf einem Stein", *TZ* 13 (1957) 523–9.

Robinson, Donald F., "Suggested Analysis of Zechariah 1–8", *ATR* 33 (1951) 65–70.

Scalise, Pamela J., "An Exegesis of Zechariah 7:4–14 in its Canonical Context", *Faith and Mission* 3 (1986) 58–65.

Schmidt, Hans, "Das vierte Nachtgesicht des Propheten Sacharja", *ZAW* 54 (1936) 48–60.

Sellin, Ernst, "Der Stern des Sacharja", *JBL* 50 (1931) 242–9.

Seybold, Klaus, "Bildmotive in den Visionen des Propheten Sacharja", *Studies on Prophecy*, ed. Daniel Lys, et al., *VT Suppl.*, Leiden, Brill, 1974, pp. 92–110.

Sinclair, Lawrence A., "Redaction of Zechariah 1–8", *BR* 20 (1975) 36–47.

Stahl, Rainer, "Das Verhältnis von Frieden und Gerechtigkeit als Theologische Problem", *TLZ* 109 (1984) 161–72.

Tidwell, N. L. A., "Wā'ômar (Zech. 3:5) and the Genre of Zechariah's Fourth Vision", *JBL* 94 (1975) 343–55.

Thomas, D. W., "A Note on MHLSWT in Zech. 3:4", *JTS* 33 (1932) 279–80.

Vanderkam, James C., "Joshua the High Priest and the Interpretation of Zechariah 3", *CBQ* 53 (1991) 553–70.

Wallis, Gerhard, "Erwägungen zu Sacharja VI 9–15", *Congress Volume, 1971, Uppsala*, ed. Henrik Samuel Nyberg, et al., *VT Suppl. 22.* Leiden, Brill, 1972, pp. 232–7.

——, "Die Nachtgesichte des Propheten Sacharja: Zur Idee einer Form", *Congress Volume, 1977, Göttingen*, ed. W. Zimmerli, et al., *VT Suppl. 24*, Leiden, Brill, 1978, pp. 377–91.

Whitley, C. F., "The Seventy Years Captivity", *VT* 4 (1954) 60–72.

Woude, Adam S. van der, "Die beiden Söhne des Öls (Sach. 4:14) Messianische Gestalten?" *Travels in the World of the Old Testament*, ed. M. Heerma van Voss, Assen, Gorcum, 1974, pp. 262–70.

——, "Seid nicht wie eure Väter! Bemerkungen zu Sacharja 1:5 und seinem Kontext", *Prophecy: Essays Presented to Georg Fohrer*, ed. J. Emerton, Berlin, New York, de Gruyter, 1980, pp. 163–73.

——, "Zion as Primeval Stone in Zechariah 3 and 4", *Text and Context: Old Testament and Semitic Studies for F. C. Fensham*, ed. W. Claassen, *JSOT Suppl. 48*, Sheffield, *JSOT*, 1988, pp. 237–48.

*On Zechariah 9–14*

Abel, F.-M., "Aṣal in Zechariah 14:5", *RB* 45 (1936) 385–400.

Botha, F. J., "Zechariah 10:11A", *ExpTim* 66 (1955) 177.

Caquot, André, "Breves remarques sur l'allegorie des pasteurs en Zacharie 11", *Mélanges bibliques et orientaux*, eds. S. Legasse, et al., Neukirchen-Vluyn, Neukirchener Verlag, 1985, pp. 45–55.

Crotty, Robert B., "The Suffering Moses of Deutero-Zechariah", *Colloquium* 14 (1982) 43–50.

Dahood, M., "Zecharia 9:1, *'ēn 'ādām*", *CBQ* 25 (1963) 123–4.

Delcor, Matthias, "Deux Passages Difficiles: Zach. XII:11 et XI:13," *VT* 3 (1953) 67–77.

——, "Les allusions à Alexandre le Grand dans Zach. 9:1–8", *VT*, 1 (1951) 110–24.

——, "Les sources du Deutero-Zacharie et ses procédés d'emprunt", *RB* 59 (1952) 385–411.

——, "Un probleme de critique textuelle et d'exegese", *RB* 58 (1951) 189–99.

Elliger, Karl, "Ein Zeugnis aus der jüdischen Gemeinde im Alexanderjahr 332 v Chr.: Eine territorialgeschichtliche Studie", *ZAW* 62 (1950) 63–115.

Ellul, Danielle, "Variations sur le thème de la guerre sainte dans le Deutéro-Zacharie", *ETR* 56 (1981) 55–71.

Hanson, Paul D., "Zechariah 9 and the Recapitulation of an Ancient Ritual Pattern", *JBL* 92 (1973) 37–59.

Harrelson, Walter, "Celebration of the Feast of Booths According to Zech. 14:16–21", *Religions in Antiquity*, Essays in Honour of Erwin Ramsdell Goodenough, ed. Jacob Neusner, Leiden, E. J. Brill, 1968, pp. 88–96.

——, "Nonroyal Motifs in the Royal Eschatology", *Israel's Prophetic Heritage*. ed. B. W. Anderson, New York, Harper, 1962, pp. 147–65.

Hill, Andrew E., "Dating Second Zechariah: A Linguistic Reexamination", *HAR* 6 (1982) 105–34.

Hoftizer, J., "À propos d'une interpretation récente de deux passages difficiles: Zach. xii:11 et Zach. xi:13", *VT* 3 (1953) 90–92.

Jones, D. R., "A Fresh Interpretation of Zechariah ix–xi", *VT* 12 (1962) 241–59.

Malamat, Abraham, "The Historical Setting of Two Biblical Prophecies on the Nations", *IEJ* 1 (1950–51) 149–59.

Redditt, Paul L., "Israel's Shepherds: Hope and Pessimism in Zechariah 9–14", *CBQ* 51 (1989) 631–42.

Rehm, M., "Die Hirtenallegorie Zach. 11:4–14", *BZ* 4 (1960) 186–208.

Saebø, Magne, "Die deuterosacharjanische Frage. Eine forschungsgeschichtliche Studie", *ST* 23 (1969) 115–40.

——, "Vom Grossreich zum Weltreich", *VT* 28 (January, 1978) 83–91.

Seybold, K., "Spätprophetische Hoffnungen auf die Wiederkunft des davidischen Zeitaltars in Sach. 9–14", *Jud.* 29 (1973) 99–111.

Thomas, D. Winton, "Zechariah 10:11A", *ExpTim* 66 (1955) 272–3.

Tournay, Raymond, "Zacharie XII-XIV et l'histoire d'Israël", *RB* 81 (1974) 355–74.

Witt, Douglas A., "The Houses Plundered, The Women Raped: The Use of Isaiah 13 in Zechariah 14:1–11", *Proceedings Eastern Great Lakes and Midwest Biblical Societies* 11 (1991) 66–74.

Woude, A.S. van der, "Die Hirtenallegorie von Sacharja 11", *JNSL* 12 (1984) 139–49.

——, "Sacharja 14:18", *ZAW* 97 (1985) 254–5.

Zolli, Eugenio, "'êyn 'ādām", *VT* 5 (1955) 90–92.

## On Malachi

Althann, R., "Malachy 2:13–14 and UT 125, 12–13," *Bib.* 58 (1977) 418–21.

Berry, Donald K., "Malachi: A Dramatic Reading", *Proceedings: Eastern Great Lakes and Midwest Biblical Societies* 4, ed. Phillip Sigal, Westerville, OH, Eastern Great Lakes Biblical Society, 1984, pp. 77–86.

Boecker, H.J., "Bemerkungen zur formgeschichtlichen Terminologie des Buches Maleachi", *ZAW* 78 (1966) 78–80.

Berquist, Jon L., "The Social Setting of Malachi," *BTB* 19 (1989) 121–6.

Bosshard, Erich, and Kratz, Reinhard Gregor, "Maleachi im Zwölfprophetenbuch," *BN* 52 (1990) 27–46.

Bossman, David M., "Kinship and Religious System in the Prophet Malachi", *Religious Writings and Religious Systems*, Brown Studies Series 1, ed. Jacob Neusner, Atlanta, Scholars Press, 1989, pp. 127–41.

Botterweck, G.J., "Jakob habe ich lieb – Esau hasse ich," *BibLeb* 1 (1960) 28–38.

——, "Ideal und Wirklichkeit der Jerusalem Priester,

Auslegung von Mal. 1:6–10; 2:1–9", *BibLeb* 1 (1960) 100–09.

——, "Schelt- und Mahnrede gegen Mischehe und Ehescheidung, Auslegung von Mal. 2:10–16", *BibLeb* 1 (1960) 179–85.

——, "Die Sonne der Gerechtigkeit am Tage Jahweh, Auslegung von Mal. 3:13–21", *BibLeb* 1 (1960) 253–60.

Braun, Roddy, "Malachi – A Catechism for Times of Disappointment," *CurTM* 4 (1977) 297–303.

Collins, John J., "The Message of Malachi," *TBT* 22 (1984) 209–15.

Drinkard, Joel F., "The Socio-Historical Setting of Malachi", *RevExp* 84 (1987) 383–90.

Dumbrell, William J., "Malachi and the Ezra-Nehemiah Reforms", *RTR* 35 (1976) 42–52.

Fischer, James A., "Notes on the Literary Form and Message of Malachi", *CBQ* 34 (1972) 315–20.

Freedman, David B., "An Unnoted Support for a Variant to the MT of Mal. 3:5", *JBL* 98 (1979) 405–6.

Fuller, Russell, "Text-critical Problems in Malachi 2:10–16", *JBL* 110 (1991) 47–57.

Glazier-McDonald, Beth, "'ēr we'ōneh: Another Look," *JBL* 105 (1986) 295–8.

——, "Intermarriage, Divorce, and the *bat-'ēl nēkār, JBL* 106 (1987) 613–16.

Hendrix, John D., "'You Say': Confrontational Dialogue in Malachi," *RevExp* 84 (1987) 465–77.

Hill, Andrew E., "Dating the Book of Malachi", *The Word of the Lord Shall Go Forth: Essays in Honor of David Noel Freedman in Celebration of His Sixtieth Birthday*, ed. Carol L. Meyers, M. O'Connor, Winona Lake, Ind., Eisenbrauns, 1983, p. 77–89.

Hoonacker, A. van, "Le rapprochement entre le Deutéronome et Malachie", *ETL* 59 (1983) 86–90.

Jones, David Clyde, "A Note on the LXX of Malachi 2:16", *JBL* 109 (1990) 683–5.

——, "Malachi on Divorce", *Presbyterion* 15 (1989) 16–22.

Keown, Gerald L., "Messianism in the Book of Malachi", *RevExp* 84 (1987) 443–51.

Kuehner, Fred Carl, "Emphases in Malachi and Modern Thought", *The Law and the Prophets: Old Testament Studies Presented in Honor of Oswald Thompson Allis*, ed. John H. Skilton, Phillipsburg, N.J., Presbyterian and Reformed, 1974, p. 482–93.

Locher, Clemens, "Altes und neues zu Maleachi 2:10–16", in *Mélanges Dominique Barthélmy*, ed. Pierre Casatti, et al., Fribourg, Editions Universitaires, Göttingen, Vandenhoeck & Ruprecht, 1975, p. 241–61.

Malchow, Bruce V., "The Messenger of the Covenant in Mal 3:1", *JBL* 103 (1984) 252–5.

McKenzie, Steven L. and Wallace, Howard N., "Covenant Themes in Malachi", *CBQ* 45 (1983) 549–63.

Meyers, Eric H., "Priestly Language in the Book of Malachi", *HAR* 10 (1986) 225–37.

Michel, Walter L., "I Will Send You Elijah", *TBT* 22 (1984) 217–22.

Ogden, Graham S., "The Use of Figurative Language in Malachi 2:10–16", *Issues in Bible Translation*, United Bible Societies Monograph Series 3, ed. P. Stone, London, United Bible Societies, 1988, p. 265–73.

Pfeiffer, Egon, "Die Disputationsworte im Buche Maleachi", *EvT* 19 (1959) 546–68.

Rehm, Martin, "Das Opfer der Völker nach Mal 1:11", in *Lex tua Veritas. Festschrift fur Herbert Junker*, Trier, Paulins, 1961, p. 193–6.

Robinson, Alan, "God, The Refiner of Silver", *CBQ* 11 (1949) 188–90.

Rofé, Alexander, "The Onset of Sects in Postexilic Judaism: Neglected Evidence from the Septuagint, Trito-Isaiah, Ben Sira, and Malachi", *The Social World of Formative Christianity and Judaism: Essays in Tribute to Howard Clark Kee*, ed. Jacob Neusner, et al., Philadelphia, Fortress, 1988, pp. 39–49.

Rudolf, Wilhelm, "Zu Mal. 2:10–16", *ZAW* 93 (1981) 85–90.

Scalise, Pamela J., "To Fear or Not to Fear: Questions of
Reward and Punishment in Malachi 2:17–4:2", *RevExp* 84
(1987) 409–18.

Schreiner, Stefan, "Mischehen – Ehebruch – Ehescheidung:
Betrachtungen zu Mal. 2:10–16", *ZAW* 91 (1979)
207–28.

Snyman, S. D., "Antitheses in Malachi 1:2–5", *ZAW* 98
(1986) 436–8.

Swetnam, J., "Malachi 1:11: An Interpretation", *CBQ* 31
(1969) 200–09.

Tate, Marvin E., "Questions for Priests and People in
Malachi 1:2–2:16", *RevExp* 84 (1987) 391–407.

Thomas, D. Winton, "The Root *sn'* in Hebrew and the
Meaning of *qdrnit* in Malachi 3:14", *JJS* 1 (1948–9)
182–8.

Vriezen, Th. C., "How to Understand Malachi 1:11", *Grace
Upon Grace: Essays in Honor of Lester J. Kuyper*, ed. James I.
Cook, Grand Rapids, Mich., Eerdmans, 1975, pp. 128–36.

Waldmann, N. M., "Some Notes on Malachi 3:6; 3:13;
Psalm 42:11", *JBL* 93 (1974) 543–9.

Wallis, Gerhard, "Wesen und Struktur der Botschaft
Maleachis", *Das ferne und nähe Wort: Festschrift Leonhard
Rost*, ed. F. Maass, Berlin, Töpelmann, 1967, pp. 229–37.

Watts, John D. W., "Introduction to Malachi", *RevExp* 84
(1987) 373–82.

Wendland, Ernst, "Linear and Concentric Patterns in
Malachi", *BT* 36 (1985) 108–21.

Woude, A. S. van der, "Der Engel des Bundes; Bemerkungen
zu Maleachi 3:1c und seinem Kontext", *Die Botschaft und
die Boten: Festschrift für Hans Walter Wolff zum 70. Geburtstag*,
ed. J. Jeremias and L. Perlitt, Neukirchen-Vluyn,
Neukirchener Verlag, 1981, pp. 289–300.

Woude, A. S. van der, "Malachi's Struggle for the Pure
Community: Reflections on Malachi 2:10–16", *Tradition
and Reinterpretation in Jewish and Early Christian Literature:
Essays in Honor of Jurgen C. H. Lebram*, ed. Jan W. van
Hentan, et al., Leiden, Brill, 1986, pp. 65–71.

# INTRODUCTION

The books of Haggai, Zechariah, and Malachi are sometimes ignored or even denigrated because those prophets are thought to have none of the reforming fire of a prophet like Amos. Instead, their concern with the rebuilding of the Temple and with priestly issues is said to mark them as defenders of an outmoded ritualism or a religio-political élite. People who study these books, however, often develop an appreciation for the prophets' messages. Such is the case with the author of this commentary.

This work will be characterized by attention to the messages of both the prophets themselves and of the redactors or editors who arranged and supplemented those messages. Where it is possible to suggest earlier versions of a book (as in connection with Zechariah 1–8) or earlier collections standing behind books (as in the cases of Zechariah 9–14 and Malachi), the commentary will discuss the meaning of the texts at each level. One difference between Haggai, Zechariah, and Malachi and most earlier prophetic books is the extent to which these books were the products of literary efforts. Both Zechariah 1–8 and Malachi may have been written originally to be read, and Haggai, Zechariah 9–14, and Malachi show extensive editorial reshaping.

This work will also be marked by attention to the social settings for each book or section of a book. The prophets Haggai and Zechariah will be seen against the background of a tiny, post-exilic community that needed desperately to work in unity. The book of Zechariah 1–8 will be traced through three editions. A first edition of Zechariah 1–8 will be seen as the appeal of Zechariah to exiles who had remained in Babylon urging them to come to Jerusalem. A "second, enlarged, revised edition" applied those visions to the events of 520, when construction of the Temple began. The third edition, prepared before the Temple was completed, was prefaced by the book of Haggai.

Zechariah 9–14 and the book of Malachi arose in the fifth century under different circumstances. The final redactor of Zechariah 9–14 will be presented as a pro-Judaite reformer, who inherited the eschatological hopes of the post-exilic period but abandoned many of them because of the perceived sins of its leaders. The book of Malachi, in turn, will be understood as the product of a non-Zadokite Levite who opposed some of the practices and some of the claims of the Jerusalemite priesthood. One of his followers edited and supplemented the words of the prophet. Eventually the messages recorded in Zechariah 9–14 and Malachi were taken over by the religious establishment, but they were not stripped of their protests against religious or political abuses. The Old Testament in general and the prophetic corpus in particular is the richer for their perspectives.

# INTRODUCTION

to

Haggai

The prophetic books of Haggai, Zechariah, and Malachi provide readers of the Old Testament with glimpses into the life and thought of the people of Jerusalem and Judah in the post-exilic period. At first glance we seem to be relatively well informed about that period, with the books of Ezra and Nehemiah providing a narrative account of the years from 538 to at least 433 BC (Neh. 13:6) if not 398 (depending on when one dates Ezra). In addition, Joel, Isaiah 24–7, 34–5, 56–66, 1 and 2 Chronicles, perhaps the Priestly source (P) and the final editing of the Pentateuch, some of the wisdom literature, and other materials scattered throughout the Old Testament derive from the post-exilic period as well.

Much of this material (e.g. P and 1 and 2 Chronicles) deals overtly with earlier periods of history and can be used only guardedly as evidence for the post-exilic period. The prophetic material rarely narrates events, though it does provide evidence for reconstructing theology, sometimes of an uncertain time frame and perhaps even from competing factions within the community. Wisdom literature likewise makes few references to historical events. Even the books of Ezra and Nehemiah were written years after the events they relate and exhibit such imprecision in details that scholars often doubt their historical reliability. Thus, the historical background for the books of Haggai, Zechariah and Malachi remains obscure in many ways. Nevertheless, the interpretation of these books is inextricably bound up with a reconstruction of the history of the post-exilic period, so it will be necessary to set forth the reconstruction upon which this commentary is based. Here the background for Haggai and Zechariah 1–8 will be discussed together, since the two were contemporaries.

## A. HISTORICAL BACKGROUND

Cyrus the Great captured Babylon in 539 BC and, according to an inscription, "returned to [the] sacred cities on the other side of the Tigris, the sanctuaries of which have been ruins for a long time, the images which (used) to live therein and established for them permanent sanctuaries. [He] (also) gathered all their (former) inhabitants and returned them to their habitations" (*ANET*, 316). Consonant with this inscription is the so-called "Edict of Cyrus" (from the year 538) in Ezr. 1:2–4, 6:3–5, which granted to the Israelites in exile the right to return to Jerusalem and rebuild the Temple. Cyrus gave to an official named Sheshbazzar a number of silver and gold vessels originally taken from Jerusalem. Ezr. 1:11 reports that he brought them to Jerusalem "when the exiles were brought up from Babylonia to Jerusalem".

Ezr. 2:1–70 (cf. Neh. 7:6–73a) contains a list of groups who returned from exile, 42,360 in number, plus 7,337 servants, for a total of 49,697. The clear implication is that these are the people with whom Sheshbazzar travelled, perhaps in 538 (see Geo Widengren, "The Persian Period", in *Israelite and Judaean History* [ed. John. H. Hayes and J. Maxwell Miller, OTL, Philadelphia, Westminster, 1977], 519). However, a migration to Palestine of such proportions seems unlikely in the year 538, because the boundaries of the Persian Empire were not secure enough to permit much movement before Cambyses conquered Egypt in 525 BC (see Karl-Martin Beyse, *Königserwartungen*, 18–23).

Consequently, Kurt Galling (*Studien zur Geschichte Israels im persischen Zeitalter* [Tübingen, Mohr, 1965], 92) and Beyse (23), among others, have argued that the list in Ezr. 2 derives from a migration under Zerubbabel just before the death of Cambyses and the fighting surrounding the coming of his brother Darius I to the throne. This suggestion too is unlikely. The entire population of Judah has been estimated at only 20,000 in the year 520 (John Bright, *A History of Israel* [3rd ed., Philadelphia, Westminster, 1981], 365, following W. F.

Albright), and a new estimate (Broshi, *BARev*, 4 [1978], 12) of the population of Jerusalem puts the total at only 4500 as late as the time of Nehemiah. Given the reference in Neh. 11:1 of casting lots to select ten per cent of the population to live in Jerusalem, the population of Judah would have been under 50,000 as late as the mid-fifth century. Thus, there can be no question of a mass migration of approximately 50,000 people in 538 or 522 or over the entire period for that matter. The list in Ezr. 2 and Neh. 7 must derive from a later period and perhaps reports the total number of people, living and dead, for whom descent from families who had been in exile was being claimed, or was a head count from the time of Nehemiah.

Alternatively, Siegfried Hermann (*A History of Israel in Old Testament Times* [2nd ed., Philadelphia, Fortress, 1981], 302) suggests that the list was a census of people from 538 or 515 who had never been in exile and argues that neither Haggai nor Zechariah spoke to repatriates. There seems to be no reason to accept such an extreme view, but their number (as well as the number of those who had never been exiled) must have been small, smaller probably than the census list in Ezr. 2 and Neh. 11.

Little is known about the organization of the Persian Empire under Cyrus and Cambyses, but, according to Herodotus, Darius established a system of thirty satrapies, which in turn were made up of smaller units called provinces. Judah belonged to the satrapy called "Beyond the River". Carol L. and Eric M. Meyers (xxxiv and 13–16) argue that Judah was established this early as an independent province with its own governors (i.e. Sheshbazzar, Ezr. 5:14, and Zerubbabel, Hab. 1:1, 14; 2:2, 20) over against the older position of Albrecht Alt ("Die Rolle Samarias bei der Entstehung des Judentum," *Festschrift Otto Procksch* [Leipzig, Delichert-Hinrichs, 1934], 5–28) that it was a subprovince under the direction of Samaria until the time of Nehemiah.

The best evidence for the position of Meyers and Meyers is the discovery of a number of bullae (clay used in sealing letters), seals, and jar handles on which the names of three "governors" have been found. Unfortunately, the dates assigned to the artefacts range from the sixth to the fourth centuries, so they offer inconclusive evidence that the office of governor continued from Sheshbazzar to Nehemiah (see Ephraim Stern, "The Persian Empire and the Political and Social History of Palestine in the Persian Period", *The Cambridge History of Judaism*, eds. W. D. Davies and Louis Finkelstein [Vol. 1, Cambridge, Cambridge University, 1984], 534, and Peter R. Ackroyd, *IR* 39 [1982] 12–13). Sean E. McEvenue (*CBQ* 43 [1981] 361–3) argues that the title "governor" (*peḥâ*) was used in the pre-exilic period, where it referred to a person who marched with an army, regardless of that person's authority. Further, the term refers to Sheshbazzar in Ezr. 5:14, to Zerubbabel in 6:7 (implied, but see Hag. 1:1, 14; 2:2, 20), and to Tattenai in 5:3, 6; 6:6, 13, people clearly of differing authority. McEvenue concludes that despite its use in Persian records as the name of an office, it is not used technically in the Bible and can refer to a governor (Tattenai) or to a lesser official (Sheshbazzar). In other words we cannot be sure that the term means the same when applied to Sheshbazzar or Zerubbabel in the sixth century and Nehemiah in the fifth (or even to different persons at one time). On the other hand the discovery of minted coins from the fifth century and afterwards suggests that Judah attained the status of a province about the time of Nehemiah.

The evidence of Ezr. 4 on this issue is inconclusive, but probably points in the direction of Alt's view that Judah was under the control of Samaria down to the time of Nehemiah. The chapter opens with an account of a friendly overture by Samaritans (i.e. descendants of persons transported to Israel by Esarhaddon in 676, and who then began to worship Yahweh) to assist with the rebuilding of the Temple. They were rebuffed by the returning exiles (v. 3), and the people who had remained in Judah during the exile showed little desire for the work (vv. 4–5). That narrative resumes in 4:24, and in between one finds references to three other times the inhabitants of Jerusalem and Judah met with opposition. The third reference is expanded by means of a narrative about a letter to Artaxerxes (reigned 464–23 BC). Listed among those who sent the letter were Rehum, Shimshai, their associates, judges, governors, officials, Persians, the men of Erech, Babylonians, Elamites and others settled in Samaria by Osnappar (Assurbanipal?). These people opposed the repair of the wall around Jerusalem, presumably at the time of Nehemiah. The import of this report for our purposes is that the book of Ezra appears to describe interference in Judaean affairs by Samaritans from the days of Cyrus until the time of Nehemiah. The most likely explanation for such behaviour is that the Samaritans were responsible to the Persian authorities for what went on in Judah.

If so, how should one understand the application of the title "governor" to Sheshbazzar and Zerubbabel? The answer is partly based on one's understanding of the passages in Ezra in which the word occurs. Sheshbazzar is specifically called "governor" in Tattenai's letter to Darius where he is quoting the Judaeans (5:14). Darius's response refers to the "governor" (Zerubbabel?) and the elders of the Jews (6:7). The two verses appear in the long segment 4:8–6:18 that was written in Aramaic. In view of the consistency between Cyrus's proclamation quoted above and Ezr. 1:2–4 and 6:3–5, it is often claimed that the Edict of Cyrus is authentic (Widengren, 522). In view of the differences between 1:2–4 and 6:3–5, however, it might be the case that the letters report the gist of the documents (see L. H. Brockington, *Ezra, Nehemiah, Esther*, Century Bible, New Series [London, et al., Thomas Nelson and Sons, 1969], 82). If the letters are summaries, they were probably summarized on the Judaean end of the transmission.

What is more, 5:5–16 purports to report a conversation between Tattenai and the Judaean leaders, but includes only the Judaean rationale for building the Temple, a most unlikely happenstance if, as reported (6:6–7), Tattenai was attempting to block the building project. Further, the name of the governor mentioned in 6:7 is not given. In the context of 5:14, one might conclude that the governor intended was Sheshbazzar, though the reference is more likely to Zerubbabel, who flourished during the reign of Darius (see Hag. 1:1, 12, 14; 2:2, 20, where Zerubbabel is called "governor"). Further, one should note that Tattenai does not himself mention speaking with a governor, but only with elders and people (5:9). In view of the above, one ought not lay much emphasis upon the occurrence of the word "governor" in Ezr. 5:14 and 6:7. The probable source of the term in both places is a Judaean author, so the word would carry no technical meaning and offers no evidence that Judah was an independent province in the time of Sheshbazzar and Zerubbabel.

Certainly, Sheshbazzar and Zerubbabel had Persian authorization to build the Temple. It is possible that the Samaritan governor thought of them as his representatives, while the people of Judah may have conceived of them as the official representatives of Persian authority. Even if these conjectures are granted, they still do not make it probable that Judah was an independent province in 538 or 520, with its own governor. All in all it seems best to follow Alt in seeing tiny Judah under the jurisdiction of Samaria in 520.

The next questions to face are the extent to which the Temple needed to be rebuilt and the roles of Sheshbazzar and Zerubbabel in that project. When Nebuchadnezzar captured Jerusalem in 586 BC, he broke down the wall of the city in places and burned the Temple along with other important buildings (2 Kg. 25:8–10). It is not clear, however, just how extensively the Temple was damaged. The fire presumably would not have destroyed the stonework, and Hag. 1:8 commands the people only to secure wood from the nearby mountains. Jer. 41:5 mentions a group of worshippers bringing offerings and incense to present to the Lord at the Temple, so presumably the altar was intact. When Cyrus issued his decree allowing the exiles to return to Jerusalem, he placed Sheshbazzar in charge of the rebuilding project. According to Ezr. 5:16 Sheshbazzar "laid the foundations" of the Temple during the reign of Cyrus. On the other hand, Ezr. 3:3 says that Joshua, the high priest, and Zerubbabel set the altar in its rightful place in the seventh month, implying that it had been dislodged (though not destroyed), and 3:8–10 says that in the second year (of Darius?) "the builders laid the foundation of the temple of the Lord." Finally, Zech. 4:9 says: "The hands of Zerubbabel have laid the foundation of this house."

How should one understand these notices? The place to begin is with the verbs used. In Ezr. 5:16 the Aramaic verb *yhb* is employed. The basic meaning of the word and its Hebrew cognate is "to give". Just two verses earlier *NRSV* translates the passive of the verb "were delivered". Only in Ezr. 5:16 is it translated "to lay". Even if one assumes the Babylonians and/or time dislodged many of the stones of the Temple walls, there seems to be little reason to assume that the foundation *per se* was destroyed and needed to be relaid. It would make more sense to translate *yhb* in 5:16 by the word "deliver" (as in 5:14) or to "give to", meaning (presumably) that Sheshbazzar transferred control of the Temple to the people in the name of Cyrus. Further, the verb *ysd*, translated "laid the foundation" in Ezr. 3:10, 12 and Neh. 4:9, 8:9, can mean "to found" and should be so translated in these verses (Meyers, 228).

If one accepts the basic authenticity of the Edict of Cyrus, one should also assume that Sheshbazzar attempted to carry out his charge, as Ezr. 5:16 plainly says. The book of Ezra does not again mention Sheshbazzar, and the books of Haggai and Zechariah celebrate the role of Zerubbabel in the building process. It is difficult, then, to imagine why anyone would invent the role of Sheshbazzar in Ezr. 1:8–11 and 5:16, so the basic historicity of those verses should be accepted.

However, to deliver Cyrus's permission to build is only to begin the project, and it cannot have progressed very far. Consequently, when Haggai (and then Zechariah) began to urge the people to complete the project, the new leader appears to have been Zerubbabel. Haggai identified him as the new Davidic leader (2:20–23), and the book of Zechariah insisted that he founded and would finish building the Temple (4:9). It is not quite clear when Zerubbabel returned to Judah, but probably after Cambyses's campaign into Egypt (523) and before the second year of Darius (520). There is no reason to doubt that Zerubbabel actually completed his task of rebuilding, but the political realities of subjugation to Persia precluded any possibility of his ever fulfilling Haggai's vision

of him as a new David. In fact, the building of the Temple
set the stage for the rise in prestige of the priesthood, a tendency already evident in the book of Zechariah.

The result of this investigation is to conclude that the
Temple had been burned and many of its stones may have
fallen or been knocked down, but it would not have been
reduced to bare ground. Worship seems to have continued at
the altar during the exilic period. Sheshbazzar returned in
538 with some funding and the permission of Cyrus to rebuild
the Temple, an activity which began but ceased before the
work progressed very far (Ezr. 5:16). The time of the stoppage
(during the reign of Cyrus) and the intervening years are
difficult to reconstruct from the book of Ezra, but in 520
Haggai instructed the people to go to the surrounding hills
and cut timber for the work (1:8). Solomon, of course, had
used cedar from Lebanon to build his Temple (1 Kg. 5:6),
but the new Temple would have timber from nearby. The
reference to laying stones (Hag. 2:15; see also Zech. 4:9) probably involved a ceremony of dedication/purification, rather
than construction of the Temple itself (see comments below
on Hag. 2:15).

In part because of interference by the Samaritans, the
rebuilding activity took about four years. During this period
the dedication/purification ceremony mentioned above
occurred on the twenty-fourth day of the ninth month of the
second year of Darius (i.e. in December) of 520. The Temple
was finished on the third day of the month of Adar (i.e.
March) of the sixth year of Darius (i.e. 515). On the fourteenth
day of the next month, the exiles observed Passover in Jerusalem. During a few months of 520, the prophet Haggai
flourished, providing the inspiration for the rebuilding of the
Temple.

## B. AUTHORSHIP

In the midst of the conflict surrounding the death of Cambyses
and the rise of Darius, Haggai began his ministry. Little is
known of the man. He is mentioned outside the book only in

Ezr. 5:1 and 6:14, which mention him along with Zechariah as the prophets responsible for prompting the people of Judah to rebuild the Temple and gain prosperity. Scholars have often attempted to derive further information about him from clues within the text. W. A. M. Beuken (*Haggai-Sacharja 1–8*, 217–23) argues that Haggai addressed Judaean farmers only (see 1:6, 10–11; 2:16–19) and should be seen as a Judaean who had remained in Palestine during the time of the exile. By contrast, Wilhelm Rudolph (84) concludes from the allusion to the pre-exilic Temple in 2:3 that Haggai was himself an old man who had recently returned to Palestine with Zerubbabel and could remember the Temple from his youth. Such vastly differing conclusions suggest that the details of the life of Haggai are irrecoverable. Even so, K. -M. Beyse (Königserwartungen, 60–5) argues that Haggai followed the thought of the exilic prophets Ezekiel and II Isaiah, making it likely that the prophet had himself lived in Babylon and returned prior to 520.

## C. LITERARY HISTORY AND STRUCTURE

In the book of Haggai one finds two voices. The first, of course, is the voice of the prophet Haggai himself. The other voice is that of the redactor responsible for editing the book. It is through his eyes that the reader sees Haggai. The redactor recognized Haggai as a genuine prophet, but he may have omitted or modified some of Haggai's characteristic emphases.

The book of Haggai consists of four edited sections (1:1–15a, 1:15b–2:9, 2:10–19, 2:20–23), each beginning with a date: 1:1, the second year, sixth month and the first day of the reign of Darius I Hystaspes, or Darius the Great (reigned 521–485); 1:15b–2:1, the seventh month and twenty-first day; 2:10, the ninth month and twenty-fourth day; 2:20, the same day. Although many scholars think the date in 1:15a originally introduced 2:15–19, there is no textual support for the suggestion. It would appear, instead, that the redactor tied the teaching of the prophet to three dates in the year 520 BC when the people of Judah were rebuilding the Temple, and the date in

1:15a belongs to the narrative of chapter one. These dates show that the book cannot have reached its present form earlier than December of 520 (the date of the last two oracles), but the redaction of Haggai's messages need not have been delayed long after that date either.

In addition to supplying dates for Haggai's messages, the redactor perhaps made other contributions. Many scholars think that he added the names of Zerubbabel and Joshua to the first (and possibly the second) of these messages, while Haggai himself addressed the people in general. Also, the redactor supplied a narrative context for Haggai's messages, including at times the people's response. Similar language and common themes suggest that the redactor also edited Zechariah 1–8. That he stood within the tradition of the Chronicler (so Ackroyd, *Exile* 154, and Beuken, *Haggai-Sacharja 1–8*, 10–20, 331–6) remains unproven. The redactor wrote in prose, but Haggai's oral prophecies may have been poetic (*BHS* prints them as such, while the *NRSV* translates them as prose). Either way in their present form they should probably be considered prose also.

## D. MESSAGE

Haggai's message is steeped in theology in the narrow sense of that word, i.e. the doctrine of God. The prophet designated God as the Lord of Hosts, a name connected with God at Shiloh in the pre-monarchical period (1 Sam. 1:3). The name appears fourteen times in Haggai, fifty-three times in Zechariah, and twenty-four times in Malachi. It seems to envision God as the "Lord of all powers, seen and unseen, in the universe . . ." (Baldwin, 45). As such, God controlled the climate and harvests and could intervene in human affairs as well. The redactor saw Haggai's message as the word of God. He presented Haggai and Zechariah as genuine prophets God was using to usher in a new age.

Haggai's own eschatology focused on the Temple and on Zerubbabel as the new David. Because Israel had failed to rebuild the Temple, God had withheld his blessings (1:9–11).

Rebuilding the Temple was the key to ushering in the new order with its abundance of crops (2:19) and a new Davidic king, Zerubbabel (2:23). The redactor also included the High Priest Joshua in his vision for the future.

## E. CONTENTS

1:1—15a    Haggai Calls the People to Work on the Temple
1:15b—2:9  The New Temple Versus the Old
2:10—19    The Founding of the New Temple as the Turning Point
2:20—23    Zerubbabel as God's Signet Ring

# COMMENTARY

## on

## Haggai

As it now stands 1:1–15a is a narrative containing the setting
(v. 1) for Haggai's first prophetic announcement, the sermon
itself (vv. 2–11), and a description of its affect on the people.
According to Karl Elliger (2.86) this first sermon consists of
two disputations (vv. 4–6 and 9–11) connected by an admonition (vv. 7–8). J. William Whedbee ("Question-Answer
Schema," 188) argues that the entire piece is a disputation,
with vv. 2b–7 defining the problem, v. 8 advancing the solution, and vv. 9–11 reiterating the problem. Since disputation
speeches are often combined with other literary types, the
difference between these two views may be more apparent
than real. In any case one is probably on good grounds in
regarding vv. 2–11 as a unit.

**1.** According to the superscription, the word of the Lord
**came by** (lit. by the hand of) **Haggai** to **Zerubbabel** and
**Joshua.** Usually a superscription gave a short genealogy of a
prophet (see Hos. 1:1, Isa. 1:1, Zech. 1:1, and especially Zeph.
1:1) or his home town (see Am. 1:1, Mic. 1:1, and Nah. 1:1)
or both (see Jer. 1:1, Ezek. 1:3), but this verse gave neither.
Instead, the redactor focused entirely on Haggai's role as the
intermediary through whom God sent his word.

The name "Haggai" meant "festal" and came from the
noun *hag*, which designated the three annual pilgrimage festivals of Passover, Weeks and Tabernacles. The name Zerubbabel was Babylonian (Zer-Babil), and meant "Offspring of
Babylon". He was **the son of Shealtiel** and the grandson of
Jehoiachin, the king of Judah carried into exile by Nebuchadnezzar in the first deportation (see 2 Kg. 24:8–16). Zerubbabel was identified as the **governor** (*peḥâ*), Nehemiah's title
in the fifth century, but it is unclear how much authority
Zerubbabel had (see pp. 5–8 above). Joshua was the **son of
Jehozadak**, who was also carried into exile by Nebuchadnezzar (see 1 Chr. 6:15). Joshua was identified as the **high** (lit.
great) **priest**, the first person so named in the *OT*. These

three people very likely embodied for the redactor the three institutions he thought belonged in the restitution: prophecy, monarchy, and priesthood. The redactor claimed that Haggai's message was for the two leaders, but the message which followed (vv. 2–11) addressed the people only, and not Zerubbabel and Joshua, whose roles were taken up by the redactor in v. 12.

**2.** The name **the Lord of Hosts** occurs two hundred and sixty-seven times in the Old Testament and a longer form, the Lord God of Hosts, another eighteen. The name is found especially in Isaiah, Jeremiah, Haggai, Zechariah and Malachi. There is fairly wide agreement that it originated at Shiloh (see 1 Sam. 1:3, 11), where Yahweh was associated with a cult god. He was thought to sit upon the cherubim on top of the Ark of the Covenant (see 1 Sam. 4:4). The hymn fragment in Am. 4:13 associated the name "the Lord, God of hosts" with the act of creation. Beyond that, however, there remain three problems in understanding the name. First, the meaning of the name Yahweh itself is unsettled; is it affirmative or causative? Second, what is the meaning of Sebaoth? Does it mean "armies"? Or does it refer to a heavenly council, the stars, or perhaps even all of these? Third, do the two words form a construct, or is Sebaoth to be understood attributively as a noun, adjective, or proper name? Despite these problems one can say that the title appears to be God's war name, and it connoted more and more power during the exile and afterwards (see M.-L. Henry, *Glaubenskrise und Glaubensbewaehrung in den Dictungen der Jesajaapokalypse* [Stuttgart, et al., Kohlhammer, 1968], 161).

The disputation speech recorded in vv. 2–11 begins by quoting the people's claim that the **time has not yet come to rebuild** (lit. build) **the Lord's house**. It is not difficult to see why they would say this. Any money the exiles might have sent with Sheshbazzar (Ezr. 1:4) would have long since been spent or have been held by Tattenai, governor of the province named Beyond the River (if that is why Darius commanded him to pay for rebuilding the Temple, see Ezr. 6:8). Further, the population of the city itself is not likely to have been very large, reaching a total of only 4500 by the time of Nehemiah (see Broshi, 12), and the surrounding rural area would have been small and poor, occupying the Judaean hill country no more than about twenty-five miles from just north of Jerusalem south to Beth-zur (G. E. Wright [*Biblical Archaeology* [Rev. ed., Philadelphia, Westminster, 1962], 202). In addition, 1:6, 9–11 and 2:16–17 mentioned crop failures and economic hardships (cf. Zech. 8:10–13).

**3–4.** More problematic is the response of Haggai that the people themselves lived in **panelled houses**, in contrast with the ruined Temple. Most commentators simply contrast the life of ease and luxury lived by the people of Jerusalem, as symbolized by richly panelled houses, with the ruined state of the worship centre. Such a contrast cannot be maintained, however, for the people as a whole, as 1:6, 9–11 and 2:16–17 make clear. Several possible solutions offer themselves. Haggai may have been referring to a subgroup within the people other than the one he was addressing, but the redactor, at least, seemed to think he was addressing the people as a whole. It is surely these same people whose work is reported in vv. 12–15. Second, he may simply have been indulging in hyperbole to urge the people to work less on their houses and more on the Temple. This view may also be combined with a third, namely that the word *sĕpûnim* should be translated "roofed" here rather than "panelled", the distinction being that the work on their own houses was further advanced than the repairs on God's house (see F. I. Andersen, *ABR* 6 [1958], 25–6). Thus, the contrast here seems not to be affluence versus poverty, but attention versus inattention.

**5–6.** Haggai told his hearers to **Consider how** they **have fared**, and directed their attention to five examples of unfulfilled expectations. (1) They had sown heavily in hopes of good crops, but reaped little. (2) They had eaten their produce, but never had enough food to fill their stomachs. (3) They had drunk wine, but never become happily sated (lit. drunk). (4) They wore clothes that could not keep them warm. (5) They occasionally saved a little money only to lose it before they could spend it for what they needed.

**7.** Whedbee thinks that v. 7 closes the first part of the disputation speech. In that case v. 7 would form an inclusion device with v. 5, to which it is very similar. On the other hand the phrase **Thus says the Lord of hosts** is an introductory phrase, not one that appears at the end of prophetic speeches. Taken in that light it probably introduced the command which follows in v. 8. In that case it is difficult to see the function of **Consider how you have fared**, which looked to the past, while the imperatives that followed look to the future. Hence, it might be best to regard the phrase as an addition due to dittography from v. 5.

**8.** Haggai's solution to the immediate past and present situation of economic depression was to **build the house** of God. Haggai gave two reasons for rebuilding the Temple. The first was that **I** (i.e. God) **may take pleasure in it**. The verb *rṣh* often meant "to accept" and was used in connection with God's acceptance of a sacrifice, which was its likely meaning here. Ackroyd (*Exile*, 160) notes that Haggai was attempting to impose no limits on God, who clearly cannot be confined to a building (1 Kg. 8:27). Rather, it is God himself who "condescends to reveal himself and to localize his presence in order that blessing may flow out." The second reason for rebuilding the Temple was that God might be **honoured**. The better future envisioned in the book of consolation in Jer. 31–2, in Ezek. 36–9, and in Second Isaiah had not come to fruition. Haggai had not come to despair over that failure, but saw that the new age was delayed and saw why: the Temple had not been finished. When it was finished, God himself would come and the previous bad fortunes of his people would be reversed. Thus Haggai's message was eschatological in the same sense that much other post-exilic prophecy is eschatological: Haggai foresaw a better future "with significant discontinuities from the present", discontinuities "that scarcely could be expected to arrive as the result of normal, or even extraordinary, human progress", but only from God's direct intervention within history (Donald Gowan, *Eschatology in the Old Testament* [Philadelphia, Fortress, 1986], 1–2). In keeping with this thinking, Haggai also expected that

God would reestablish the Davidic kingship in the person of Zerubbabel (2:20–23), who would reign in harmony with God.

**9–11.** O. H. Steck (*ZAW* 83 [1971], 357–8, 368–70) argues that vv. 9–11 addressed those who recently returned from Babylon and were concerned about acquiring housing, whereas vv. 2–8 addressed people who already had houses, namely the Judaeans who had stayed behind. The problem with his hypothesis is that both v. 4 and v. 9 seem to level the same charge, namely that people were more concerned with their own houses than God's house. Granted, Haggai expressed his concern slightly differently in the two verses, but one must question whether those differences warrant postulating two different groups. Further, one must question whether the number of exiles who had returned by 520 was sufficiently large to constitute a significant subgroup (see pp. 4–5). It seems better to proceed on the assumption that vv. 9–11 addressed the same group as vv. 2–8.

**9.** In this verse Haggai drew a contrast between **much** and **little**. The people Haggai addressed had held great expectations or waited anxiously for the future, a circumstance easily understood if they included returnees from the exile. There they had been filled from the start with false hopes of a short exile (see Jer. 29:8–10), and later Second Isaiah had announced the end of their punishment and the start of their exaltation. These hopes had not yet materialized. When they brought their produce **home**, it did them no good. God said: **I blew it away**. One might more graphically translate the phrase: "and I snorted on it." Mal. 1:13 reads similarly: "But you say: 'Behold, what is this weariness?' And you have snorted at it . . ." The verb in both verses is *nph*, which means to blow or gasp. *BDB* (656) translates Mal. 1:13 "and ye have sniffed at it (in contempt)." In Hag. 1:9 it is God who snorted!

**10.** Since the people of Judah had not rebuilt the Temple and, thus, God would not receive their offerings and glorify himself among them, they were forfeiting his blessing and enduring instead the conditions of a curse. According to v. 10 **the heavens . . . have withheld dew**, with the result that the crops failed. In Palestine it rarely rains from May to October, so farmers depend on dew to sustain their crops after the "latter rains" in April/May or in places where there was little rainfall. If the dew failed also, produce would be badly hurt.

**11.** If God further **called for a drought** and withheld the autumn rain, the damage would be worse. The **grain** crop was planted in the autumn after the "early rains" wet the soil, making planting possible, and was harvested after the "latter rains" in April gave it the last real growth spurt. The **new wine** was the sweet wine obtained first, when the grapes were put through the wine presses. It was kept separate from wine obtained subsequently by trampling. The **oil** was olive oil pressed from olives harvested in October-November. A failure of both dew and rain would blight everything **the soil produces**, and would frustrate the labours of **human beings and animals** as well as cause them to suffer thirst.

**12.** Having reported the words of Haggai, the redactor next turned to its effect, namely that **the people feared the Lord**. To fear God they **obeyed** (lit. heard or harkened to) **the voice of the Lord their God**, which was understood as **the words of Haggai the prophet**. Thus the redactor emphasized the prophetic role of Haggai as the legitimate spokesperson for God to his people. (See the same connection between Zechariah and God emphasized in Zech. 2:8–9, 11; 4:9; 6:15.) Since the redactor's focus was upon Zerubbabel and Joshua, he listed them first among those who had heard Haggai's sermon. The phrase **all the remnant of the people** presumably included the entire Judaean population, and not some subgroup within it, even if not every person in the post-exilic community heard Haggai preach. The term **remnant** probably reflected the small population of Jerusalem and Judah in contrast with their pre-exilic numbers.

**13.** Next the redactor summarized the import of Haggai's preaching: **I am with you, says the Lord** (see 2:4). The phrase expressed God's care for his people articulated in his promise to bless them (Gen. 26:24), in his promise to Jeremiah to guard him from his enemies (15:20) and twice in an oracle of salvation as the basis for the command "Fear not" (Isa. 41:10, 43:5). Having called Haggai a prophet in vv. 1, 3, and 12, the redactor called him God's **messenger** in v. 13. Claus Westermann (*Basic Forms of Prophetic Speech* [Philadelphia, Westminster, 1967]) argues that the prophets are best understood on the model of the messenger dispatched by a king to convey his word to others. The redactor clearly presented Haggai in terms of that model in this verse.

**14.** The result of Haggai's preaching was that the Lord stirred up the **spirit** of the leaders and the people. The word "spirit" often referred to the life principle of a person or to his emotions (e.g. a spirit of bitterness), but here and elsewhere it referred to God's enabling a person to perform a specific task such as rebuilding the Temple (see Ezr. 1:5).

**15a.** They resumed building the Temple twenty-three days later on the twenty-fourth day of the sixth month. Many, perhaps most, scholars see v. 15a as the date for an allegedly undated oracle found in 2:15–19. There is no textual support for changing the text; moving the half-verse would break the chronological sequence; and (as will be shown later) there is good reason for viewing 2:10–19 as a unit. Hence, it seems best to consider the date as an inclusion device, rounding off the first narrative in the book of Haggai.

### THE NEW TEMPLE VERSUS THE OLD
### 1:15b–2:9

The second section of the book of Haggai begins with a date following the same pattern as 1:1: **the second year of Darius, the seventh month, the twenty-first day**, i.e. October, 520 BC, and concludes with 2:9, the date in 2:10 marking the beginning of the third section. Elliger (2.92) classifies vv. 3–5 as a warning and promise, vv. 6–9 as pure promise. Ralph L. Smith (156) calls the entire unit a word of encouragement. Overall, Smith's judgment is probably correct that the passage contains one form (a prophecy of salvation), though the speech opens with questions vaguely reminiscent of a disputation speech, and includes injunctions in v. 4 to take courage, which are reminiscent of an admonition.

**1:15b–2:2.** The redactor was clearly responsible for 1:15b–2:1. Again, Haggai appears to have addressed the people as a whole, so the mention of Zerubbabel and Joshua in vv. 2 and 4 may have been his handiwork again, continuing his concern with the two leaders exhibited in 1:1–15a.

**3.** It is clear that the building operation was underway, but that the new Temple suffered in comparison with Solomon's Temple. Haggai asked: **Who is left among you who saw this house in its former glory?** Despite the claims of some scholars, this question yields evidence neither for nor against the possibility that Haggai himself had seen the first Temple. On the other hand, it probably does yield evidence that the group addressed included people who had not gone into exile. Persons old enough in 586 (or 597) to remember the Temple would have surely been too old to return to Jerusalem after the exile. Thus, Haggai's question, at least, was pointed at the eldest members of the Jewish community and suggested that they had begun to oppose or at least ridicule the building project. Very likely, the builders relied on these people's memory of what the old Temple looked like, and their objections to the new Temple would have carried significant weight.

Further, the term **glory** carried economic and even political connotations (see Myers, 73). The glory of the first Temple had been associated with the wealth of Solomon and the breadth of his empire. Possibly the term in Haggai's day would have conjured the image of a wealthy king as the new temple's patron. Haggai dealt with some economic and political implications in this sermon, but he did not discuss the new king until two months later in 2:20–23. Haggai conceded the old men's point with the question: **Is it not in your sight as nothing?**

**4–5.** Verse 4 exhibits two themes associated with the redactor: an emphasis on Zerubbabel and Joshua and the phrase **I am with you** (cf. 1:13). Even so, it is altogether likely that Haggai would have told the people to **take courage** and it is possible he addressed Zerubbabel. Also v. 5 may have come partly or wholly from the redactor, in particular the reference to God's spirit residing among the Judaeans, a thought which clearly paralleled the promise that God was with them. R. A. Mason (*VT* 27 [1977] 419) notes that the idea was also consistent with P's image of God's "tabernacling" among his people. If the redactor were drawing upon the P tradition, whether oral or written, that would explain as well the reference to the exodus in this verse. The meaning seems to have been that if the people were faithful to God he would be faithful to them.

**6–7.** Haggai answered the old men's objection that the new Temple exhibited no splendid appointments. God himself promised to beautify the building when **the treasure of all nations** would flow in and God would **fill this house with splendour**, surely promises with political ramifications. God promised **I will shake the heavens and the earth and the sea and the dry land; and I will shake all the nations**, . . . Again the image was eschatological, the shaking resulting in the reversal of the present with Judah's being elevated and the nations brought down, the rich being stripped of their treasures and the house of God in poor Judah being filled with riches.

**8–9.** Furthermore, the Judaeans themselves would participate in the Temple's new wealth: **in the place I will give prosperity** (v. 9). This reversal of fortunes was possible because God owns everything anyway: **The silver is mine, and the gold is mine.** Consequently, the new Temple would not merely equal Solomon's Temple: **The latter splendour of this house shall be greater than the former**, . . .

## THE FOUNDING OF THE NEW TEMPLE AS
### THE TURNING POINT
### Haggai 2:10–19

The limits of the third pericope in the book of Haggai are hotly debated. Many scholars (e.g. Elliger, 2.89–90, and Ernst Sellin, 454–9, who includes 1:13) associate the date in 1:15

with 2:15–19. The reasons for this suggestion are clear. Even a casual reader can see the difference between the issue of clean/unclean in vv. 10–14 and the issue of the founding of the Temple in vv. 15–19. In addition, the question/answer format stops with v. 14, where the prophet draws his conclusion; vv. 10–14 speak of "this people" in the third person, while vv. 15–19 address them in the second (see May, *VT* 18 [1968], 190). The real question, however, is whether there is an integral connection between the two passages. If such a connection can be shown, there is no need to associate 1:15a with 2:15–19; the date in 2:10 would cover the entire passage 2:10–19. The issue will be decided in connection with vv. 15–19.

**10–11.** About mid-December (**the twenty-fourth day of the ninth month**), 520 BC, Haggai preached his last two recorded sermons. The redactor reported in the third person a dialogue between Haggai and the priests dealing with the issue of ritual pollution.

**12–13.** The question asked is whether holiness can be transmitted by accidental contact. Meyers and Meyers (78) point to Lev. 10:10–20 as the background for Haggai's question. Lev. 10:10–11 commanded the priests to distinguish the holy from the common, the unclean from the clean, and to teach the people the statutes which Yahweh spoke by the hand of Moses. The verbal harmony between those verses and Haggai is unmistakable.

Haggai set the context (v. 12): if a person was carrying meat for his sacrifice in the **fold of his garments**, and the fold touched something ordinary, did the sanctity of the holy meat "rub off" on the common object? The priests answered in the negative. Next, v. 13, Haggai asked if the sanctified meat touched anything defiled, did the sacrifice become contaminated? The priests answered in the affirmative. It would appear that Haggai had simply ascertained that while holiness was not contagious, pollution was. However, what Haggai really had in mind was an accusation against the people that their prior worship had been unclean.

Before turning to that accusation, however, a point of

translation in v. 13 requires attention. *NRSV* translates Haggai's question: **If one who is unclean by contact with a dead body touches any of these, does it become unclean?** The difficulty lies with the Hebrew phrase *temê' nepeš*. The word *temê'* is an adjective in the construct state, and it means "unclean of". The word *nepeš* can mean "corpse", as it does in Num. 5:2, 9:6, 7, and 10, but those cases employ the preposition *le* and not the construct. One wonders, then, if Haggai did not have a broader meaning in mind than such a specific case of defilement as touching a corpse. Perhaps one should simply translate the phrase "unclean of being", i.e. anything unclean.

**14.** Haggai was asking questions whose answers he and his hearers already knew. Starting on the basis of shared opinions, he attempted to take his hearers to new ground by applying the verdict of **unclean** to a new subject: **this people . . . this nation**. Scholars offer two suggestions identifying the people in question: Jews or Samaritans. Challenging near unanimity that the people were Jews, Johann Wilhelm Rothstein published a small volume (*Juden und Samaritäner*, BWAT 3, ed. R. Kittel [Leipzig, Hinrich, 1908]), arguing that "this people" designated the Samaritans. Sellin adopted Rothstein's thesis in his commentary of 1922; both were followed by an impressive array of German scholars (including Rudolph, Hans Walter Wolff, F. Horst, Elliger, Beuken, Martin Noth, and Gerhard von Rad) as well as others (e.g. Bright and Aage Bentzen). In independent studies Klaus Koch (*ZAW* 79 [1967], 52–66) and May (*VT* 18 [1968], 190–7) successfully challenged Rothstein's view. One key to Rothstein's theory was the contention that vv. 15–19, which obviously spoke to Jews, originated independently of vv. 10–14, so the people in v. 14 need not have been Jews at all. Koch's contribution was to show on form-critical grounds that the passage was a prophecy of salvation, a literary type which includes (1) a review of the past defining the difficult situation confronting the prophet and his hearers (2:11–14), (2) a claim that the present is the moment God will act to change things (2:15), and (3) a depiction of the changed future (2:16–19).

A second key to Rothstein's theory was his contention that Haggai would not have called Jews unclean, a claim May refutes on the grounds that the people were lax in rebuilding the Temple. More importantly, May argues that the word *goy* in 2:14 refers to the Jews, corresponding to its use in Hag. 1:2 and elsewhere in the Old Testament (see also Aelred Cody, "When Is the Chosen People called a Goy?" *VT* 14 (1964), 1–6, and Ronald E. Clements, "Goy," *TDOT*, 2. 426–33).

If Haggai was addressing fellow Judaeans and not Samaritans, how were they "unclean"? Haggai's answer was that **every work of their hands** (i.e. their produce; see David Petersen, 83) **they offer there** (i.e. at the Temple) **was unclean**. Here is the point of Haggai's questions to the priests: the offerings the people brought there were rendered unclean by contact with something defiled. Since there is no charge against the priests for being polluted, and since the word **there** can only refer to the Temple ruins, Haggai must have been saying that the Temple itself was polluted. It is possible he had in mind the altar. Petersen (84) notes that Ezekiel denied any need to cleanse the Temple, but gave instructions for cleansing the altar (43:18–25). Two considerations militate against this conclusion. For one thing the altar had been repaired and put in use earlier (Ezr. 3:1–5). More importantly, Haggai never attacked the altar; his concern lay exclusively with the unfinished Temple. On the other hand, Ackroyd (*Exile*, 168–70) agrees with this interpretation, but goes further to say that Haggai meant that the people themselves were unclean, due to unspecified moral failures. To that suggestion one can only say that the people may well have been guilty, but Haggai does not say so and we have no grounds for crediting him with such a charge. Hence, one should probably conclude that Haggai was saying it was the Temple that was defiled.

**15.** The reader now gains a first hint of the context for these remarks. Haggai mentioned **this day** as the turning point in God's dealings with Judah, a day the redactor identified for the reader in v. 18 as the day the Temple was founded (see comments on Zechariah 4:9). The verb used in 2:18 (*yśd*) usually meant "to lay a foundation" (see 1 Kg. 6:37), but could have a broader meaning. One example is 2 Chr. 24:27, where *NRSV* translates the verb *yśd* "rebuild", presumably on the grounds it makes no sense to speak of Joash's laying the foundations of Solomon's Temple. This means that it is possible to found a temple more than once and that "founding" a temple may involve patronage by a king, a topic which Haggai broached the same day in 2:20–23. It seems to make most sense, then, to assume that Haggai was delivering his sermon on the day of a ceremony "founding" the unfinished Temple. (See Ezr. 6:15, which gave the third day of the twelfth month of the sixth year of Darius [i.e. March, 516] as the date for finishing the Temple.) Petersen (88–90) argues that the ceremony was similar to a Babylonian *kalû* ceremony and was "designed to achieve ritual purification and cultic continuity" (90; see also Petersen, *CBQ* 36 [1974] 366–72, esp. 369–70). Regardless of whether Petersen is correct, Haggai interpreted this founding as a consecration and their previous worship and sacrifices as unclean.

Haggai's prophecy of salvation (v. 19) was based on a two-fold injunction (v. 15 and v. 18) to **consider (what will come to pass) from this day onward**, i.e. the change about to occur. Verse 15 appears to address them as they are about to lay stones in the Temple. Many scholars see the reference as a retrospective to the time they began to lay stones, and that cannot be ruled out, though the claim that the word *māʿlāh* referred to the past seems to be without merit and was rejected by *NRSV*. The better alternative is to see the reference to stone laying as part of the founding ceremony itself.

**16–17.** Whichever is correct, v. 16 opened with the rhetorical question: **How did you fare?** Haggai answered with three examples. **When one came to a heap of twenty measures, there were but ten**. *NRSV* reads the first verb here, and in the next question as well, as an imperfect, when the MT has an imperative. Either way, the point was the same: food was scarce. The same was true of the wine. The person wanting to draw **fifty measures** from his wine vat could draw only **twenty**. The cause for this shortage was **blight, mildew, and**

**hail** (v. 17) sent by God. A blight is normally caused by drought, mildew by excessive moisture, and hail is a constant summer threat to crops. Since blight and mildew are not both likely to occur in the same growing season, one should probably assume Haggai was talking about a series of crop failures, not an unusual occurrence in Palestine where rainfall was marginal. David J. Clark (*BT* 34 [1983], 434–5) notes that the two terms appeared together elsewhere (Deut. 28:22, 1 Kg. 8:37, 2 Chr. 6:28) and probably described the extremes of dampness and dryness.

God's purpose in sending these hardships upon his people was to cause them to return to him. Haggai echoed the message of various other prophets, such as Amos 4:6–12, where God said that he sent famine, drought, blight, mildew, and pestilence to warn Israel to repent and return to God. Since Israel had refused, she must prepare to meet God for punishment. According to Exod. 9:14–16 (which may have been an addition to J), Pharaoh had suffered at the hands of God who could have killed him, but God warned him instead through the plagues. Haggai, thus, stood in a line of theological reflection that interpreted crop failure and other natural disorders as warnings from God.

**18.** The repetition of the admonition to **consider** has been obscured somewhat by the redactor's addition of the date, **the twenty-fourth day of the ninth month**. Haggai's audience did not need to be told the date. Nor did they need to hear that the Temple was being founded; they were present for a ceremony to do just that.

**19.** Haggai's own words probably resume in v 19. *NRSV* translates the first sentence, a question, thus: **Is there any seed left in the barn**? The question actually consists of only three words with an interrogative *he* prefixed to the first. Literally, the question might be translated: "Yet seed in the granary?" As such it seems quite cryptic; so scholars often assume that a verb has dropped out and supply one. Or, they translate as *NRSV* does and attempt to make sense of the question. Haggai might have been reminding them that either they were late planting for some reason or they had run out of food.

*NRSV* treats the second question similarly. "**Do the vine, the fig tree, the pomegranate, and the olive tree still yield nothing?**" This understanding of the two questions seems to give reasonable sense. The last part of the verse, however, predicted a change for the better: **From this day on** (i.e. the day of the founding ceremony) **I will bless you**.

Haggai had made the point that in the past the Judaeans had experienced crop failure because God was warning them against misconduct. The founding ceremony would mark the transition, rendering the Temple site holy once again. The future would be characterized by sufficiency. Grain, grapes, figs, pomegranates, and olives, which comprised the basic staples of the Palestinian diet, would again be abundant. The future was assured because God would now bless his people. Zech. 8:9–13 made the same promise.

ZERUBBABEL AS GOD'S SIGNET RING
**2:20–23**

In the first two sermons, Haggai had spoken to the people, but the redactor had named Joshua (not otherwise mentioned in the book) and Zerubbabel as the major recipients. In this last sermon, however, it was clearly Haggai himself who addressed Zerubbabel on the day of the founding (purification) ceremony itself. Petersen argues (*CBQ* 36 [1974], 366–73) that Zech. 4:9 shows Zerubbabel actually laid a ceremonial stone in that ceremony. It is tempting, therefore, but not necessary, to understand this sermon also as part of the founding ceremony. We have already seen in connection with 2:3 that Haggai's programme for the future had economic and political ramifications. Now, the last of these, namely that founding a temple is a royal act, is spelled out. Not surprisingly, God told Haggai to **speak to Zerubbabel**, the descendant of David.

**21–2.** The message opened by repeating the threat in 2:7 to shake the heavens and the earth, but where that message focused primarily on the economic implications of that threat, this one focused on the political. Specifically, v. 22 said God would **overthrow the throne of the nations and destroy the strength of the kingdoms of the nations**. The phrase "throne of the nations" was presumably a reference to Darius, certainly a conceivable threat in the light of the turmoil surrounding his rise to the throne. The "kingdoms of the nations" might have meant simply Persia, but the phrase more likely had in view all Gentile nations that would be impacted by God's reversal of Judah's fortunes.

**23.** Equally important was the restoration of the Davidic kingdom in Judah under Zerubbabel. Haggai called him God's chosen, his **signet ring**. A signet ring was used by the king to seal official documents. As such, it was worn by the king and would have been guarded to prevent its being stolen or copied. When Jeremiah condemned Coniah (King Jehoiachin), he said in the name of God: "though Coniah . . . were the signet ring on my right hand, yet would I tear you off and give you into the hand of . . . Nebuchadnezzar . . ." (22:24–5). Further, no descendant of Jehoiachin would ever occupy the throne (v. 30). There can be little doubt that Haggai had this very verse in mind as he reversed the prophecy of Jeremiah and proclaimed Zerubbabel, the grandson of Jehoiachin, God's signet ring. Whereas Jeremiah had seen Nebuchadnezzar as the king wielding the sword for God, Haggai instead saw Zerubbabel as the king (Georg Sauer, "Serubbabel in der Sicht Haggais und Sacharjas", 203). Ackroyd (*Exile*, 165–6) argues on two grounds that the term was primarily non-political. (1) The Persians saw no reason to recall Zerubbabel. Presumably Ackroyd has in mind Ezr. 6:7, which, however, did not name the governor. (2) The point of the passage was clearly the reversal of Judah's fortunes by God himself. How the reversal of fortunes envisioned here could fail to have political ramifications Ackroyd does not say. It would seem better, therefore, to say that the passage was both political and theological.

Haggai also called Zerubbabel God's **servant**, which was certainly reminiscent of David as God's servant (see e.g. 1 Kg. 11:34) and Ezekiel's picture of the restored monarch as servant (34:23–4) associated with the new Temple (37:24–8). This designation most likely reflected the estimation of Jehoiachin and his family held by the exiles in Babylon and those who had returned (whether under Sheshbazzar, Zerubbabel, or someone else). Further, the political programme of Haggai anticipated the restoration of the Davidic monarchy under God. Zerubbabel was to be the ring on God's hand, the seal of God's authority, but not an oriental despot (see Klaus Seybold, *Jud.* 27–8 [1971–72], 71–73, and Beyse, *Königserwartungen*, 66–7).

## SUMMARY

The prophet Haggai has emerged as an eschatological prophet, who saw the rebuilding and consecrating of the new Temple as necessary to bring in the new age. He addressed his first two, perhaps three, sermons to the people at large, while his final sermon was addressed directly to Zerubbabel. His message included not just cultic concerns, but economic and political considerations as well. He looked forward to a reversal of the relative fortunes of Israel and the surrounding powers. Instead of tribute money going out, it would come in and enrich both Temple and people. Zerubbabel, a leader of the exiles with a Persian office, would become the new David. This would be possible because he was a descendant of David through Jehoiachin. Thus in the post-exilic period, Jeremiah's condemnation of Jehoiachin's progeny was reversed, along with the status of Judah itself. A new day was being born, precisely with the "founding" of the Temple.

The redactor, obviously working at least a little later, in a period in which the prestige of Joshua was rising, introduced Haggai's first two sermons as messages directed primarily at the two leaders. The redactor saw both men as responsible for the work on the Temple. His inclusion of Joshua in the project suggests some priestly leaning on his part. Further, the redactor emphasized that Haggai the prophet was the messenger, the mediator through whom God spoke. Thus, he saw no conflict between the two roles of prophet and priest.

As a prediction of things about to happen in the sixth century, the book of Haggai seems to have been too optimistic. When the Temple was finished, gifts from the nations did not pour in to beautify it. Nor did Zerubbabel become the new Davidic king. That the economic conditions of the people improved is unlikely as well. Nevertheless, the message of the book did continue to speak to the post-exilic community. This was probably so because it kept alive a meaningful hope for a reversal of fortunes. It also spoke and continues to speak in more general terms of God's care for his people. On the basis of his nature, his people are called to remain faithful.

# INTRODUCTION

to

Zechariah 1–8

The opinion that Zechariah 1–8 (often called First or Proto-Zechariah) arose separately from Zechariah 9–14 (Second or Deutero-Zechariah) goes back at least to the sixteenth century scholar Joseph Mede, who observed that Zech. 11:12–13 apparently is attributed to Jeremiah in Mt. 27:9–10. From the early eighteenth century on, scholars have articulated a number of differences between the two parts of Zechariah (see the review in Otzen, *Studien* 11–34; or Baldwin, 62–70), the most telling of which are the following.

(1) In Zechariah 1–8, references to the prophet as well as other persons and events from the sixth century appear frequently, whereas none appear in Zechariah 9–14. To be sure Greece and Judah's neighbours are mentioned in Second Zechariah, but in such a way that no widely accepted inference about the date of the chapters can be drawn. In terms of allusions to historical persons and events, Zechariah 1–8 appears much more similar to the book of Haggai than to Zechariah 9–14. Indeed, the styles of Zechariah 1–8 and the book of Haggai are in places so similar that scholars often conclude that the materials were edited by the same person.

(2) Zechariah 9–11 and 12–14 appear to have very similar superscriptions, which in turn are so similar to the superscription of the book of Malachi that scholars have sometimes concluded all three were anonymous oracles added to Proto-Zechariah (see O. Eissfeldt, *The Old Testament: An Introduction* [New York and Evanston; Harper and Row, 1965], 440).

(3) Zechariah 12–14 exhibits stylistic features very unlike Zechariah 9–11 (see Y. T. Radday and D. Wickman, "Unity of Zechariah", 30–55), suggesting that more than one hand is responsible for Zechariah 9–14.

This commentary, therefore, will adopt the typical scholarly judgment that chapters 1–8 and 9–14 arose separately from each other and underwent very different redactional histories. Such similarities as do exist between First and Second Zechariah are best explained as the result of the deliberate use of motifs in Proto-Zechariah by Deutero-Zechariah (see Mason, *ZAW* 88 (1976), 227–39). In this chapter attention will be focused only on First Zechariah.

## A. AUTHORSHIP

The prophet Zechariah was a contemporary of Haggai. The two are named in Ezr. 5:1 as the prophets who urged the rebuilding of the Temple in 520. Zechariah was the son (Ezr. 5:1) or grandson (Zech. 1:1) of a man named Iddo. One person with that name was a priest mentioned in Neh. 12:4, 16 as someone who had returned to Judah under Zerubbabel and Joshua. Most scholars assume Zechariah was descended from him, though that is not certain, and Robert R. Wilson (*Prophecy and Society in Ancient Israel* [Philadelphia, Fortress, 1980], 289) suggests that Zechariah might have descended from the Iddo mentioned in 2 Chr. 9:29, 12:15 as a prophet and visionary. The book says little else about the prophet, but his association with the rebuilding of the Temple and with the repatriates Zerubbabel and Joshua make it likely that he himself had returned from Babylon.

## B. LITERARY HISTORY AND STRUCTURE

As in the case of the book of Haggai, the reader must reckon with the presence of a redactor who edited the work of Zechariah. As First Zechariah now stands, it consists of three sections (1:1–6; 1:7–6:15; 7:1–8:23), each provided with a date and various formulae characteristic of the style of the redactor of the book of Haggai. David J. Clark (*BT* 36 [1985], 334) concludes that Haggai is the only *OT* book to show close structural similarities with Zech. 7:1–8:23. In addition, the redactor of Zech. 8:9–13 is familiar with Hag. 1:6–11; 2:18, i.e. with the final form of the book. Finally, the third section shows such similarity to the first that some scholars (e.g. R.

Press, *ZAW* 54 [1936], 44) suggest they originally circulated independently of the second section. While that opinion may be extreme, it does point to differences within First Zechariah which show that the book had a literary history.

To trace this history, one should begin with an analysis of the various types of literature in Zechariah 1–8. The most conspicuous material is a series of eight visions, found between 1:7 and 6:15, that Zechariah is said to have seen on the night of the twenty-fourth day of the eleventh month of the second year of Darius (i.e. January of 519). In addition to visions, the book contains a number of prophetic oracles, which appear in the introduction to the book (1:1–7), interspersed within the visions (1:14–17; 3:7–10; 4:6b–10a), at the end of the visionary section (6:15), and again in the last section of the book in 7:4–14 and chapter eight. The book also contains two exhortations, in 2:6–13 (Heb. 2:10–17) and 6:9–15.

Given the indications that 1:1–6 and 7:1–8:23 achieved their present form from the redactor, one should look to the second section (1:7–6:15) for the earliest materials. All three types of material appear here. Some scholars routinely eliminate the oracles and exhortations as additions, but visions frequently include oracles (see Burke O. Long, *JBL* 90 [1971], 359–64), and later apocalyptic literature characteristically combined visions with exhortations. The real issue is whether all the material in the second section is self-consistent.

One passage, 4:6b–10a, is so inconsistent with its context (the vision of a candlestick flanked by olive trees) that translators of the *JB* and the *NEB* rearrange the text, and scholars are overwhelmingly of the opinion that the verses constitute a later addition. Without those verses the explanation of the vision introduced in 4:4–5 continues in v. 10b: the seven lamps on the lampstand are the seven eyes of the Lord, and the two olive trees beside the lamp are the "sons of oil". The intruding verses report two oracles to Zerubbabel, rather than to Zechariah.

Scholars sometimes exclude the exhortation at the end of the night visions (6:9–15) on form-critical grounds, but that is unnecessary. Even so, one may ask whether the passage is

internally consistent. Again, the answer is no. As the passage
stands, God commands Zechariah to collect silver and gold
from three newly returned exiles, have Josiah the son of
Zephaniah fashion crowns from the metals, and place them
in the Temple as a memorial. Scholarly attention has been
drawn to the term "crowns", primarily because of 6:11b,
which commands Zechariah to place it/them(?) on the head
of Joshua. There are two problems with v. 11b. (1) There is
no direct object for the verb set (i.e. no pronoun corresponding
to the word "it" in the *NRSV*). (2) While God tells Zechariah
to crown Joshua in v. 11b, vv. 12–13 originally referred to
Zerubbabel, whom 4:9 emphatically charged with building
the Temple.

These two problems will be dealt with in the commentary.
Here it is sufficient to note that vv. 12–13 thus contradict v.
11b. More importantly, however, the three verses also interrupt the exhortation, though scholars seem not to have
noticed. If a reader simply jumps from 6:11b ("and make a
crown", literally "crowns") to 6:14, the meaning of the original text becomes quite clear: the entire exhortation originally
spoke of crowns for the three returning exiles and for Josiah.
That means that 6:11b–13 (like 4:6b–10a) were added and
the coronation of Joshua (or Zerubbabel) is secondary.

A third passage within 1:7 to 6:15 often suspected of being
secondary is 3:1–10, a vision of the cleansing of the high priest
Joshua (see, among others, Seybold, *Bilder zum Tempelbau*, 16–
17; and Elliger, 2.103, 119–22). Several features distinguish
this vision from the other seven. (1) In the others Zechariah
does not understand the visions, so an angel interprets them
for him, while in 3:1–10 Zechariah both understands what is
happening and participates in the procedure. (2) There is no
interpreting angel in 3:1–10. (3) The other seven visions use
stereotypical introductory phrases missing from 3:1–10. (4)
In the third vision, the interpreting angel leaves Zechariah,
but is told by another angel to return to **that young man**
(2:4, Heb. 2:8) and speak. The man might be the one going
to measure Jerusalem, but it could as easily be Zechariah. If
so, the phrase would be important for this discussion. The

interpreting angel does not return in 3:1–10, but he does in 4:1.

Either way it would appear that 3:1–10 did not belong to the original sequence of visions, which would have consisted of seven. The structure of these visions was as follows.

IV.

(4:1–6a, 10b–11, 13–14)

God at the Centre

| III. | V. |
|---|---|
| (2:1–5) | (5:1–4) |
| Measure | Cleanse |
| Jerusalem | Jerusalem |
| | |
| II. | VI. |
| (1:18–21) | (5:5–11) |
| Destroy | Send wickedness |
| Babylon | to Babylon |
| | |
| I. | VII |
| (1:7–17) | (6:1–8) |
| Coloured horses; nations | Horses and wagons; God |
| at rest | at rest |

In the first three visions, Zechariah saw God's turning toward Jerusalem with compassion and promising to rebuild the Temple (1:7–17), his punishment of those who had exiled God's people (1:18–21, Heb. 2:1–4), and the rebuilding of Jerusalem (2:1–5, Heb. 2:5–9). The first admonition (2:6–13, Heb. 2:10–17) drew out the implications of those visions for the readers, namely that they should return from Babylon in light of God's returning to Jerusalem. The fourth vision (4:1–6a, 10b–14, perhaps minus v. 12), which symbolized God's presence by means of a lampstand, stood at the centre of the series. The last three visions depicted God's banishment of sins and sinners from Judah (5:1–4) to Babylon (5:5–11) and God's rest (6:1–8) in light of all he had done to correct the evils Zechariah complained about in the first vision. The closing exhortation (6:9–15) showed that returning exiles had a stake in rebuilding the Temple and predicted that they would return to help with the rebuilding project.

It seems safe to conclude, then, that the exhortations belonged originally to the series of night visions. If that is true, they identified the original audience to whom the visions were directed: the exiles in Babylon. Assuming that Zechariah had already returned to Jerusalem, this original series would have been committed to writing and sent back to the exiles.

What should one make of the three passages (4:6b–10a, 6:11b–13, 3:1–10) excluded from the visions in 1:7–6:15 as secondary? The most obvious feature they have in common is their interest in Zerubbabel and Joshua and their part in the rebuilding of the Temple, i.e. the events of 520. Most likely, then, someone (quite possibly Zechariah himself) issued a "second, revised and enlarged" edition of the night visions by adding the three passages about the Davidic prince Zerubbabel and the high priest Joshua. This version would have been aimed at the Jerusalem community itself. It was intended as a programme for the restoration of the cult centre on Mount Zion. Its special concern was to show continuity between the first and second Temples (see Seybold, *Bilder zum Tempelbau*, 107). The structure of the visions was not significantly affected, since the cleansing of Joshua (3:1–10) stood next to the centrepiece, the vision of God. The date of this edition may well have been the date given in 1:7, the twenty-fourth day of the eleventh month of the second year of Darius. If so, the date of the original edition would have been earlier (see the suggestions of G. A. Smith, *Twelve Prophets*, 2.255–6; Kurt Galling, *VT* 2 [1952], 18–36; and Lawrence Sinclair, *BR* 20 [1975], 36–47), though how much earlier is impossible to say.

The latest date given in Zechariah 1–8 is the fourth day of the ninth month of the fourth year of Darius, i.e. November 518. The final redaction of the book probably occurred between that date and the time of the completion of the Temple in April of 516. (See comments on 7:1.) The editor of Haggai/Zechariah 1–8 was responsible for that edition, which involved adding sections one and three as well as

attaching the book of Haggai. Section one (1:1–6) may well
have been a creation of the redactor. It was written in the third
person and intended to establish Zechariah as the legitimate
successor of the pre-exilic prophets.

The third section (7:1–8:23) is framed by a question and
answer narrative reminiscent of the narrative context the
redactor provided for the message of Haggai (1:2–15a). In
7:1–3 messengers arrived in Jerusalem to ask Zechariah
whether people should continue to fast in observance of the
destruction of the Temple in Jerusalem in 586. The reason
for the question was, presumably, the progress toward
rebuilding the Temple under Zerubbabel. If the question was
answered at all, the answer came in 8:18–19. The balance of
chapter seven consisted of a discussion of fasting. Chapter
eight apparently was edited to include ten oracles, mostly
prophecies of salvation, at least one of which was 8:18–19.
The oracles in chapter 8:2–8 cohered nicely with the hope for
Jerusalem expressed in the night visions. They may well have
been authentic utterances of Zechariah, but the present form
of section three derived from the hand of the redactor of
Haggai/Zechariah 1–8. *BHS* prints the oracular material in
section three (indeed in all sections) as poetry, while *NRSV*
prints all of Zechariah 1–8 as prose.

## C. MESSAGE

The message of Zechariah 1–8 echoed much of what Haggai
said. Once again, God took an interest in human affairs,
directing them, as it were, from off-stage. The foreign powers
had exceeded God's intention in destroying Judah (1:15), a
theme reminiscent of Isa. 10:13–19 and 40:1–2. The time of
eschatological reversal was now at hand (1:16–17; 2:18–21
[Heb. 2:1–4]). God would purify his people (5:1–11), who
would live again in Jerusalem (1:17; 8:2–8). About the other
nations Zechariah said nothing, but the redactor included
them in his vision of the future (8:20–23, so Elliger, 2.142).

Like Haggai, Zechariah clearly thought Zion was God's
special place, and the rebuilding of the Temple was a pre-

requisite for ushering in the new age. Assuming Zechariah added the materials in 4:6b–10a, 6:11b–13, and 3:1–10, he thought Zerubbabel and Joshua were God's special people. He insisted (4:9; 6:12–13) that Zerubbabel, the Davidic prince, had founded the Temple, would complete the project, and would take his place on the throne of David. Going beyond Haggai, Zechariah predicted that Joshua the high priest would rule over the Temple (3:7), in harmony with Zerubbabel.

Christian scholars in particular have written about the messianism of First Zechariah, indeed of the whole book. (See, for example, Robert T. Siebeneck, *CBQ* 19 (1957), 312–28; and Smith, 175–180). Elliger (2.131–2) even argues that late interpolations turned Zechariah's specific references to Zerubbabel into general predictions about the Messiah and that the LXX construed the "Branch" of 3:8 and 6:12 as a priestly king on the model of Ps. 110. Baldwin (*VT* 14 [1964], 93–7) suggests that the term "Branch" was used often in the *OT* to designate a priest-king.

There can be no doubt that Zechariah saw Zerubbabel as the new David, the messiah in the typical Old Testament sense of the anointed king. Further, the mission of Zerubbabel to rebuild the Temple was eschatological in the sense that it would usher in a radically improved future here on earth, especially for Israel. It is difficult to find anything more specifically messianic than this. The fact that in 3:8 and 6:12 the term "Branch" designates the high priest Joshua suggests that a non-regal reinterpretation of Zechariah's hopes for Zerubbabel emerged in light of the rise to prominence of the high priest in the post-exilic community.

Recently several scholars have investigated the relationship of Zechariah 1–8 to the apocalyptic movement. Hartmut Gese (*ZTK* 13 [1957], 38) has argued that Proto-Zechariah exhibits such apocalyptic features as a presentation of two aeons, otherworldly hope, a uniting of universal and individual eschatology (at least in the additions), angels, spiritual beings, messianism, the place of salvation, and the state of the unsaved. Other scholars (e.g. S. Amsler, "Zacharie et l'origine de l'apocalyptique", 227–31; and Robert North, "Prophecy to Apocalyptic via Zechariah", 47–71) argue that the chapters constitute only a precursor to apocalyptic. Clearly they exhibit some of the literary characteristics of apocalyptic literature, but they do not exhibit the theology characteristic of apocalyptic literature. Specifically, apocalyptic literature thinks of the end of this world, not simply the end of the exile as one finds in Zechariah.

## D. CONTENTS

1:1–6      Do Not Be Like Your Fathers
1:7–17     Vision of the Horsemen: God's Return to Jerusalem
1:18–21    Vision of the Horns and the Smiths: the End of Foreign Control
2:1–5      Vision of a Man Measuring Jerusalem: the Return of Prosperity
2:6–13     Exhortation to the Exiles: Return Home
3:1–10     Vision of the Cleansing of Joshua
4:1–14     Vision of the Lampstand and Olive Trees: God's Presence
5:1–4      Vision of the Flying Scroll: the Cleansing of Jerusalem
5:5–11     Vision of a Woman in a Basket: Wickedness Sent to Babylon
6:1–8      Vision of the Four Chariots: God at Rest
6:9–15     Exhortation to Returned Exiles: Make Crowns as a Memorial
7:1–14     The Question about Fasting
8:1–23     Ten Words about the Future

# COMMENTARY

## on

## Zechariah 1–8

# DO NOT BE LIKE YOUR FATHERS
## 1:1-6

These verses are dated **in the eighth month, in the second year of Darius**, i.e. mid-October to mid-November, 520 BCE, about a month or so before the last two oracles of Haggai (2:10–19, 20–23). The date is unusual for Haggai and Zechariah 1–8 in that it omits the day of the month. If 1:1–6 belonged to the latest edition of First Zechariah and came from the redactor's hand in its present form, the date may have been a redactional device making the career of Zechariah overlap with that of Haggai's. The structure of the passage is intricate. It opened with a superscription (v. 1) and a historical retrospect (v. 2). Next, at the heart of the passage, came a warning to the post-exilic communities to avoid the mistakes of their ancestors and an admonition to return to Yahweh (vv. 3–4a). The remainder of v. 4 summarized the message of the pre-exilic or former prophets. Verses 5–6a drew an object lesson from the historical experience of the pre-exilic community, who had to learn the hard way to obey the word of God that came through the prophets. The passage ended by quoting their confession that God was justified in carrying out the threats he had made.

**1.** The name "Zechariah" meant "Yah(weh) has remembered". The inclusion of his genealogy is typical (cf. Hos. 1:1, Isa. 1:1, Jl. 1:1, and Zeph. 1:1), and contrasts with the designation of Haggai simply as "the prophet".

**2.** This verse set the context for all that would follow. In the past, God had been angry with the ancestors of the people (Heb., your [plural] fathers). His anger, of course, had resulted in the overthrow of the Davidic kingdom and the exile to Babylon, events in whose aftermath the people still lived. Nor could those ancestors plead ignorance; v. 4 reminded the reader of the series of prophets God had sent to warn the people of his wrath and the coming punishment.

**3–4a.** God commanded Zechariah to address **them**. Strictly speaking, the antecedent for the pronoun would appear to be the ancestors mentioned in v. 2. It makes no sense to tell Zechariah to address his dead ancestors (v. 5), however, so the instruction must have meant that Zechariah should address his own generation. The message to his community was introduced with the same solemn formula as the warnings of the former prophets: **Thus says the Lord of hosts**. (See the comments on Hag. 1:2 for a discussion of the title Lord of hosts.) The term **former**, used only here and in Zech. 7:7, 12, did not refer to the section of the Hebrew Bible by that title (Jos., Jg., Sam., Kg.), but to the pre-exilic prophets seen as a group.

The message was comprised of two elements. The first is the admonition to **return** to God, coupled with the promise that he would return to the people. It is not quite clear what was meant by returning to God. Was this sentence a warning that the people were living in disobedience of God? If so, did this verse have in mind the delay in rebuilding the Temple? Or was this sentence a warning against the more widespread violation of God's law of which the pre-exilic ancestors were thought to be guilty? Either way, God next promised to return to the people. In the visions of Zechariah and in the book of Haggai, the full realization of this promise was conditioned upon the rebuilding of the Temple, but the return to Jerusalem itself was expressed as a certainty based upon God's anger with the nations for their excesses in punishing Judah (1:16).

**4b–5.** The result of God's sending his message by the prophets to the ancestors was their refusal to hear and heed. Neither they nor the prophets themselves were still alive in Zechariah's day (v. 5). By contrast, God's word to the prophets was still alive and operative. The words of the prophets had clearly become something much more than the words of men to their own contemporaries; they had become the abiding word of God valid over generations.

**6.** The disasters about which the pre-exilic ancestors had been warned came to pass. They had repented too late and could only confess that God had done to them as he had warned. They had no one to blame but themselves for what had happened. Though this verse did not actually mention the destruction of Jerusalem and the exile, those events were almost surely what was meant. Thus, the opening section of Zechariah functioned to exonerate God from any blame for the events of 586 and to fix the blame squarely on the ancestors themselves. This section also carried a warning to its post-exilic audience: **do not be like your ancestors**. They must heed Zechariah's message or they would suffer a fate like that suffered by their ancestors.

## VISION OF THE HORSEMEN: GOD'S RETURN TO JERUSALEM
### 1:7–17

The second major section of First Zechariah opened with a vision of a man riding a red horse with horses of other colours behind him. When Zechariah asked the meaning of his vision, he was told the horses had been patrolling the earth. They reported to the interpreting angel that all the earth **remains at rest**, that is, that God had not yet begun the eschatological reversal. The interpreting angel then commissioned Zechariah to proclaim that Yahweh was jealous for Jerusalem, angry with the nations, and was returning to Jerusalem with compassion and with the intention to rebuild and to repopulate the city. Verses 14–17 constitute an oracle, which many scholars regard as secondary. To be sure, v. 13 would make a suitable ending to the vision, but would leave the interpreting angel's question of when God would act essentially unanswered. The concluding verses appear to report the content of the **gracious and comforting words** mentioned in v. 13. The verses also appear to supply the entire passage with the overtones of a call vision (cf. Long, *JBL*, 90 [1971], 361).

**7.** The vision was introduced by a second superscription, this one including the date. May suggests (*JBL* 57 [1938], 173–5) that the date was significant for its proximity to the spring New Year. May attempted to interpret the visions as a unit preparing his audience for that day. It seems more likely, however, that the redactor chose the date because it is precisely two months after Haggai's last two recorded oracles, given at a public ceremony. Thus the "second, revised and enlarged" edition of the night visions would have carried forward the programme announced in Hag. 2:10–19, 20–23.

**8.** Zechariah saw his visions **in the night**. Generally speaking, the *OT* distinguished dreams from visions, though several verses (e.g. Isa. 29:7, Job 33:15, Dan. 2:28, 4:7, 7:1) used the terms interchangeably. Either could be a medium of God's revelation. Zechariah's visions were not presented as dreams, though his state of mind when he received them could be compared to sleep (4:1). Situating the visions at night functioned symbolically, indicating that the rest of humankind remained in the dark, while Zechariah sees God's future with clarity (M. Bič, *Nachtgesichte*, 10). The phrase also calls to mind the image of the prophet as God's watchman waiting for the dawn (Mason, 31).

Zechariah saw **a man riding on a horse**. The man was not named, allowing May to identify him with God (*JBL* 57 [1938], 174, n. 8). Verse 11 designated the same being as an angel. He is further to be distinguished from the interpreting angel, who is invariably identified as the angel who spoke with Zechariah (see Clark, *BT* 33 [1982], 213–16).

Zechariah noted the colours of the horses, which would be possible in a vision but not at night in the phenomenal world. The first horse was identified as **red**. Other horses were described as **red**, **sorrel**, and **white**. The repetition of the colour red, plus some differences in the versions, led W. D. McHardy (*ZAW* 103 [1968], 179) to make the speculative suggestion that here and in chapter 6, the author abbreviated names for colours, which originally would have been red, yellow, black, and white. There is, however, no compelling reason to make the colours in 1:8 and 6:2–3 the same. In terms of colours used of horses, one might suggest that the colour red probably designates a roan, while the term sorrel (Heb. *śĕruqîm*) suggests a bright chestnut. Meyers and Meyers (113) note that the Heb. word represents a mixture of red and white. The *KJV* reads "speckled", and *NEB* offers "dappled", based on the Vulg. and Pesh. "Dapple", however, is not a colour, but a description. It would seem less likely than "sorrel" in view of the colours specified for the other horses. The number of horses is not given, but commentators often assume there were four because of parallels to 6:1–8.

The man/angel was **standing** (or perhaps waiting) **among the myrtles in the glen**. The myrtle was an evergreen shrub, whose branches were cut for use in building booths for the Feast of Tabernacles (Neh. 8:15). It is mentioned among the trees that would flourish in the prosperity of the Messianic age (Isa. 41:19, 55:13; see Mitchell, *Haggai-Zechariah*, 118). The LXX apparently read *hehārîm* (mountains) instead of *hah-ădasîm* (myrtles). Either way, scholars often interpret the setting as the gateway to heaven, which may well be correct. Van der Woude ("Söhne des Öls, 267) points to the Gilgamesh Epic, in which the Eastern entrance to heaven was marked by trees. Others argue, however, that Zechariah had in mind a garden in the Kidron Valley outside Jerusalem where myrtles grew in pre-exilic times, but the phrase seems too general to have such a specific place in mind.

**9–10.** Zechariah asked the interpreting angel, who had not been mentioned previously, to explain what he was seeing. The angel agreed, but the angel on horseback actually made the explanation. The horses had been sent to **patrol the earth**. The verb translated **patrol** is a Hithpael infinitive construct, meaning "to walk to and fro" (cf. Gen. 3:8; Job 2:2). The horses crisscrossed the whole earth, their riders gathering information to report to God or his angel (v. 11). Baldwin (95) suggests that they functioned like the mounted messengers in the Persian Empire, who kept the monarch abreast of all that was happening throughout the Empire. The abruptness with which the interpreting angel was introduced and the lack of precision about the identity of the two angels led Mason (36) to suggest that the vision had been recorded earlier and brought into the series of night visions when the others were written. Two other considerations make this suggestion seem possible. (1) The vision seems to reflect an earlier time period than 520, and (2) it combines elements of a call vision with elements similar to the last vision (6:1–8).

**11.** After the man/angel explained to Zechariah that the horses had been patrolling the earth, **they** spoke to him. In a vision it would be possible for horses to speak, and that may be what Zechariah had in mind. More likely, however, Zechariah intended for the reader to understand (though he did not say so) that all the horses had riders, who did the talking, perhaps through the angel who had been explaining their role. They reported the result of their patrolling the earth: **the whole earth remains at peace**.

The phrase poorly described the year 520, when Darius was still attempting to secure control of the Persian Empire. Consequently, Mitchell (*Haggai-Zechariah*, 121–3) argues that the first vision constituted a retrospective. As shown above, it is more likely that the vision was originally composed prior to the events of 520 and enlarged and reapplied to that year. (Indeed, Zechariah could have received his call before the fall of Babylon in 539.) Regardless, the phrase reported that conditions had not changed. As this vision and the next made clear, the decisive defeat of the enemies lay yet in the future; Cyrus's defeat of Babylon had had little real impact on the lives of the exiles who remained far from home.

**12.** The angel of the Lord responded to the news with the question on the heart of Zechariah and his people: **how long?** The question carried with it the conviction that bad conditions had already continued too long. The heart of the issue was that God had failed to show **mercy** or compassion on Jerusalem and Judah. Simply put, the city still lay uninhabited and in ruins, with its population still in Babylon. World kingdoms and emperors were not the cause for Judah's continuing state of affairs. Rather, the cause was God's continuing anger. As First Zechariah now stands, the reader knows that God was justified in punishing his people for their sins. No less for the final redactor than for Zechariah, however, the time for God to act had arrived.

The duration of God's anger was given as **seventy years**. C. F. Whitley (*VT* 4 [1954], 63–4) argues that this phrase was added by a later editor, who had in mind the time from 586–516, i.e. the time between the fall of the Temple and its reconstruction. While his view is not impossible, it is more likely that the term was taken from Jer. 29:10 (rather than vice versa, as Whitley contends), which spoke of the duration of the Neo-Babylonian Empire. The phrase then would have been turned into a general designation for the duration of the exile, Zech. 1:12 being the earliest surviving example of the reapplication of the number. Indeed, 2 Chr. 36:21 (which cited the prophet Jeremiah as its source) gave the reason the number caught the post-exilic imagination: so that the land might have its Sabbath rest. Seventy years, of course, is ten Sabbath years. Finally, Lipinski (*VT* 20 [1970], 38) thinks the number may also agree with ancient Mesopotamian expectations about the duration of divine wrath against a sanctuary or city. He points to an Assyrian inscription that says Marduk should have been angry with Babylon for seventy years, but relented much earlier.

**13.** God responded to his angel's question with **gracious** (good, pleasing, agreeable) and compassionate words spoken to the interpreting angel. The response was reported in vv. 14–17 in the form of a charge commissioning Zechariah to proclaim God's message. Verses 13–17, therefore, functioned like a call vision.

**14a.** The interpreting angel repeated God's answer, conveying it to Zechariah. The first component was a command to **Proclaim this message**. Actually, this specific injunction was rare in prophetic speech, but instructions to preach were integral to call visions. Next came the messenger formula so characteristic of prophetic speech: **Thus says the Lord**. The formula was repeated in vv. 16 and 17. In v. 17 the command to **proclaim** was repeated, introducing a second, short oracle.

**14b–15.** The first oracle moved in two directions. On the one hand God reported that he was **jealous for Jerusalem and Zion**. The term "jealous" implied an exclusive relationship between God and his people. They had failed to keep their commitments, so God had allowed other nations to conquer them. Now, since he was dependable, he was about to act on Jerusalem's behalf. This act, however, would have consequences for other peoples, specifically the nations reported to be **at ease**. God said that he was **only a little angry** with the pre-exilic ancestors, but the nations carried God's punishment to excess (cf. Isa. 10:5–11). The implication was that they would be punished for making the disaster worse than God intended, or Jerusalem deserved.

**16.** The first oracle concluded with a message of salvation. In view of the excesses of the nations, God would return to Jerusalem with compassion. The consequences of his turning would be positive in two ways that represented a radical improvement for his people. First, the Temple would be rebuilt. Second, a **measuring line** (used by builders) would be stretched over the city, signifying that it too would be rebuilt and repopulated.

**17.** The second, short oracle completed the thought of v. 16. Not only would God rebuild the Temple and Jerusalem, it and his other cities would once again receive his blessing and **overflow with prosperity**. The prophecy of salvation concludes with another promise that God would **comfort Zion** and **choose Jerusalem**. The word *'ôd* (**again**) appears four times in the verse (though *NRSV* translates the first occurrence by "further"), emphasizing the renewing of an already existing bond between God and the people.

### VISION OF THE HORNS AND THE SMITHS: THE END OF FOREIGN CONTROL
### 1:18–21 (Heb. 2:1–4)

Overall, the second vision portrayed foreign conquerors who had defeated Judah being defeated themselves by agents under God's control. It continued the basic thought of the oracles in the first vision. The imagery of the verses, however, is difficult to understand, which will become obvious in the discussion that follows.

**18–19.** Zechariah saw **four horns**, which were identified as those who scattered **Judah and Jerusalem**. (The name **Israel** does not appear in the LXX and may be a gloss.) The number need not signify four separate kingdoms. It may instead indicate completeness, i.e. all the nations who fought against Judah. Whoever was meant, the Babylonians were certainly included; and Galling (*VT* 2 [1952], 21) argues that Zechariah intended only the Babylonians, whose king took the title of "Lord of the four quarters".

The word *qĕrānôt* (horns) usually designated animal horns or projections at the corners of altars. Meyers and Meyers (135) argue that Zechariah saw horns on a metal headpiece, symbolic of divine or political power. R. M. Good (*Bib* 63 [1982], 58) suggests that the "horns" represented the whole animals which were seen by Zechariah. According to v. 21 the horns were **struck down**, but the verb used is anything but clear and provides no further information about what Zechariah saw. In view of the use of the term "horn" as a symbol for aggressive power elsewhere in the *OT* (e.g., Ps. 75:10, 92:10; Jer. 48:25; Dan. 7:7–8, 11–12), it is not necessary to press further for the particular type of horn.

**20–21.** Next, God showed Zechariah four **blacksmiths** (*ḥārāsîm*) coming toward him. Actually, the term could designate workers in wood, metal, or stone, so the translation "craftsmen" might be better. When Zechariah inquired about their mission, God told him they had come to **terrify** and to **strike down** the nations who had oppressed (literally, lifted a horn) against Judah. The verb *lĕyadôt* is usually treated as a Piel infinitive construct of the root *ydh* (to throw or cast), but both the form and the meaning have been challenged. A similar verb *gd'* ("cut down") appears with *qarnê* (horns of) in Ps. 75:10 (MT 75:11). If v. 21 is similar, it would mean that the craftsmen were coming to cut off the horns. Interpreted politically, that image would probably mean that God was about to disarm his enemies.

The second vision, therefore, points to a coming political reordering. It is not clear whether the craftsmen should be identified with any particular power (e.g. the Persians). The point was that God was acting through natural or supernatural means to liberate his people.

## VISION OF A MAN MEASURING JERUSALEM: THE RETURN OF PROSPERITY
### 2:1–5 (Heb. 2:5–9)

In the third vision Zechariah saw a man (presumably another angel) holding a builder's measuring line. In this vision (as in 3:1–10) Zechariah entered into the action by asking him directly what he was doing. The angel replied that he was going to measure Jerusalem. The interpreting angel appeared, walking toward Zechariah, and he was told by yet another angel to run to Zechariah and carry him a message from God. Once again the message was conveyed in a short oracle at the end of the vision (vv. 4b–5). The setting for this vision was clearly not Jerusalem, since that was where the angel was going. Since the setting of the first vision was heaven, the setting for this vision was probably heaven also.

**1–2.** Mitchell (*Haggai, Zechariah*, 137) recalls that the measuring line had been used by Amos as a symbol of the partition of Samaria by foreigners (Am. 7:17) and that the author of 2 Kg. 21:13 employed the same symbol for the destruction of Jerusalem. On the other hand, Ezekiel 40–48 spoke of a man who measured the temple area and the city prior to its rebuilding. Hence, the prophet was really asking whether the angel's visit was for woe or weal, and it was not until the prophet heard the oracle in Zech. 2:4–5 that he learned for sure that this visit was positive. Here he learned only that the angel was going to Jerusalem to measure the city.

**3.** The angel with the measuring line could not have been the interpreting angel, for he appeared here for the first time in the vision. He was met by yet a third angel, who conveyed to him a message for Zechariah.

**4–5.** The heart of the vision was once again given in an oracle, this time to someone identified as **that young man**. If the referent was Zechariah, the verse supplied a hint as to his age. However, the "young man" might have been the angel going to measure Jerusalem. The oracle, a prophecy of salvation, included two components. First, Jerusalem would once again teem with so many people it could not be walled in.

Obviously, that expression of hope stood in marked contrast to the actual appearance of Jerusalem at that time. Indeed, as late as the time of Nehemiah, inhabitants for the city had to be drafted from the populace of Judah (Neh. 11:1–2). Second, the absence of a secure wall would not leave the populace threatened, because God himself would surround the city as a wall of fire. As such he would protect it from external foes. Further, he would once again fill it with his glory, surely a reference to his Temple from which the glory of God had been driven by the sins of God's people, according to Ezek. 11:22–3.

## EXHORTATION TO THE EXILES: RETURN HOME
### 2:6–13 (Heb. 2:10–17)

Because 2:6–13 interrupted the series of visions, many scholars consider these verses an addition. However, later apocalyptic work was characterized by exactly this juxtaposing of visionary and hortatory materials. It seems better, then, to see these verses as an exhortation drawing out the implications for behaviour of the first three visions. In light of God's turning toward Jerusalem in mercy (1:8–17), the disarming of his enemies (1:18–21), and his intention to repopulate Jerusalem, the prudent and moral thing for the exiles to do was return and participate in the glorious future.

**6–7.** The exhortation opened with the twofold occurrence of the word *hoy*. Verse 7 also began with the word. Usually translated "woe," here it is rendered **Up, up!** by *NRSV*, and "Away, away" by *NEB*. Petersen (172–4) prefers "Listen, listen." *Hoy* carried a sense of warning, a potential threat if the following was not heeded.

The **land of the north** (v. 6) was Jeremiah's designation for Babylon, and it was clearly identified as such in v. 7. God called the exiles to **flee** from that land to which he had sent them. Indeed, God had scattered them abroad **like the four winds of heaven**, that is, all over the ancient world. In v. 7 God addressed Zion directly: "Away, O Zion, who dwells (with) the daughter Babylon." The verse was parallel in meaning to v. 6, which commanded the exiles to flee from Babylon. *NRSV*, however, construes the sentence quite differently, understanding **Zion** as the destination to which the exiles should flee: **Escape to Zion**, **you that live with daughter Babylon**.

**8.** Verse 8 opened with the transitional particle *ki* and the messenger formula. The next phrase, however, has caused much difficulty. (See the review by Kloos, *VT* 25 [1975], 729–31.) *NRSV* translates it: **after his glory sent me**, construing the word *'aḥar* as a conjunction and *kābôd* as the subject. The pronoun **me** presumably refers to Zechariah, but there can be no question of his having been sent to the **nations who plundered** Judah. *NRSV* properly takes the phrase **after his glory sent me** as parenthetical. The main sentence reported God's word **regarding the nations who plundered** Judah. These nations were clearly the same as those represented by the horns in the second vision.

God uttered a warning about those who have **touched** Judah. The word could be used of non-violent or violent touching. Here violent touching, i.e. striking or harming, was clearly intended. Whoever struck Judah was guilty of striking the **apple** of God's **eye**. The apple was the pupil, so whoever struck Judah was striking God in the pupil of his eye (Petersen, 177). The phrase connoted a very close relationship between God and his people.

**9.** Because the plunderers have struck God's pupil, he has raised his hand to punish them (literally "waved his hand over them"). The punishment will consist of their becoming plunder for their own slaves. The basic idea was that the plunderers will receive what they deserve; they will be plundered. The verse also carried overtones of Exod. 3:21–2, 11:2–3, and 12:35–6, all of which spoke of the Egyptians' paying their Israelite slaves to leave after God sent the plagues. Such a comparison would speak volumes to exiles trying to decide whether to return to Judah.

The prophecy of salvation ended on a note of victory. The remainder of the verse consisted of the statement by the prophet that **you** (the exiles) **will know that the Lord of Hosts has sent me**, a phrase repeated three times (2:11; 4:9; and 6:15). Elliger (2.118) argues that all four instances were additions, attempting to shore up belief in Zechariah's failed, very specific prophecies. This argument is not convincing, however. It would be just as important for Zechariah's first audience to believe him as for a later one. So Zechariah promised them that God would provide for them as he had their ancestors when they prepared to escape from Egypt. A phrase that does sound as if it might have been added to bolster sagging faith is found at the end of 6:15: **This will happen if you diligently obey the voice of the Lord your God**. This phrase placed the blame for any failure of the prophet's message on the audience.

**10.** In 2:10 God spoke again. The command to **sing and rejoice** is reminiscent of a cultic shout in the Temple. Indeed, God promised that in the new age he will dwell in the midst of his people, perhaps an allusion to 1:16, where God promised to rebuild his Temple. Further, in this verse Zion was called a daughter, balancing the use of the same epithet for Babylon in 2:7. In v. 11 the verb and the pronoun in the phrase **and you shall know that the Lord of Hosts has sent me to you** are both feminine singular, continuing the personification of the people as the daughter Zion from v. 7.

**11.** Zechariah announced next that many other people would join themselves to God. Elliger (2.119, 142) questions whether this verse and 8:20–22 derived from Zechariah, whom Elliger considered nationalistic. Yet there is nothing in these verses inconsistent with Zechariah's general emphasis on Judah, provided that one assumes the nations referred to here did not include the plunderers. Zechariah was not focused on which nations belonged to which group, but on Babylon and Judah.

**12.** The verb *nāhal*, translated **inherit** by *NRSV*, here meant to "take possession", and the word *ḥelqô*, translated **his portion**, can also designate one's share of booty. Hence, the sentence can be translated: "And the Lord will take possession of Judah as his booty upon the holy land". Both the

verb *nāhal* and the noun *helqô* were characteristically used of
Israel, who would inherit the land from God as her portion,
so Zechariah was employing conventional thinking with an
ironic twist. In the last phrase of the verse, Zechariah said
God **will again choose Jerusalem**. The verb "choose" (*bḥr*)
is the same one used to speak of God's choosing or electing
Abraham or Israel in the first place. The election of his people
remained valid.

Only here in the *OT* was Judah referred to as the **holy
land**, but Baldwin (111–2) notes that the idea is an extension
of the concept of Jerusalem or Zion as God's holy mountain
(cf. Ps. 2:6, 15:1, 48:1, 99:9). Even so, the extension deserves
notice for two reasons. (1) The city itself was in all likelihood
so sparsely occupied that a more inclusive geographical designation seemed necessary to Zechariah. (2) The phrase indi-
cates a lack of the conflict between Jerusalem and Judah that
can be discerned in Second Zechariah, specifically in 12:6–7,
10–14; 13:1.

**13.** The concluding verse in the exhortation clearly employed liturgical language, like v. 10. The verse was ominous.
God had stirred himself **from his holy dwelling**, heaven.
He was about to leave there to reinhabit his earthly dwelling
in Jerusalem.

### VISION OF THE CLEANSING OF JOSHUA
### 3:1–10

There are good reasons to think that the series of night visions
originally numbered only seven and that this vision was added
later, perhaps by Zechariah himself, as part of a revised edition to reapply the visions to the Palestinian community in
light of the events of 520 (see pp 39–43). The vision itself,
however, might not constitute a unity. The first five verses
were set in the council of God, where Joshua the priest
was cleansed. Verses 6–7, 9 fit the scene admirably. In
them Joshua was perhaps installed as high priest over his
people. Verses 8 and 10, however, sound messianic; certainly

the title **Branch** would fit Zerubbabel better than Joshua. Further, the two verses seemed to interrupt (like 4:6b–10a and 6:11b–13) rather than to interpret what was being said. Therefore, these two verses will be treated as additions, perhaps by the redactor of Haggai/Zechariah 1–8, who showed a tendency in Haggai to include both men in his editorial work. A number of scholars (e.g., Blocher, *ETR* 54 [1979], 265; Eichrodt, *TZ* 13 [1957], 509; and Petitjean, *ETL* 42 [1966], 40) argue that 3:8–10 together form a separate passage, but v. 9 seems to fit the scene of Joshua's cleansing.

**1.** The vision opened with the high priest Joshua **standing before the angel of the Lord**. The scene was the council of God, whose members included **Satan**, the Accuser or the Adversary. In Job 1–2 Satan appeared as a member of the divine council, whose function was to accuse sinners before God. That was his function in Zech. 3:1 also.

**2.** Before Satan could even speak, God demanded his silence with a rebuke. The time for accusing was past; the time for absolving had arrived. Instead of serving as the judge, God was serving as the attorney for the defence! The same God who had chosen Jerusalem (2:12) had also chosen Joshua. Commentators often suggest that Joshua represented all the exiles, and perhaps he did. More importantly, however, he stood before the angel as a priest. If the Temple was to be rebuilt, it would need a high priest.

God called Joshua **a brand plucked from the fire**. This may be an allusion to Am. 4:11, where God called the people of the northern kingdom a brand snatched from the fire. The image was graphic. A brand is a charred piece of wood. If snatched from a fire, a brand would be spared certain destruction. So it was with Joshua; he had been plucked from the "fire" of exile.

**3–4.** Zechariah reported that Joshua **was dressed with filthy clothes**. The word translated "filthy" designated human excrement. This filth was symbolic of some unspecified guilt (v. 4). The angel ordered the filthy clothes replaced with **festal apparel**. Horst (227) says the filthy clothes symbolize sorrow (which could be caused by sin), while the festal clothes symbolize joy. If v. 2 referred to the exile, v. 3 implied that it was both sorrowful and defiling.

**5.** Zechariah himself entered the action by ordering that a clean turban be placed on Joshua's head, and the scene reached its climax when Joshua was reclothed and received a turban for his head. Scholars have long noted the dependence of this verse on the investiture of priests described in Lev. 8:1– 9. In particular, priests received new clothes and a turban. It is fairly clear, then, that Zechariah meant to depict the investiture of Joshua as high priest.

**6–7.** The ceremony continued with the angel of the Lord delivering a charge to Joshua. He laid down certain conditions for Joshua to follow, but there is a question about the number of those conditions. *NRSV* translates the particles *'im. . . 'im* as **if . . . if**, and the particles *wĕgam. . . wĕgam* **then . . . then**. It is not clear, however, that the *wĕgam* clauses began the protasis (Beuken, *Haggai-Sacharja 1–8*, 290; Petersen, 203–6). Petersen offers the following translation (206):

> *If you walk according to my ways,*
> *and if you keep my charge,*
> *if you administer my house,*
> *and if you oversee my courts, then . . .*

In this case all four phrases belonged to the charge given to Joshua. Actually, though, it is not clear that *gam* can mean "if" either. More typically the particles meant "also", "moreover", or even "yea". Thus the clauses read more like strong affirmations: "and also you will . . ."

Perhaps another suggestion for understanding the text is in order. The first two clauses clearly functioned as commands to Joshua. The first phrase commanded him to walk in God's ways, a phrase from Deuteronomy meaning to obey his commandments. The word *mišmeret* could designate priestly service, but it also carried the broader meaning of injunction or charge. A scribe might have wished to make more explicit the high priest's right and responsibility to oversee the Temple

(God's house) and its courtyards and added the third and fourth clauses.

The verse concluded with a promise in the last half of the verse. If Joshua faithfully fulfilled all of these obligations, both moral and ritual, God would give him the right to stand among the angels in whose presence he was commissioned. This would appear to grant Joshua the right to stand in the divine council, where Jeremiah claimed the true prophet stood before he spoke God's word (Jer. 23:18–22).

**9.** The continuation (and original completion) of the vision appeared in v. 9. God spoke of a stone he set before Joshua, **a single stone with seven facets**. It is not clear, however, what that stone might be. Many scholars want to equate it with the **top stone** in the hands of Zerubbabel in 4:7. There is, however, no compelling reason to equate the two, even if one sees both 3:9 and 4:7 as additions to the original series of visions. The stone in 4:7 had to do with Zerubbabel and the rebuilding of the Temple, while the stone in 3:9 appeared in connection with Joshua's investiture. Nor were the seven lamps (4:2) and seven eyes (4:10b) related to the stone in any way.

The stone in 3:9 was described as being a single stone having seven facets. God promised to engrave the stone himself. In the context of Joshua's investiture, it makes most sense to try to understand the stone as something he would receive during such a ceremony. Exod. 28:36 spoke of inscribing a gold rosette for the priest's turban with the words "Holy to Yahweh". Exod. 28:9 spoke of engraving two onyx stones with the names of the tribes of Israel for Aaron's ephod. Exod. 28:17–21 spoke of setting twelve stones, one per tribe, in the breastpiece of the priest. Presumably, the stone in Zechariah 3:9 drew its inspiration from this chapter. One suggestion along these lines is that of J. C. Vanderkam (*CBQ* 53 [1991], 568–9), who argues that the dual noun *ênayim* (pairs of eyes), combined with the number "seven", denoted the same fourteen "stones of remembrance" seen in Exodus 28 and that the one stone of Zech. 3:9 corresponded to the single remaining tribe, Judah.

**8, 10.** Verses 8 and 10 constituted a messianic addition to the rest of the chapter. Two features of the addition were messianic. The first was the term *ṣemaḥ* (cf. 6:12), the root meaning of which was "to sprout". The closest parallels to its use in First Zechariah are found in Jer. 33:15 ("I will cause a righteous Branch [*ṣemaḥ*] to spring up ['*aṣmîaḥ*] for David") and Isa. 11:1 ("A shoot [*ḥōṭer*] shall come up from the stump of Jesse"). The second messianic feature of these verses was the image of people inviting each other to sit under their vines and fig trees. In a time of drought, both vine and fig tree wither (Jl 1:12). In a time of plenty, a person would eat from his own vine and fig tree (1 Kg. 4:25; Isa. 36:16). In the messianic period, each person would sit under his own vine and fig tree (Mic. 4:4). According to Zech. 3:10, people would even share with each other under their vines and fig trees.

Who was this Branch? The most obvious answer is Joshua, though 3:8 did not quite identify Joshua with the Branch (see Harrelson, *EI* 16 [1982], 120). In 6:12 the term Branch appeared again, where the referent was more clearly Joshua, but the task specified for the Branch is to build the Temple, a task emphatically reserved to Zerubbabel in 4:9. It seems quite likely, then, that the two verses originally designated Zerubbabel as the Branch, but were modified by a later hand to refer to Joshua in light of the rising influence of the high priesthood. It is possible, though on the whole it seems less likely, that the reference is to some future, unspecified person.

Not only is it difficult to discern the identity of the Branch in v. 8, but also the opening address of God to Joshua is problematic. Who were the **colleagues who sit before** Joshua? Were they priests? Members of the repatriated community? Members of God's court? (This would not be the first time in First Zechariah that celestial beings were called "men".) Whoever they were, they were **omens**, or persons of portent. They pointed to the divine blessing God was about to pour out on his people, the only aspect of which that was mentioned was the coming of the Branch.

## VISION OF THE LAMPSTAND AND OLIVE TREES: GOD'S PRESENCE

### 4:1–14

At the heart of the night visions stood this vision of a lampstand flanked by two trees. The lampstand most likely symbolized God himself. While Zechariah nowhere identified the lamp, the vision contained two statements that lead to this conclusion. (1) The lampstand had seven lamps (v. 2), which were interpreted as the seven **eyes of the Lord** (v. 10b). (2) The two olive trees were said to be the two "sons of oil" that **stand by the Lord of the whole earth**.

It was shown in the Introduction to Zechariah 1–8 (p. 39) that this vision was not a unity. A redactor, possibly Zechariah himself, added vv. 6b–10a. It is so jarring in its context that scholars have suggested moving it, sometimes to the end of the chapter, sometimes to chapter 3. There is, however, no evidence to suggest that the verses ever appeared anywhere else. It would seem better to assume that they were composed for their present position. The interpretation of the vision will begin with the presumed original version of the vision and then proceed to the current modified version with its focus on Zerubbabel.

**1.** In v. 1 the interpreting angel, missing from 3:1–10, reappears and **wakens** Zechariah, **as one is wakened from a sleep**. While Zechariah compared the visionary state to sleep, he did not equate the two.

**2–3.** First, Zechariah saw a golden menorah or lampstand. On top of the lampstand was a bowl. The word *gullāh* designated a basin or a bowl, which presumably held the oil for the lamps. The lamps numbered seven, each having seven niches, allowing seven wicks to be placed in each lamp. (See R. North, *Bib* 51 [1970], esp. his reconstruction on 201). Beside the lampstand were two olive trees, one on each side. No function was ascribed to the trees in v. 3, but v. 12 said that they transmitted oil (literally gold) through pipes to the lampstand, presumably into the *gullāh*.

**4–6a.** A conversation ensued between Zechariah and the

interpreting angel, in which Zechariah confessed twice that
he did not know what the vision meant. At the point in v. 6a
where the angel was about to disclose the meaning, two oracles
about Zerubbabel have been inserted.

**10b.** The original vision continued in 10b with the interpretation of the seven lamps. They were identified as **the eyes of
the Lord, which range through the world**. Elliger (2.110)
argues that the background for the number seven is Babylonian astrology, which knew of seven planets. Whether that
is true or not, he is correct to say that they symbolize God's
omniscience.

**11-12.** Next Zechariah asked about the meaning of the
olive trees on each side of the lampstand. In v. 12 he supplied
additional information about them, namely that they poured
gold through golden pipes, presumably into the *gullāh*, though
that was not actually said. He asked more particularly about
the two **branches** of the olive trees. The term translated
"branches" (*šibbălê*) usually referred to ears of grain, which
would make no sense here. Consequently scholars have suggested more specialized meanings like spikes or twigs. The
extra details not in the original vision suggest that v. 12 was
an addition, the specific function of which is unclear.

**13-14.** The angel told Zechariah that the trees were the
"sons of oil". *NRSV* translates the word *yiṣhar* **anointed**, a
meaning it has nowhere else in the *OT*. Instead, everywhere
else *yiṣhar* is referred to as an agricultural product which signi-
fied God's blessing (cf. Jl 2:19, 24) and which should be
brought as tithes (cf. Deut. 12:17, 14:23; Neh. 10:38, 40). The
closest parallel to the phrase in Zech. 4:14 was Isa. 5:1, where
a hill was designated "a son of oil" (*šāmen*). There the phrase
clearly designated the hill as fertile. The phrase *běnê hayiṣhar*
in Zech. 4:14 also designated the olive trees as "sons of fat-
ness", i.e. symbols of bounty. Bounty was associated with
the presence of God. Not surprisingly, then, the trees flanked
Yahweh, reminiscent of the myrtles on each side of the
entrance to heaven.

**6b.** The addition to the vision in 4:6b-10a directed the vision
toward the rebuilding of the Temple under Zerubbabel. The

addition opened with an introductory statement: **This is the word of the Lord to Zerubbabel**. That statement was followed by a denial that human instrumentality was at work; instead the task to be done would be accomplished by God. The task in question was not disclosed, but the context shows that it was the building of the Temple.

**7.** Verse 7 opened with an entirely enigmatic question: **What are you, O great mountain?** A few examples will illustrate the lack of scholarly consensus in identifying the mountain. Petersen (239–40) suggests that the "mountain" was none other than Joshua, or perhaps the Samaritan governor Tattenai, while Galling ("Serubbabel und die Wiederaufbau des Tempels", 84) thinks it was the Temple ruins. Elliger (2.126) has a better suggestion, namely to understand it as a symbol for all of the difficulties Zerubbabel will have to face. Van der Woude ("Zion as Primeval Stone", 240) translates: "Whatever you are, great mountain". The question is followed by a verbless clause which can be translated: "Before Zerubbabel as a level plain". In light of the assertion in v. 6b that God's wind or spirit would perform the coming task, this verse assured Zerubbabel that no obstacle could prevent the completion of the rebuilding of the Temple.

If so, the last part of the verse fitted quite well also. It affirmed that Zerubbabel would **bring out the top stone**. The phrase *hā'eben hārō'šâ* occurred only here in the *OT*, and is variously understood as a foundation stone, cornerstone, head stone or boundary stone. It has also been interpreted as a symbol for the Persian Empire. Petitjean (*ETL* 42 [1966], 40–71), Lipinski (*VT* 20 [1970], 30–33), Meyers and Meyers (246–9) and Petersen (240–2) argue that the background for this sentence is a ceremony in which a stone from an earlier temple was transferred to a new temple. Such a ceremony may well have taken place on the day the new Temple was founded (see comments on Hag. 2:18), but Baldwin (121–2) argues correctly that the context demands that this stone was a completion stone.

Verse 7 predicted that when Zerubbabel completed the rebuilding of the Temple, the laying of the last stone would be met with shouts of **Grace, grace to it**. The word *hēn*, translated "grace" or "favour", can also mean "beauty". The word is sometimes understood, therefore, as signifying that the stone is made of rare minerals, but there is no other indication in the text that leads to such a conclusion. Its state of favour derived from its function as the last stone to be put in place. The eschaton could then begin!

**8–9.** The addition continued with a second oracle. Its heart is the prediction in v. 9 that just as the **hands of Zerubbabel** had founded the Temple (see comments on founding a temple in connection with Hag. 2:18), **his hands shall also complete it**. At a minimum Zechariah was offering a word of hope that the rebuilding of the Temple would be completed. It is likely the prediction said even more. Since Zechariah laid such heavy emphasis on the role of Zerubbabel throughout the entire building process, one might well assume that the prince's leadership was not recognized by the whole community. This supposition is corroborated by several other passages. Haggai 1:2, 4; 2:3 bore witness to dissension within the community over building the Temple, and Ezr. 5:3 described official opposition from Tattenai. It is not possible to say whether Zechariah was urging people to follow Zerubbabel instead of some other leader, or whether opposition to the building project itself was the problem.

Verse 9 ended with the phrase **Then you will know that the Lord of hosts has sent me** (cf. 2:9, 11). The antecedents for the pronouns in this sentence are unclear. The sentence is usually understood to mean that the people would recognize the divinely-given authority of Zechariah. That meaning would be consistent with 2:9, 11. Actually, however, the sentence was spoken by the interpreting angel, and might have been a word on his own behalf. The verb *weyāda'tā* (you will know) is second masculine singular and could designate Zerubbabel (or even Zechariah) as the one who would know, but scholars routinely add a final *mem* to the suffix, making it second masculine plural to agree with the pronoun **you** at the end of the verse. In that case it would be the whole community that would recognize the angel.

**10a.** The addition concluded with one last prediction, which is as enigmatic as anything else in these verses. *NRSV* translates the first phrase quite plausibly: **For whoever has despised the day of small things.** The word for day has a *lamed* as a prefix, which can be construed as the sign of the direct object. Meyers and Meyers (252) argue instead that the *lamed* constitutes an emphatic article to be translated "such". The reference was presumably to the rebuilding of the Temple, which people in the community scoffed at as being insignificant (Hag. 2:3). People who held that opinion would nevertheless be won over and rejoice. The occasion of this rejoicing would involve seeing something called the stone of tin (*hā'eben habbedîl*) in Zerubbabel's hand. Meyers and Meyers (253) argue that the phrase designated a tin object used in constituting new buildings. Alternatively, the word for "tin" might be emended slightly to a form of the root *bdl*, which means "to separate", resulting in the phrase "separated stone". Such a stone might have been a stone removed from an older temple to use in the foundation of a newer temple. Finally, *NRSV* translates the phrase by the single word **plummet**. Scholars have objected that a plummet would have been needed early in a construction project, not at the end as the context demands. One is left then with two possibilities. (1) The term might have designated an object made of tin, which Zerubbabel used in a ceremony, perhaps placing it in the wall of the Temple. (2) The term might have designated the "completion stone" mentioned in v. 7.

Despite some uncertainties it is possible now to state the purpose of vv. 6b–10a. They applied the vision of the lampstand to the rebuilding of the Temple. If the original vision depicted bounty in the presence of God, the new version tied that bounty to the reconstruction of the Temple under Zerubbabel.

## VISION OF THE FLYING SCROLL: THE CLEANSING
## OF JERUSALEM
### 5:1–4

In the sixth vision (fifth in the original series), Zechariah saw a scroll flying through the air. The scroll represented a curse spreading across the land. The writing on one side condemned thieves, and on the other those who bore false witness. These were the two sins most often associated with taking an oath. Scholars often suggest that the curses were levelled against those who had remained in Palestine during the exile and would not relinquish control of their land to repatriates returning from Babylon. If the original vision was directed toward the exiles, it would have functioned to assure them that people who had remained behind would not take advantage of them. In the second edition, addressed to the community in Judah, it would have warned everyone in the Holy Land against undermining the confidence people needed to have in one another and would amount to a plea for the people to deal with each other with integrity.

**1–2.** The scroll seen by Zechariah measured **twenty cubits** (about thirty feet) in length and **ten cubits** (about fifteen feet) in height. Scrolls thirty feet or more in length were quite common, but they were typically no more than a foot high. A scroll fifteen feet high would be incredibly unwieldy. The size of the scroll suggested a vast number of transgressions and of God's punishment upon thieves and liars.

**3–4.** The background of these verses was the practice of oath-taking. In case someone was accused of stealing or otherwise breaking an oath, that person was brought before God in the Temple and required to take an oath of innocence (Smith, 208). If the person was in fact guilty, the oath would amount to a self-curse. According to v. 4, the curse would fall upon the physical house of a guilty person, another indication that disputes over the possession of real estate might have stood in the background of this vision.

## VISION OF A WOMAN IN A BASKET: WICKEDNESS SENT TO BABYLON

### 5:5–11

The next vision was coupled closely enough with the one of the flying scroll that scholars sometimes count the two as one. It was, however, distinct. It consisted of two parts, the first being the vision of an ephah or basket with a woman trapped inside by a heavy lid. Since an ephah held a little less than ten gallons in dry measure, the basket would have been too small to hold an adult. The image appears, then, to have resembled a genie in a jar. The woman was said to represent wickedness. In the second part of the vision, she was carried by two women with storks' wings to Babylon, where she was placed in a temple and worshipped. The house for wickedness in Babylon should be seen as the foil for the house of God to be built in Jerusalem. The removal of wickedness from Jerusalem continued the theme of cleansing the Holy Land begun in the previous vision.

**5–6.** The interpreting angel initiated the action in this vision by asking Zechariah what he saw coming toward him. The author built the reader's suspense by not identifying the ephah immediately, but he did employ feminine singular pronouns, anticipating the feminine singular noun "ephah". The ephah was identified as iniquity. The Hebrew word *ʿăwōn* (iniquity) is actually an emendation. The MT reads *ʿênām*, "their eyes", which yields little sense. Petersen (255–6) notes the frequency with which the *OT* speaks of an "unjust ephah", making Zechariah's identification of the basket with iniquity a natural association.

**7–8.** The basket had a lid made of lead. No other passage in the *OT* spoke of such a lid, nor have archaeologists unearthed examples of one. Perhaps the mention of lead served to assure the reader that the contents of the basket would not spill out. Zechariah next said that the lid was lifted (presumably just enough to allow him to peek inside). There sat a woman, who was identified as *rišʿâ* (wickedness). Since "wickedness" could be either a masculine or a feminine noun, one might assume that this identification is an example of anti-feminine bias on the part of Zechariah, but that conclusion is not necessary. In the second part of the vision, two women with storks' wings play a positive role. Commentators have offered a number of explanations for the gender of "wickedness". One suggestion is that Zechariah had in mind Asherah, whose worship had permeated pre-exilic Israel. Another is that he had in mind the Queen of Heaven mentioned by Jeremiah (7:18; 44:17–19, 25), or even Queen Athaliah, who was called "wickedness" in 2 Chron. 24:7. It seems quite possible that the feminine gender of wickedness was suggested by the gender of the word "ephah". Anyway, the angel thrust "wickedness" back into the ephah and covered the basket with its heavy lid.

**9–11.** At this point the second part of the vision commenced. Zechariah saw two women advancing toward him. They had wings like storks. The two seized the ephah and rose in the air with the wind. They flew toward **the land of Shinar**, i.e. Babylon. Their mission was twofold. First they would build a house (a ziggurat) for it. Then they would set the ephah upon **its base** or pedestal. Once it was in its temple, the people of Babylon would surely worship it. The contrast between the house of wickedness in Babylon and the house of Yahweh in Jerusalem could hardly be more stark. This wickedness was the opposite of the righteousness required by God. It probably included all sin and sinful conditions. The original readers were faced with a decision: should they stay in Babylon where people worshipped wickedness, or return to Jerusalem where people worshipped God? The readers of the enlarged version would be challenged to complete the house for God.

### VISION OF THE FOUR CHARIOTS: GOD AT REST
### 6:1–8

The final vision had two clear points of contact with the first: the use of horses and the idea of rest. Once again Zechariah saw horses, this time pulling four chariots. These horses came into view from between two bronze mountains, which flank the entrance to heaven (cf. the myrtles in 1:8, which some scholars emend to read "mountains", and the olive trees in 4:3). The horses, identified as the four winds (*ruḥōt*) of heaven, went out from the presence of God to patrol the earth. Those who patrol the north country (Babylon) set God's *rûaḥ* (spirit) **at rest**. Galling (*VT* 2 [1952], 30–1) accepts Ewald's view that **rest** refers to God's turning in grace to the exiles in Babylon. More to the point, this vision reversed conditions in the first vision, where the nations were at rest, but God was jealous and angry with them. In this last vision God was at rest, because the north country (Babylon) has been defeated (1:18–21) and the Holy Land cleansed (5:1–11).

**1.** In third millennium Mesopotamia the sun-god Shamash was depicted as rising between two mountains (*ANEP*, 863–5). This scene provides a likely background for the setting of Zechariah's vision. The mountains in Zechariah's vision consisted of copper ore or (more likely) its alloy bronze, its shiny surface perhaps suggesting dawn. Instead of the sun's rising – or God's appearing (see Mal. 4:2) – four chariots pulled by horses emerged.

**2–3.** Apparently each of the chariots was pulled by a matched team of horses. To the three colours mentioned in 1:8 (red, white, and sorrel), these verses add the colour black. Scholars have often speculated about the meaning of the colours. Elliger (2.113) thinks that red represents the dawn while black represents midnight. Smith (214) notes that the book of Revelation interprets white as victory, red as bloodshed, black as famine, and pale as death. Other commentators interpret the four colours as kingdoms. No agreement on the matter seems in the offing.

**4–5.** When Zechariah inquired about the horses and chariots, he was told that the horses were the four winds of heaven, which would present themselves to God and then set forth to patrol the earth. In the first vision the horsemen had completed patrolling the earth and reported to the angel of the Lord that the nations were at rest. In this vision the horses

were impatient to set out on their mission to patrol the earth
(v. 7).

**6.** The chariot with black horses was sent toward the **north
country**, i.e. Babylon. According to *NRSV* the white horses
**go to the west country**, but the MT reads "after them".
Since there are four colours of horses identified with the four
winds, the slight emendation by *NRSV* makes sense. However,
there is no mention of the roans going east. Given the position
of Palestine between the Mediterranean Sea and the Arabian
Desert, the significant horses were those going north and
south. The omission of the fourth set of horses is incon-
sequential.

**7–8.** When the horses emerged from between the bronze
mountains, they were anxious to patrol, so the Lord sent them
on their way. Actually, the one dispatching them might have
been the angel, but the nearer antecedent is the Lord and the
context suggests it was he that commanded the horses. There
was no mention of a battle in this vision, the breaking of the
power of Babylon having been described in the second vision.
Those who patrolled in the north country apparently conveyed that message, which set God's spirit at rest (see above).

### EXHORTATION TO RETURNED EXILES: MAKE CROWNS AS A MEMORIAL
### 6:9–15

While scholars often agree that these verses were not
composed at the same time as the night visions, some (e.g.
Eichrodt, *TZ* 13 [1957], 517; Ackroyd, *Exile*, 197) date them
earlier and others (e.g. Sellin, 469–70, 520; Mason, 63) see
them as later additions. At issue is the relationship between
these verses and the final vision, which brings the night visions
to a very satisfying conclusion with God at rest. This exhortation, like the one at the end of chapter 2, urged the people
to take action based on what Zechariah had reported. Its
function was to assure those **far off** that they too had a role
in building the Temple (v. 15a).

The original version of the exhortation included vv. 9–11a (through the phrase "and make crowns") and vv. 14–15a (through **you shall know that the Lord has sent me to you**). The intervening materials constitute an addition, probably by Zechariah, in the "second, enlarged" edition aimed at people in Jerusalem. The last clause betrays the concerns of the final redactor, who also added chapters seven and eight.

**9–11a.** The exhortation began with an introduction typical for an oracle, rather than one for a vision. Then God told Zechariah to **collect silver and gold** from three returned exiles, **Heldai, Tobijah, and Jedaiah** and to take the metals to the house of a craftsman named **Josiah son of Zephaniah**. From the metals Josiah was to make crowns. As noted in the Introduction to First Zechariah (pp 39–40), the word *'ăṭārôt* (crowns) was plural, both in v. 11 and in v. 14. To be sure the word was used with a singular verb in v. 14, but it was not unusual for names of objects to be used with feminine singular verbs (*G-K*, 464, §k).

The word *'ăṭārâ* was one of three Hebrew words designating a royal crown, and was used in that sense in 2 Sam. 12:3 (cf. 1 Chr. 20:2), Jer. 13:18, Ezek. 21:31 (probably), Ps. 21:4, Lam. 5:16 and in Ca. 3:11 as a crown for the king on his wedding day. However, the meaning of *'ăṭārâ* was not limited to a royal crown. In Isa. 28:3 and Est. 8:15, it designated a crown worn by persons other than a king. In Ezek. 16:12 God adorned Israel with jewellery, including a crown. The word could also be used symbolically as a reference to God himself (Isa. 28:5), wisdom (Prov. 4:9), grey hair (16:31), or even grandchildren (17:6). In Zech. 6:11, therefore, the crowns could have been intended for anyone.

**14.** The discussion of the crowns originally continued in 6:14, which says that the crowns would be "for Helem, Tobijah, Jediah, and Hen, son of Zephaniah". While these four names are not identical to the four in 6:10, scholars routinely emend Helem to Heldai and Hen to Josiah. *NRSV* translates the preposition *le* with the phrase **in the care of**, implying that the four would retain Joshua's crown for safekeeping. No such inference is warranted, however; the four men were to make the crowns for themselves, presumably one per person.

The crowns were to be placed in the temple as a *zikkārôn* (a memorial or reminder), which often designated something material (e.g. phylacteries in Exod. 13:9, burnt offerings in Num. 10:10, plundered gold in Num. 31:54, and even the stones in the priest's ephod in Exod. 28:12, 29). The purpose of these objects was to cause one to remember some person, object, or event. The term was used in the same way in this verse: the four were to place their crowns as memorials in the Temple when it was complete, thus staking their claim in the new Temple.

**15.** Nor was the Temple complete yet. Verse 15 promised that people far off (in Babylon for sure, and perhaps elsewhere) would return and help with the building project. If so, it could not yet have been complete, though scholars often argue that these verses constitute a late addition. The promise to the exiles would have given hope as well to the recipients of the second version, the builders in 519, who must have been happy to hear that help was forthcoming. As v. 15 now stands, it continues with the assurance that you (masculine singular) **shall know that the Lord of hosts has sent me to you** (masculine plural), but most scholars emend the verb to read *wida'tem* (second masculine plural). In that case, the coming of the exiles would prove that God had sent Zechariah as his messenger.

**11b–13.** The addition began with the statement: **and set it on the head of the high priest Joshua son of Jehozadak.** There was no pronoun corresponding to the English word "it" in the MT, so v. 11b offers no help on the issue of the number of crowns. The first issue that can be addressed is that of the recipient of the crowns. Since the noun *'ăṭārâ* could refer to various types of crowns, one can conceive of someone's making crowns for Joshua, but the context militates against that conclusion. Verse 12 specifically calls the recipient the Branch, which is a messianic title (see comments on 3:8). Further, the verse specifically said that the Branch would build the Temple, a task reserved exclusively for Zerubbabel in 4:6b–10a. It is difficult to avoid the conclusion argued by many scholars that the name Zerubbabel originally stood in the text, either alongside Joshua or (more likely) alone. Either way, the prophet employed a word play based on the root ṣmḥ: "Branch ... will branch out". Verse 13 continued to insist that he would build the Temple, a claim not even a later generation could make for Joshua. In addition, the Branch would **bear royal honour, and sit and rule on his throne**.

Joshua did enter the picture at the end of the addition. Beside the throne of the Branch there would be a priest. **Peaceful understanding** (or counsel) would characterize their relationship. This vision of unity by Zechariah might have stood in marked contrast to the actual relationship between the two men. To what extent the high priest was already encroaching on royal rights (or vice versa) is impossible to say. Or Zechariah might simply have expressed the wish that the good relations that did exist would not deteriorate once the building project was finished.

Whatever Zechariah may have meant, Zerubbabel did not fulfil the hope that he would rule as a Davidide. Indeed, chapters 7 and 8 never mention him. Ironically, once the Temple was completed, it was the high priest who rose in status in the absence of any indigenous, secular authority. Not surprisingly, the same scribe who removed Zerubbabel's name from 3:8 must have substituted Joshua's name in 6:11b as well. Suggestions that Zerubbabel was removed from office by the Persians are mere speculation, though they might be correct. The further suggestion that his name was removed from 6:11 out of fear of the Persians is incorrect since his name remains in 4:7, 8, and 10.

## THE QUESTION ABOUT FASTING
### 7:1–14

The third section of First Zechariah was framed by a question (7:1–3) about fasting in the fifth month (over the destruction of the Temple), which was answered in 8:18–9. This answer was embedded in a series of ten short predictions about the future that bring First Zechariah to a positive conclusion. The apparent answer in 7:4–14 was actually an indictment for insincerity on the part of the community in connection with four different fasts, followed by an admonition to show mercy and justice. Indeed, the admonition agreed substantially with the first section (1:1–6) and with 8:16–17, whose author undoubtedly penned these words as well.

**1.** The third section opened with its own superscription. It is dated on the fourth day of the ninth month (**Chislev**) of the fourth year of Darius, i.e. about November of 518. The final edition of the book of Zechariah could have been prepared any time after this date. Suggestions that Zechariah 1–8 was finished in the fourth century are based on similarities to the books of 1 and 2 Chronicles. The night visions, however, would have lost much of their impact after the completion of the Temple on the third day of the twelfth month (Adar) of the sixth year of Darius (Ezr. 6:14), i.e. about April of 516. While a later date for these chapters cannot be disproved, it would seem best to date the final edition of Zechariah 1–8 (with Haggai placed before it) between November of 518 and April of 516.

**2–3.** The occasion for Zechariah's message about fasting was the appearance of a delegation to ask the priests and the prophets of the Lord whether people should continue to observe the fast in light of the near completion of the Temple. The text of v. 2 is far from clear. *NRSV* translates: **Now the people of Bethel sent Sharezer and Regem-melech and their men**, . . . There is, however, no sign of the definite article before the name Sharezer, so F. S. North (*ZAW* 66 [1954], 192–3) understands Bethel as the place to which inquirers were sent, but the name is not preceded by a preposition, nor does it end with a *he* locale. Many scholars suggest that the name Sharezer would have been preceded by the name of a god, e.g. El, Bel, or even Bethel. Hyatt (*JBL* 56 [1937], 387–94) finds the name Bit-ili-shar-usur on a tablet from ancient Erech and argues that it is the same name and perhaps even designates the same person. He translates the phrase: "Now Bethel-sar-ezer had sent Regem-melek and his men to propitiate the Lord." Alternatively, the name of the person dispatching the delegation may have dropped out and Bethel-Sharezer may have been a member of the delegation. (Either suggestion requires the addition of the sign of the definite article.) Thomas ("Zechariah," *IB* 6.1082, cf. Ackroyd, *Exile*, 206) thinks the name Regem-melech itself might be a corruption of the title of an office: *rb mg hmlk*, "the chief officer of the king".

If, indeed, Bethel was part of the name of a person, the place of residence of those sending the delegation is unclear, but it is possible that they came from Babylon, inquiring on behalf of the exiles (Elliger, 2.133). It seems less likely that they were sent by Darius (Lipinski, *VT* 20 [1970], 37). Regardless of where they were from, they appear to have been Jews inquiring on behalf of a larger group of Jews. This conclusion can be drawn from v. 2, which notes that they also came to **entreat the favour of the Lord**, i.e. to seek God's help in a time of difficulty. The fact that Zechariah answered them perhaps suggests that they came to him as a recognized prophet, specifically the author of the first edition of the night visions.

The question of whether to mourn and abstain from food was asked in the first person singular, presumably by the head of the delegation. While the question does not state the purpose for mourning, it was almost surely a rite in memory of the destruction of the Temple in the fifth month of the year.

**4–5.** Whether the priests or any other prophets answered the question, Zechariah did. His answer was to abandon all fasts, ones in the fourth, seventh, and tenth months as well as the fifth, since they would be replaced by festivals of joy in Judah. That answer has been displaced to 8:18–19 by other material. Thus the original short dialogue now serves as the framework for a much larger collection of materials. The answer which begins in v. 5 is secondary, and derives from the hand of the redactor; it is addressed to **all the people of the land and the priests** rather than the delegation that asked the question. It begins with a rhetorical question: when

you fasted and lamented in the fifth month and the seventh,
for these seventy years, was it for me that you fasted? (On
the seventy years, see comments on 1:12.) The redactor
thought that the fasts were self-centred, rather than God-
centred.

**6.** The same was true with the eating and drinking mentioned in v. 6, probably a reference to feasts rather than to
the eating of daily meals. In the Pentateuch, Israel was commanded to celebrate God with three pilgrimage festivals
(Passover/Unleavened Bread, Weeks, and Booths). Verse 6
accused the people and the priests with observing them without proper consideration for God.

**7–8.** *NRSV* places v. 7 at the end of the paragraph that
began in v. 1, and treats the formula in v. 8 as the beginning
of a new paragraph. This arrangement leads to the conclusion
that the redactor thought that fasting and feasting formed the
centre of the preaching of the pre-exilic prophets. The contents
of vv. 9–10, however, qualify much better than do vv. 5–6 as
a summary of their message (see Beuken, *Haggai-Sacharja 1–
8*, 121). Consequently one should see v. 7 as the redactor's
narrative framework for the last seven verses of the chapter.

As in 1:4, here also he appealed to the time before the fall
of Jerusalem, which he could describe as a time of prosperity,
both for it and the towns around it. In addition, he referred
to the Negeb (an area south of the Dead Sea) and the
Shephelah (an area of low hills between the Judaean hill
country and the coastal plain). Both of these areas had been
strategic to the defence and prosperity of Judah, but were lost
to her in the war with Babylon and were probably devoid of
Judaean inhabitants in the late sixth century. The pre-exilic
conditions, therefore, stood in marked contrast with the conditions of 518.

**9–10.** Verses 9–10 constitute an admonition introduced
by the messenger formula **Thus says the Lord of Hosts**. The
admonition taken as a whole called the people of Israel to
maintain a just society, one in which the widow, the orphan,
the resident alien, and the poor would be treated humanely
and could get a fair trial. The treatment of these very classes

had been a special concern in the Covenant Code (Exod. 22:22, 24) and the book of Deuteronomy (10:18; 14:29; 16:11, 14; 24:17; 26:12–13), and had constituted a "litmus test" among the pre-exilic prophets for determining whether the society was just (see Isa. 1:17; Jer. 7:6, 22:3). Rendering true judgments included hearing cases on their merits, rather than submitting to bribes. More than that, showing kindness (loyalty to those with whom one had entered covenants) and mercy (compassion to one's subordinates) had been required of all Israelites.

**11–12.** The narration resumed in vv. 11–12. The pre-exilic ancestors had refused to obey the word God had sent through the prophets (cf. 1:4). The redactor described their reaction in what moderns would call body language (Petersen, 292): they refused to hear by turning their shoulders away and by stopping their ears. Further, they hardened their own hearts. Their sin was all the more grievous in view of their knowledge of what they should do. God sent his message directly (**by his spirit**) to the former prophets and through them (literally by their hand) mediated it **to the people**. Despite all God had done to warn them, the people refused to hear his message. Consequently, God had released his wrath upon them. By mentioning the outcome of the failure of the ancestors to heed the message of God through the prophets, the redactor was warning his own audience of the danger in failing to heed their new representative Zechariah.

**13–14.** When God's wrath fell upon the ancestors in the form of the Babylonian army, they cried out to God for help. However, he acted toward them as they had acted toward him: he refused to listen and act. Instead, he **scattered them with a whirlwind**. The point was that God employed the Babylonians as his instrument for punishment. In saying this the redactor was employing a typical prophetic explanation of disaster upon God's people. Isaiah had claimed that God used the Assyrians to punish Israel in the eighth century (10:5–6), and Jeremiah had warned God would use the Babylonians (4:6). The fall of Jerusalem was not a sign of the powerlessness of God before the Babylonians and their gods, but the just recompense for their failure to heed God's prophets. They were scattered among the nations, principally Babylonia. The land was left desolate. The claim that no one moved about in the land was either hyperbole or was limited to the upper classes, who had been exiled.

### TEN WORDS ABOUT THE FUTURE
### 8:1–23

In the last chapter of First Zechariah, the redactor collected or composed ten short oracles, each introduced with some variation on the formula **Thus says the Lord of hosts**. The series built to a climax in which foreigners grasped the garments of Jews, begging to go to Jerusalem to participate in its new glory. Verses 2–8, which spoke of the return to Jerusalem, cohered well with the thought of the night visions and were probably authentic. Verses 9–17 just as clearly repeated the themes of the redactor and should be ascribed to him. Verses 18–19 recorded Zechariah's answer to the question posed in 7:2–3, namely that fasts would turn into joyous celebrations. At the end of the chapter, vv. 20–23 continued the theme of the return to Jerusalem, except that foreigners were said to join in. This verse and 2:11 were the only places in First Zechariah that envisioned people other than Judaeans coming to Jerusalem, unless 6:15 included them. If the thinking was that the Babylonians (and any others guilty of abusing Judah) had been punished already (1:18–21), nothing in Zechariah's thought would contradict his saying other peoples would come to Jerusalem.

**1–2.** The first oracle simply repeated 1:14 to the effect that the Lord was jealous for Zion. Two ideas were implicit here. First, God's wrath will be poured on Zion's enemies. Second, their punishment will allow Zion to receive the blessings God had in store for them.

**2.** The second oracle is a prophecy of salvation. It repeats the emphasis of 1:16 and 2:10–12 that God would return to Zion. In 1:16 God had promised that his house would be rebuilt, a project now almost completed. When completed it would be the place God would reside. The consequence of his resuming residence in Jerusalem would be entirely positive. Jerusalem would be called the faithful city. The prophet Isaiah had drawn a contrast between Jerusalem the faithful city (*qiryâ ne'emānâ*) and Jerusalem the prostitute (1:21). Zechariah could see a day when it would again be called the faithful city (*'ir-ha'ĕmet*). At the heart of the holy land (Zech. 2:12) would be the holy mountain capped by the new Temple.

**4–5.** Third, Jerusalem would be repopulated (cf. 2:4, 8;8). No longer would people die prematurely; **old men and old women shall again sit in the streets**. Normal family life would return; the city **shall be full of boys and girls playing in its streets**.

**6.** Zechariah's audience must have been incredulous, questioning whether and how the city, so devastated by Babylon and so long reduced in residents, would be repopulated. Indeed, their scepticism proved well-founded. As late as the time of Nehemiah, it was necessary to draft inhabitants for the post-exilic city (Neh. 11:1). The prophet answered with a rhetorical question placed on the lips of God: **Even though it seems impossible to the remnant of this people in these days, should it also seem impossible to me, . . . ?** Petersen (300) notes that a weak people are likely to think in terms of a weak God, but God himself will allow no such doubts about his ability to deliver his people.

**7–8.** One of the means by which God would repopulate the city was to bring back his **people from the east country and the west country**. The city had been decimated by the deportations of 597 and 586. 1 Kg. 24:14 said ten thousand were carried away in 597 (v. 16 mentioned only eight thousand) and 25:11 said the rest of the populace was carried away in 586. Jer. 52:28–30 listed a total of four thousand six hundred in three deportations, but scholars sometimes suppose this number did not include women and children and at times guess that the number of deportees (including those from other towns) may have reached much higher. Many inhabitants, of course, had died in the siege, but a number

had fled to Egypt or elsewhere, reducing the city from an
estimated population of 25,000 in the time of Josiah (Broshi,
*BARev* 4 [1978], 12) to nearly nothing during the exile and
immediately afterwards.

Whether the number of deportees was over ten thousand
or less than five, many (probably thousands) of their descendants still lived in Babylon. To those people Zechariah had
addressed the first edition of his night visions, and upon their
return primarily he placed his hopes for repopulating Jerusalem. Ultimately, Zechariah's hope for the future lay in the
nature of God, who promised to be the God of the returnees
**in faithfulness and righteousness**. Those very traits had
been called into question by the destruction of Jerusalem. The
fault lay, he said, not with God but with the people. They
could depend on God to dwell among them.

**9–13.** Overall, vv. 9–13 constitute a prophecy of salvation,
but they opened with the admonition to **Let your hands be
strong**, i.e. get to work. In vv. 9–10 the redactor made explicit
reference to the ceremony of founding the Temple in a manner
reminiscent of Hag. 2:15–19. Beginning with that ceremony,
a new day had dawned (v. 11; cf. Hag. 2:19: **From this day
on I will bless you**). Further, the desolate land of 7:14 would
be made fertile again (v. 12). In the past there had been
neither reward for hard labour nor safety from foes, external
or internal. Those days, however, lay behind. God would now
treat his people differently (v. 12). The people who had been
a curse among the nations (v. 13) would become a blessing,
probably an allusion to God's promise to Abraham (Gen.
12:2–3). The passage closed with a phrase characteristic of
the oracle of salvation (or *priesterliche Heilsorakel*): do not be
afraid. Then the redactor repeated his opening admonition to
**let your hands be strong**, forming an inclusion device and
emphasizing the people's role in bringing in the new day.

**14–17.** Verses 14–17 also contain the characteristic phrase
of the oracle of salvation **do not be afraid** (v. 15) and admonitions characteristic of the redactor (vv. 16–17). Like vv. 9–
13 they also drew a contrast between the days before and
after. This time he distinguished between the pre-exilic days

when the ancestors failed God and the future days when God would keep his promises to his people (vv. 14–15). There were conditions, however, attached to that new day. The conditions had to do with speaking the truth, particularly in legal contexts (judgments in the gates and swearing oaths, v. 16). Further, the people were warned not to **devise evil in your hearts against one another**, perhaps in an effort to take property from a neighbour (v. 17). In the vision of the flying scroll (5:3), Zechariah warned that all who stole and swore falsely would be punished. In 8:16–17 the redactor revealed that these moral failures were still very much a problem in the post-exilic community and would postpone the arrival of the new day in all its glory. This delay came, according to the Lord, because **all these are things that I hate**.

**18–19.** Zechariah's own answer to the question about fasting (7:1–3) appeared next in this collection of oracles. F. S. North (*ZAW* 66 [1954], 193) omits the reference to the fasts of the fourth, seventh, and tenth months as additions, and he may be correct; the verb *yihyeh* is singular. On the other hand, compound sentences often take a singular verb when the first subject mentioned is singular (*G-K*, 468 § f). It may be, then, that Zechariah's answer was more exuberant and far-reaching than the question: not just the fast of the fifth month, but all other fasts being observed would be turned into seasons of joy. (The origin and purpose of the other three fasts is not known.) Finally, the phrase at the end of v. 19, which reads **therefore love truth and peace**, would fit in better with the admonitions in vv. 16–17 and may have become misplaced through scribal error.

**20–2.** The ninth oracle made explicit the inclusiveness of the new order. It would not be for Judaeans only, but for **the inhabitants of many cities** (v. 20). **Many peoples and strong nations** would come to the Temple in Jerusalem to **entreat the favour of the Lord**. This prediction will find its echo in Zech. 14:16–19, but 8:20–22 need not be considered late because of that. The point of such a prediction was that God's own people in those countries ought to come home themselves.

**23.** Not only should they come home, they should bring with them any neighbours who wished to come. The picture that emerged in vv. 20–23 was of peoples of all backgrounds (though not necessarily all people) streaming to Jerusalem, along with the Judaeans themselves. The people would be stimulated to come when they heard that the God of the whole world (Yahweh) was once again with his people.

## SUMMARY

At each stage of development, First Zechariah presented a plan of action for the community of God. The initial tract, containing seven night visions and two exhortations, envisioned a return of the exiles to Jerusalem. God had already moved into the midst of the exiles (called Zion in 2:7) and would resettle them at home around his Temple (1:16). Zechariah depicted Judah overflowing with prosperity (1:17) and Jerusalem teeming with people (2:4). Purged of sin (5:1–11) and safe from the punishment upon Babylon (1:18–21; 6:8), Judah would be the home for Judaean and Gentile alike (2:11). Zechariah's was – if nothing else – a vision of unity. To be sure, the nations who had exceeded God's plan to use them to punish the ancestors would not participate. Indeed, the Babylonians would become plunder for the enslaved exiles.

The second edition of the book continued to envision unity. It interpreted the original tract in religio-political terms of 520/19. First, 3:1–7, 9 reported a vision of the investiture of Joshua, son of Jehozadak, as the High Priest. Second, the interpretive addition in 4:6b–10a named Zerubbabel as the one who had founded the Temple and would finish the (re)building project. The implication was probably this: as Solomon, son of David, had built the first Temple, Zerubbabel, son of David, would build the second. Finally, the addition in 6:11b–13 envisioned the two men working together harmoniously, any statement of who was more powerful left out of the picture. This "revised and enlarged" edition of Zechariah's night visions advocated carrying forward two of the basic institutions of pre-exilic Judah: the priesthood and the monarchy. The full restoration foreseen in the night visions was tied to the reestablishment of these institutions.

The third edition enlarged upon the second. Zechariah and his contemporary Haggai (whose work was attached to the front of Zechariah's) were presented as the authentic successors of the pre-exilic prophets (1:1–6; 8:9), thus carrying forward the third great institution of the pre-exilic period, namely prophecy. In this recension the theme of unity involved all classes of God's people: old men and women (8:4), boys and girls (8:5), people already in Jerusalem and those still in exile (8:7–8), and Judaeans as well as people of other nationalities (8:20–23). These promises were based upon the righteousness of God (8:8). Further, the founding of the Temple marked the beginning of the promised but delayed prosperity (8:9–13). Even so, reaping the benefits of the new day depended upon complying with the ethical (6:15b; 7:9–10; 8:16–17) and ritual (3:7) requirements of the Lord.

After the crushing military defeat at the hands of the Babylonians and the hardships of the exilic period, Judah needed to revitalize itself. To do so it needed visionaries with programmes for a new age. Haggai and Zechariah stepped forward with their ideas of what was needed. The redactor belonged to a community which heard them. The vision of Zechariah in particular was widely inclusive, but the failure of the post-exilic community to gain even a measure of political independence and to establish the monarchy meant that much of that programme could not be carried out. It nevertheless remained alive as a hope for the future.

# INTRODUCTION

## to

## Zechariah 9–14

The view that Zechariah 9–14 (all or in part) arose separately from chapters 1–8 has been argued for three centuries and has been adopted in this commentary. (See the Introduction to Zechariah 1–8.) The last six chapters distinguish themselves from the first eight especially in that they mention neither Zechariah nor any other identifiable person or event of the sixth century. Second, the existence of the second Temple is presupposed (9:8; 11:13; 14:16–21), rather than anticipated as the event that would usher in the new day. In addition, the two parts of the book differ markedly in literary type. Specifically, there are no visions in chapters 9–14 in contrast with chapters 1–8.

It is also true, of course, that the two sections of the book exhibit similarity in the themes they discuss. Mason (78–9) lists five: the centrality of Jerusalem and the sharing of the Zion tradition (9:8, 9–10; 12:1–13:6; cf. 1:12–16; 2:1–130); the cleansing of the community as part of God's final act (10:9; 12:10; 13:1–2; 14:20–21; cf. 3:1–9; 5:1–11); a place for all nations in God's kingdom (9:7; 10:14; 14:16–19; cf. 2:11; 8:20–23); an appeal to the authority of earlier prophets (numerous; cf. 1:2–6; 7:12); and a concern with the problem of leadership (9:9–10; 11:4–17; 13:7–9; cf. the emphasis on Joshua and Zerubbabel). Brevard Childs (*Introduction to the Old Testament as Scripture* [Philadelphia, Fortress, 1979], 482) adds other elements: the return of paradisal fertility, the use of covenant and curse language, and an emphasis on worship. Nevertheless, he also cautions against overstating the similarities. Thus, despite some overlap in themes and very general similarity in style, Zechariah 9–14 reveals itself to be a later addition to the work of the sixth century prophet Zechariah.

## A. AUTHORSHIP, DATE AND HISTORICAL BACKGROUND

*Authorship.* If Zechariah did not compose these six chapters, their author, of course, is unknown. Modern scholars routinely distinguish chapters 9–11 from 12–14, calling them Second and Third Zechariah respectively, but the number of contributors may be even higher. Rudolph (161–4) sees three separate collections (9:1–11:3, 11:4–13:9, 14:1–21), and Saebø (*Sacharja 9–14*, 313) sees four prior collections (chapters 9–10, 11, 12–13, and 14) standing behind the final composition.

Since these collections often seem contradictory, one should probably conclude that they arose from different hands and perhaps at different times. Many commentators, for example, see chapters 9–11 (and perhaps 13:7–9) arising about the same time, whether by one author or more, followed by chapters 12–13 (or to 13:6), with chapter 14 being the latest material. Actually, the presence of 13:7–9 (the third shepherd passage) in the last half of the book suggests that the shepherd materials (10:1–3; 11:1–17; 13:7–9) might have come later than most or all other traditions in chapters 9–13, perhaps even later than chapter 14, and that their author was the redactor of chapters 9–14 (see below).

*Date.* The date of Zechariah 9–14 has been widely contested. For convenience one may classify the dates under three general headings. Some scholars (e.g., E. J. Young, *An Introduction to the Old Testament* [Grand Rapids, Eerdmans, 1950], 273; and R. K. Harrison, *Introduction to the Old Testament* [Grand Rapids, Eerdmans, 1970], 956) still hold to the traditional view that the prophet Zechariah wrote the last six chapters. Others, beginning as early as Joseph Mede in 1653 and Archbishop Benedict Flugge in 1784, argued that chapters 9–14, all or in part, stemmed from the pre-exilic period. More recently Abraham Malamat (*IEJ* 1 [1950–1951], 149–59) has renewed this position, arguing that 9:1–8 alludes to the accomplishments of Sargon II ca. 720 BC. Benedikt Otzen (*Studien*) places

9:1–8 in the time of Josiah (117–18), the remainder of chapters 10 and 11 at the same time (145), 11:4–17 in the time of Zedekiah (165), 12:2–13:1 (with 13:2–6, 7–9 added) from the early exilic period, and chapter 14 from the post-exilic period (212). While not arguing that any of Zechariah 9–14 was pre-exilic, Hanson (*Dawn*) does date the earliest sections before Zechariah: 9:1–8 from the mid-sixth century (324), 10:1–12 slightly later (334), 11:4–16 from the end of the sixth or beginning of the fifth centuries (353), 12:1–13:6 from the fifth century, about 475 (368), and 14:1–21 from 475 to 425 (400).

Most scholars, however, have opted for a time of origin in the post-exilic period after Zechariah. Even here, however, one finds disagreement. Paul Lamarche (*Zacharie i-xiv*, 121) dates all four chapters to the lifetime of Zechariah, i.e. about 500, and Jones (*VT* 12 [1962], 241–59) argues that chapters 9–11 stem from the first half of the fifth century. Some scholars, represented particularly by Sellin (542–3), place the materials at the opposite end of the post-exilic period during the time of the Maccabees.

By far the majority, however, date Zechariah 9–14 at or about the time of Alexander the Great's invasion of the Mediterranean coast (332 BC). Elliger (2.143; cf. Delcor. *VT* 1 [1951], 110–124; Horst, 247; and Rudolph, 162–4) places most of chapters 9–11 at that time and 12–14 later (in two stages), but not as late as the Maccabean period. Mitchell (*Haggai-Zechariah*, 258–9) argues that 9:1–10 was written soon after the battle of Issus in 333 BC, and was expanded by 9:11–11:3 in the time of Ptolemy III (247–222 BC), and by 11:4–14:21 about the same time.

Such a bewildering variety of dates calls into question the method used by many of these scholars: namely, the attempt to date materials by interpreting passages as historical allusions, sometimes even as prophecy after the fact. Three passages in particular are used. The first is 9:1–8, which refers to the defeat of a number of cities. Otzen notes that several of them were destroyed before the exile and concludes that the verses must therefore be pre-exilic. Elliger and many others view the same passage as an account of the invasion of Alexander. Sellin finds parallels in 9:2 to the opposition of Tyre and Sidon to the Maccabean revolt (cf. 1 Mac. 5:15). However, after the battle of Issus he marched down the seacoast to Egypt in 332, besieging Tyre and Sidon along the way. He did not campaign at Damascus, though he did send Parmenion there to secure his eastern flank. He rested during the winter of 332/1, and returned through desert area to the Euphrates at Thapsacus (P. Jouguet, *Alexander the Great and the Hellenistic World* [Chicago, Ares, 1985], 21–31). Hence, his campaign is not accurately reflected in 9:1–8. Rudolph, despite arguing for a Greek date, notes that if the text were describing an actual invasion from north to south Hamath would come before Damascus and Sidon before Tyre (171–7).

The suggestion that Zechariah 9–14 reflects the Greek period is buttressed in the second place by appeals to 9:13, which these scholars claim presupposes the Greek Empire and suffering at the hands of the successors of Alexander. One may ask, however, whether their contention is really correct. No doubt the word *yawan* in v. 13 refers to the Greeks, despite Baldwin's contention (169) that the word sometimes referred to distant, unknown people. However, Hanson (*Dawn*, 298) and others are certainly correct that the phrase "over your sons, O Greece" does overload its line in comparison with the next line with which it is parallel. It would indeed make perfectly good sense to read the two lines thus:

> *I will arouse your sons, O Zion,*
> *and wield you like a warrior's sword.*

In fact, *JB*, *NEB*, and *NAB* treat the allusion to Greece as an insertion. Dentan's claim ("Zechariah," *IB*, 6.1097) that "The passage requires the mention of a definite enemy" flies in the face of the following line and the rest of the chapter, which mention none.

Nevertheless, the reference to Greece does appear in the text, whether original or a later gloss. The question yet to be answered is whether it necessarily denotes the Greek Empire and harm the Greeks directed against Jerusalem after the invasion when relationships between Judah and Greece went sour. To be sure Judah suffered at the hands of the successor states as early as 320. After Alexander's death and the division of his empire, Ptolemy, son of Lagus, captured Jerusalem and, according to Josephus (*Ant.* 12.1.1. § 1–7), carried away exiles to Egypt. Van der Woude (*JNSL* 12 [1984], 148) points to this time as the date. On the other hand Mitchell argues that 9:9–11:3 was written during the time of Ptolemy III (247–222). Even so, Zech. 9:13 simply listed *yāwān* as one more enemy God would punish, and Joel 3:6 (Heb. 4:6) condemned Greece for selling citizens of Jerusalem and Judah into slavery. Since Ezek. 27:13 also mentioned Greeks among those who sold slaves to Tyre, it is probably safe to say that she did so as early as the exile. Thus, again, it is not necessary to look to the Greek period as the only time such a threat would be meaningful.

Rudolph (198) claims that the line in 10:11b **The pride of Assyria shall be laid low** referred to a currently existing kingdom and proved that the name Assyria had been transferred to Syria. The best parallels for Zech. 10:11b, however, are Isa. 11:11 and 27:13, which speak of God's bringing home those exiled to Assyria and Egypt. It would appear that both texts looked to the return of all exiles (Isa. 11:11 adds a number of additional places to which God's people had been exiled) and that language about the return of exiles from Assyria and Egypt had become traditional and was intended to include all who had been carried off from Israel or Judah, to the north (Assyria) or to the south (Egypt) and anywhere else. In Zech. 10:8 God signals for the exiles to return (cf. Isa. 11:12–16), and Zech. 10:11a clearly employs exodus language to speak of their return. Verse 11b simply continues this traditional language. It would appear, then, that there is little reason to see allusions to the invasion of Alexander the Great and the eventual struggles between his generals in 9:13 or 10:10–11, and the mention of Greece in 9:13 offers too flimsy a basis for dating Zechariah 9–14 during the Greek period.

The third passage often used is 11:4–17, the so-called

Shepherd Allegory. Verse 8 states that in one month God's shepherd deposed three other shepherds. Here the identifications range even wider. Otzen (*Studien*, 156) claims that the shepherds were Saul, David, and Solomon, and Sellin thinks that they were the second century Tobiads Simon, Menelaus, and Lysimachus (562). Indeed, suggested identifications also include Moses, Aaron and Miriam; the kings Zechariah, Shallum, and Menahem; three world empires (Assyrians, Babylonians and Persians, or Persians, Greeks and Romans); and even the Pharisees, Sadducees, and Essenes (Smith, 270). Those scholars dating Zechariah 9–14 in the Greek period also claim that 11:14 (where the Shepherd breaks the staff of union) has in mind the Samaritan split. Since the "Greek" interpretation itself is debatable, since it is difficult to pinpoint the time for this "split", and since scholars disagree over whether 11:14 is a genuine prediction coming before the split or is a prophecy after the fact, this suggestion too is of little or no help in dating Zechariah 9–14.

Not surprisingly, scholars lately have sought other means to date these chapters than by interpreting allusions. The most ambitious attempt has been that of Hanson, who arrived at his dates (sixth and fifth century; see above) by developing a chronology of styles in Isaiah 56–66 and tracing the same chronology in Zechariah 9–14. Another attempt to date the materials by studying styles employs computer-assisted research. Hill (*HAR* 6 [1982], 130–2) argues that Zechariah 10–14 exhibits considerable linguistic continuity with Haggai and Zechariah 1–8, and, while conceding a date as early as 600 cannot be ruled out, prefers a date of 515–458 for their origin. This continuity does not, however, prove identity. Radday and Wickman (*ZAW* 87 [1975], 54) conclude that the odds of chapters 12–14 stemming from the same hand as 9–11 (or 1–11) is no better than one in five hundred.

Four conclusions seem to emerge from this review of scholarship. First, it is impossible to date the chapters on the basis of historical allusions. Hanson (*Dawn*, 291) is almost certainly correct that 9:1–8 did not describe a past invasion, but employed traditional language to depict the future.

Second, despite the radical disagreement about the absolute date of Zechariah 9–14, most scholars see a chronological development through them. That is, by and large earlier materials appear in Second Zechariah and later materials in Third Zechariah. Third, the shepherd materials were the latest material in the collection. The allegory in 11:4–17 was clearly later than chapters 9–10, and the similarity between the allegory and 13:7–9 has elicited debate about whether to place them together. Fourth, the studies of Hanson, Hill, and Radday and Wickman seem to suggest that Zechariah 9–14 fit well the Persian period.

Three other considerations seem to support the Persian period broadly as the time of origin. First, the authors of Zechariah 9–14 made frequent allusions to earlier prophetic books, especially Jeremiah and Ezekiel (Delcor, *RB* 59 [1952], 385–411), and even First Zechariah (Mason, *ZAW* 88 [1976], 227–39), suggesting a date somewhat later than Zechariah 1–8. On the other hand, 11:12 mentioned weighing out thirty shekels. Since coins became increasingly plentiful in the Greek period, this verse might suggest that the Persian period is more likely than the Greek. (Such a conclusion is at best tentative. Metal was not coined in Palestine until the Maccabean period, so it is impossible to say when the use of silver coins replaced weighing silver as a matter of course.)

The third indicator of a Persian date is the description of the future Jerusalem in 14:10–11. The verses predicted that eschatological Jerusalem would stand above the surrounding, flattened landscape. The boundaries of the city were described in pre-exilic terms. In particular the description mentioned the Benjamin Gate and the Corner Gate, two gates on the badly damaged north wall which were not repaired by Nehemiah. Such a description is quite understandable as the projection of a prophet who flourished while they were in ruins, but not of one who worked after they had been replaced by other gates. The author of vv 10–11, therefore, would have flourished before the career of Nehemiah. So, in the discussion of the historical background which follows, the assumption will be made that the book contains much material from the first half of the Persian period, though it may have reached its final form some time after the career of Nehemiah.

*Historical background.* Scholars who base their understanding of Zechariah 9–14 upon their interpretation of historical allusions describe a particular time frame, e.g. the campaign of Alexander the Great, the battles among his successors, or the trials of the Maccabean period. In view of the more general date adopted above, it will be necessary to set forth here a more general historical background. The problem, of course, is the very limited nature of available sources. The Bible itself reports only a few incidents between the completion of the second Temple in 516 (Ezr. 6:15) and the coming of Alexander in 332: the return of Ezra in 458 or later (Ezr. 7:1–8:36), the return of Nehemiah in 445 and the repair of the breeches in the wall of Jerusalem (Neh. 1:1–7:1), a draft of inhabitants for Jerusalem (Neh. 11:1–2), and Nehemiah's return to Susa in 433 and subsequent second mission to Jerusalem (Neh. 4:6–7). Beyond that one learns of a ceremony where a law code was read (Neh. 8:1–9:37) and of reforms carried out by Ezra and Nehemiah. The picture emerging from these accounts is that of a small community struggling to maintain itself against all odds, including the possibility of disintegration from within.

The glimpse into life around Jerusalem at the time of Haggai and Zechariah (see the Introduction to Haggai, pp. 4–10) revealed an extremely small community comprised of people who had remained behind and some repatriates from the exile. As time passed other exiles returned home. The books of Ezra and Nehemiah reported that groups returned with Ezra and Nehemiah themselves, so it is a fair assumption that other groups did too. As the southern population grew, their neighbours in the old northern kingdom, especially the rulers in Samaria, would have taken increasing interest in them. The reports in Ezr. 4 represented those contacts as negative. At any time, therefore, a group of southerners might have abandoned the hope of reuniting north and south.

The alarm of the Samaritan governor of Judah at the

rebuilding of the wall around Jerusalem in the fifth century is well documented in Neh. 2:9 and 4:1–22. The account of the drafting of one-tenth of the population of the surrounding countryside as inhabitants for Jerusalem (Neh. 11:1–2) indicated that rural life was still the rule, not the exception, not only by those who had remained behind in Judah during the exile but also by those who returned from Babylon. After the draft the population of Jerusalem would have become a commercial and political city large enough to subjugate the surrounding countryside. Neh. 5:12 made it clear that the wealthy had taken economic advantage of the people in the aftermath of rebuilding the wall and a concomitant drought.

The lines of division within the Judaean community were now drawn. The most important division was between those who had experienced exile versus those who had not. The most obvious areas for struggle were over landownership and public office, including the priesthood. Even the repatriates, however, were a diverse group that had returned over time, probably with different agendas and competing claims. The next division was between the inhabitants of Jerusalem and of Judah. As administrative and trade centres, cities always live off their surrounding towns and villages. Sooner or later friction results. The last division was geographic, between north and south, and particularly over who would rule, Jerusalem or Samaria. It is precisely these factional issues, not ancient empires (whether pre- or post-exilic), with which Zechariah 9–14 is primarily interested.

Recently, scholars have explored factionalism within post-exilic life. Plöger (*Theocracy and Eschatology*) claims that the last half of Joel, Zechariah 9–14, and Isaiah 24–27 formed the literary deposit of successive eschatological groups who opposed a theocratic majority. Hanson (*Dawn*) also distinguishes an apocalyptic group, comprised of priests responsible for Isaiah 56–66 and Zechariah 9–14, from the hierocratic Zadokites. While their specific conclusions have met opposition, their general thesis seems correct: the post-exilic community was not monolithic. Indeed, if anything these two studies understate the factionalism of the period. Clearly there was a dominant party in charge of the Temple after 516, but splinter groups may well have been numerous. A study of the literary history of Zechariah 9–14 will help understand where these chapters fit in.

## B. LITERARY HISTORY AND STRUCTURE

Zechariah 9–14 opened with a chapter of diverse literary genres depicting God's recapturing the old Davidic empire (9:1–8), an address to Jerusalem promising her a king under God's protection and the reunion of Judah and Ephraim under her (9:9–13), and further assurance of military victory (9:14–17). The next extended discussion, found in 10:3b–12, employed war language very similar to 9:13–17. In addition, 10:6, 8–10 promised the return of northern and southern exiles. Standing between these two collections are two and a half verses which unite them redactionally and introduce the shepherd motif. This motif appeared in three places (10:1–3a; 11:4–17; 13:7–9), and articulated God's abandonment of his people to worthless shepherds (instead of his sending a Davidic king) and specifically rejected the hope of the reunion of Israel and Judah.

Next one finds a collection of materials in 12:1–9 that promised God's protection of Jerusalem in a time of war. The motif of the protection and elevation of Jerusalem in 12:1–4a, 5, 8–9 was countermanded by supplementary materials that insist Jerusalem would not outrank Judah (12:6–7) and that she herself needed cleansing from sin (12:10–13:6). The final shepherd piece (13:7–9) concluded this articulation of Jerusalem's sin. In chapter 14 one finds another pro-Jerusalem collection that foresaw an attack upon the city. It differs from the account in 12:1–9, however, in that many of the inhabitants of the city would be abused and half would be exiled (14:2; cf. 13:8, where two-thirds of the people would be scattered). It also differs from chapter 9 in that God himself, not a human king, would rule (14:9).

Zechariah 9–14, then, seems to have been made up of

four collections of traditional eschatological hope (9:1–17; 10:3b–12; 12:1–4a, 5, 8–9; and 14:1–13, 14b–21), which have been accurately described as variations on the theme of Holy War (see Ellul, *ETR* 56 [1981], 55–71). Of the collections, the first three included hopes vital during the first half of the Persian period. The fourth collection (chapter 14) seems to have arisen later than the other three (though still before the time of Nehemiah) and expressed much more pessimism. These variations were then supplemented (1) by a collection (12:6–7; 12:10–13:6) that is pro-Judaean vis-a-vis Jerusalem and (2) by the shepherd materials, which contradict the hopes of the first two collections. This final stage probably arose after the time of Nehemiah, i.e. after the city grew strong enough to raise the ire of Judahites outside the power structure.

It is plausible to conclude, therefore, that the redactor of Zechariah 9–14 assembled the four collections and revised them by means of the supplements in 12:6–7, 12:10–13:6 and the shepherd materials. He was probably responsible as well for the redactional connection in 11:1–3. (Mitchell [*Haggai-Zechariah*, 219–20] pointed out that 10:1–3, 11:1–3, and 13:7–9 exhibited similar literary characteristics.) The redactor and his faction would likely have been rural Judaeans as opposed to the urban élite in Jerusalem. They could not foresee a future without Jerusalem, but its role would have been limited and its leadership cleansed, even purged. The redactor and his community also had given up on any hope of reunion with the north. Like all the other groups contending against the Jerusalemite power structure, they would have been a peripheral group with a sectarian vision for the future. Like the others, they would have defined their position vis-a-vis the Zadokites, not against other peripheral groups.

## C. MESSAGE

This factionalism in the post-exilic community raised a crucial question: who was Israel? Was it the priests and those who were loyal to them? Was it the Davidides and those loyal to them? Was it the urbanites in Jerusalem? Was it those who had returned to Judah under this or that leader? Or even those who had never been exiled? All of these groups raised claims that they belonged to the real Israel. Each group based its claim on some part of the inherited tradition. Perhaps no one group could speak for them all. In pressing their own case for inclusion, they inevitably slighted one group and excluded some other. None of them had the full truth; all saw it dimly. Therein lies one lesson for today (Redditt, *CBQ* 51 [1989], 641).

Zechariah 9–14 should, then, be read through the eyes of the redactor. This person apparently thought of himself as the legitimate interpreter of the prophetic tradition, which he quoted extensively. On the other hand there were only six places where he drew upon the Pentateuch (see Ina Willi-Plein (*Prophetie am Ende*, 93), suggesting little real concern with priestly matters. Despite his identification with the prophetic tradition, 13:3–6 reveals his deep suspicion of contemporary prophets. He apparently felt more confident in the written word of the earlier prophets.

He drew selectively from the Davidic tradition. It was not the David of old he discussed, but the David of the future. He passed on without comment the idea that the future king would be righteous and lowly (9:9–10). Where his inherited tradition spoke of the future David as god-like in war (12:8–9), the redactor insisted the house of David would not outrank Judah (12:7). Indeed, he included one tradition (14:9) that said God would rule directly, with no intermediary king. The redactor was disappointed in the contemporary Davidides, whose conduct had seriously compromised their future. For that future to come about, they and the other leading families of Jerusalem would have to repent and be cleansed (12:10–13:1).

The shepherd materials made it clear why this cleansing was necessary. The leaders of the people were nothing other than bad shepherds, who themselves devoured and sold the sheep. In the so-called Shepherd Allegory (11:4–17), the prophet portrayed their abuse of the sheep and their struggles against each other. Because of them, God had no choice but to delay the future he had promised and scatter his sheep again.

Jerusalem itself had to be purged of its sinful inhabitants (13:8–9; 14:2, 5) before it could play its role as the future worship centre for all nations (14:16–19). Even so, all of Judah and not just Jerusalem would be holy land, and all the cooking pots and horses of the countryside would be holy too (14:20–21). The Temple itself was mentioned twice (11:13 and 14:21), but there was no suggestion that the redactor's community should take over the Temple (contra Hanson). Instead, he saw the need for the priesthood to be cleansed (cf. 3:1–10).

## D. CONTENTS

9:1–17      The Davidic Empire Restored
10:1–12     The Reunion of the Homeland
11:1–17     The Treachery of the Shepherds
12:1–9      The War against Jerusalem, Version I
12:10–13:9  The Cleansing of Jerusalem
14:1–21     The War against Jerusalem, Version II

# COMMENTARY

## on

## Zechariah 9–14

The first major section of Second Zechariah comprised 9:1–17. The chapter opened with the description of a sweeping military campaign, in which the traditional enemies of Israel were conquered. In typical holy war thinking, the success of the whole operation was attributed to God (vv. 1, 4), who spoke in vv. 6b–8 (except for 7b). In v. 8b God promised to protect his house and by implication his people, who were referred to by means of a third masculine plural pronoun. In vv. 9–13 God addressed Jerusalem directly, employing second feminine singular pronouns, except for addressing **prisoners of hope** (masculine plural) in v. 12a. In v. 9 he promised to restore the kingship. Then he would reunite Judah and Ephraim (vv. 10, 13) and punish aggressors. Third person narrative resumed again in vv. 14–17. Once again Yahweh would lead his hosts into holy war to protect his people (v. 15) and also would restore the productivity of the land (v. 17).

The shifts between the second and third person have led scholars to posit various hands or sources behind this chapter, and that could be correct. Even so, the whole chapter makes perfectly good sense taken as a whole, and recent scholarship has tended to treat the chapter as a redactional unit. Accordingly, the shifts will be understood to mark the natural movement within the chapter.

Hanson (*Dawn*, 300–24) argues that this chapter constitutes a Divine Warrior Hymn, with the following structure:

Conflict . . . victory (1–7)
Temple secured (8)
Victory shout and procession (9)
Manifestation of Yahweh's universal reign (11–13)
Theophany of Divine Warrior (14)
Sacrifice and banquet (15)
Fertility of restored order (16–17)

Rudolph (176–7) considers the designation impossible

because in no other *OT* hymns did God sing about himself as
in vv. 6b–8, 11–13. It will be preferable, then, to identify
individual forms within the chapter rather than to accept Hanson's form-critical analyis of the whole chapter.

**1–8.** The chapter opened with an enumeration of the cities
God would conquer. As such it seems comparable to earlier
prophecies of disaster against foreign nations (cf. Saebø, *Sacharja 9–14*, 144), at least down to v. 7a. Verses 7b–8 constitute
short prophecies of salvation. As seen in the introduction to
Zechariah 9–14, many scholars have attempted to interpret
9:1–8 against the background of Alexander's march to Egypt,
especially the reference to Tyrè's building a rampart. However, his campaign fits neither the details nor the spirit of 9:1–
17. Hanson (*Dawn*, 316–9) is almost certainly correct that the
action depicted was not that of Alexander or any other human
conqueror, but that of God restoring the traditional boundaries of Israel.

**1.** The word *maśśā'*, translated **oracle** in the *NRSV* and
"burden" in the *KJV* appeared in twenty-four other places in
the Old Testament as a technical term for a message delivered
by a prophet, often with a negative overtone. It derived from
the root *nś'*, to lift up, and referred in many places to a burden
placed on someone or on an animal. Jer. 23:33–40 contained
an extended word play on this basic meaning: when the people
asked, "What is the burden of the Lord?" Jeremiah was to
reply that they were. Apparently, then, a *maśśa'* was a burden
placed on the people by the Lord. In Zech. 9:1 *maśśa'* appeared
with the phrase **word of the Lord**, a combination that
emphasized that the burden to be borne was nothing other
than the following word of God.

The combination of words *maśśa' děbar Yahweh* appeared
elsewhere only in Zech. 12:1 and Mal. 1:1. Consequently,
scholars have long held that the three words introduce originally separate passages editorially combined by a redactor of
the Minor Prophets. By contrast, Beth Glazier-McDonald
(*Malachi*, 26) argues that the word *maśśa'* alone constituted
the superscription in 9:1, that the entire first half of 12:1 served
that role, and that Mal. 1:1 was similar to other prophetic

passages where the addressee was named. Hence, one should not simply assume that the three words constituted a redactional superscription from one hand. This one-word superscription probably stood at the head of 9:1–17 even before that chapter was incorporated with the rest of Zechariah 9–14.

The verse opened with the announcement that **the word of the Lord is against Hadrach**. Hadrach was apparently a city-state in northern Syria, probably the city Hatarikka mentioned in a few Assyrian texts, and perhaps to be identified with Tell Afis southwest of Aleppo (W. S. LaSor, "Hadrach," *ISBE*, 2.592). The verse continued with a *waw* prefixed to a proper noun (and Damascus) and a participle (his resting place). *NRSV* translates the two words with the phrase **and will rest upon Damascus**. The thought may have been that God or his word would pause in Damascus after taking possession of the land.

Verse 1b continued that line of thinking, but the Hebrew is difficult to understand. Literally, one could translate it: "for the eye (or spring) of man and all of the tribes of Israel belong to Yahweh". The crux is the two words translated "eye of man", which seem to make little sense in this context. The simplest solution is the one taken by the *NRSV*, namely to adopt the slight emendations of the word *'îr* (city, understood to be the capital city) for *'ên* (eye) and *'ărām* (Aram) for *'ādām* (man). In that case v. 1b asserted that God owns Damascus, the capital city of the Aramaeans, the same as he did the tribes of Israel. A slightly different emendation, *'ārê* for *'ên* "eye", would result in the plural construct form "cities", which might balance better with "tribes" and assert that Yahweh owned all the cities of Aram. The two assertions would probably be equivalent anyway. If he owned the capital, he would own the others also.

**2.** The thought of v. 1 continued, namely that Yahweh owned Hamath, Tyre, and Sidon as well. Hamath was an ancient Hittite city, located on the Orontes River, midway between Aleppo and Damascus. It remained as one of the most important city states after the demise of the Hittite empire. During the period of the Assyrian empire, it stubbornly resisted Assyrian hegemony, with mixed success. While Hamath lay outside the territory of Israel, its ideal boundaries were said to reach to the territory of Hamath (Num. 34:8; Josh. 13:5; Ezek. 47:13–21), and Jeroboam II was credited (2 Kg. 14:28) with extending his borders there as well (H. F. Vos, "Hamath," *ISBE*, 2.602–3).

Tyre and Sidon were situated on the Phoenician coast. Both cities had long histories as independent kingdoms, though in the last half of the seventh century Sidon came under the control of Tyre. Under the Persians it became a leading city. The reference to the wisdom of the cities is troublesome because the verb *hokmah* (she is wise) is singular. However, that difficulty provides insufficient reason to emend the text.

**3–4.** Tyre itself was heavily fortified from the fourteenth century on, and the rampart mentioned in this verse was likely a breakwater built in the time of Hiram, king of Tyre (Baldwin, 160). Tyre's position on the coast, its reputation in crafts and architecture, and other favourable conditions allowed it to amass great wealth. During its history Assyrian kings exacted heavy tribute from it, Babylon conquered it, and then Persia made of it an important city again, though inferior to Sidon. The prophet of Zech. 9:4 saw its wealth and predicted a reversal in its fortunes. Also in v. 4 the prophet made explicit for the first time what was probably implicit from the beginning, namely that Yahweh himself, like a great conqueror from the North, was moving southward recapturing the ideal boundaries of Palestine.

**5–6a.** The scene shifted in vv. 5–8 to the Philistine coast. Ashkelon, Gaza, and Ekron were three of the five Philistine cities, along with Ashdod (v. 6a) and Gath (which was probably destroyed in the pre-exilic period). Defeated first by David (2 Sam. 5), they all lay within the ideal boundaries of Israel. They apparently gained a measure of freedom from Israel from time to time, sometimes becoming the object of prophetic attack (e.g. Jer. 25:20; Zeph. 2:4–7). According to Zech. 9:5–6a the cities would tremble in fear before Yahweh. The reference to Gaza's "king" has sometimes been used as a key to dating these verses, but the city flourished in so many periods that this allusion is as ambiguous as all the others in 9:1–8. Nor is it crucial for dating that Herodotus presented Gaza as separate from the Philistine cities; it was always considered Philistine in the *OT*. The specific predictions about the cities were traditional punishments: the king will perish (Gaza), the city will become uninhabited (Ashkelon), **a mongrel people** will be brought in to resettle a city (Ashdod). Literally, the Hebrew word *mamzēr* (mongrel) designated an illegitimate offspring (cf. *KJV* "bastard"), even one born of incest (*BDB*, p. 561; cf. Deut. 23:3, 23:2 MT). Here the whole population was called illegitimate; hence, *NRSV*'s translation.

**6b-7.** In vv. 6b-13 the prophet spoke for God, employing first person singular pronouns, instead of the third, masculine singular pronouns used in reference to God in vv. 1–6a, 14–17. Verses 6b-7 continued the discussion about the Philistines. The point was that the real agent behind these changes would be God himself. In v. 7 God declared that he will remove the uncleanness from their mouths. Such defilement would have come from eating meat that (1) had not been properly drained of blood (Gen. 9:4) and/or (2) that belonged to classes of unclean animals (see Lev. 11:2–47 and Deut. 14:3–21). The violation of dietary regulations obviously stood as a representation of their sinful lifestyle. This lifestyle would be changed by God himself, who would then treat the Philistines like a clan of Judah or the city of Jerusalem. The thought is remarkable that traditional enemies within the land would be accepted on a par with ethnic Israelites, and Ekron would become like the city of the Jebusites, i.e. Jerusalem itself (2 Sam. 5:6–10).

**8.** Jerusalem too received good news. The destination of God's march would be Jerusalem, where he would encamp at the door of his house (the Temple) like a guard. Never again would an oppressor overrun its precincts (as the Babylonians had). The phrase **that no one shall march to and fro** is similar to 7:14, which said that no inhabitants had been left in Jerusalem to walk to and fro. Here, the same words meant that no foreign conqueror would do so. The last

phrase is translated **for now I have seen with my own
eyes** (*NRSV*), which seems awkward enough that various
emendations have been offered (cf. *BHS*). However, the verb
can be construed as a "prophetic perfect" (I will see). Then
the phrase would mean that God would look out for Jerusalem
in the future, a meaning perfectly consistent with the verse as
a whole.

**9–13.** God's march had brought him to his destination,
Jerusalem, which he addressed in vv. 9–13 in the form of a
prophecy of salvation. Verses 9–10, which Elliger (149) calls
a *Heroldsruf* (a herald's cry), promised Jerusalem a new king,
while vv. 11–12 spoke of the return of her inhabitants from
exile, and v. 13 promised victory over the Greeks.

**9–10.** *NRSV* correctly treats the Hebrew constructs in v.
9a as appositives: **O daughter Zion** and **O daughter Jerusalem**. The city was commanded to greet her coming king with
shouts of joy. The *NRSV* translation **triumphant and victori-
ous** suggests a military conqueror, which the Hebrew does
not require. The king was called "righteous" or "just" (*ṣaddîk*)
and "saved" (*nôšāʿ*, a Niphal participle). In the context of
God's march from Hadrach to Jerusalem, the king's position
was more likely to be a result of God's prowess than his own.
Further, he would be "humble" or "poor" and would ride on
a colt, **the foal of a donkey**.

The pronouns in v. 10 cause a little trouble. The MT reads
"I will cut off" the chariot and the horse. The LXX reads a
third masculine singular. In the second half of the verse, the
MT employed a third masculine singular verb **and he shall
command peace**. *NRSV* follows the lead of the LXX, making
the king the one who both cuts off the horse and chariot and
who proclaims peace to the nations. It may be, however, that
the MT is to be preferred, that it was God himself who would
cut off the chariot and horse (and the battle bow as well) and the
king who would proclaim peace. This understanding is more
consistent with what was said earlier in 9:1–8 and with the
emphasis to follow on God's action in Holy War. True, the king
would rule, but over a kingdom subjugated by God.

As Mitchell (*Haggai, Zechariah*, 275) notes, the boundaries of this kingdom are ambiguous. For certain they would include both Ephraim and Jerusalem. The phrase **from sea to sea** might have meant the whole (known) world, but in light of the limited territory God captured in vv. 1–8 the phrase might have something much smaller in mind. Similarly, the next line might have referred to a river thought to surround the earth, but it might have designated a much smaller area. **The River** in the *OT* was usually the Euphrates, and the word for earth (*'āreṣ*) can mean simply "the land". Hence, the verse might well have in mind the Davidic empire, which stretched from the Euphrates to the ends of the land.

The motif of the future protection of Jerusalem by God and the inclusion of the Philistines among his people perhaps led to the placement of 9:1–17 at the beginning of these materials and, thus, immediately after First Zechariah. Zechariah 1–8 concluded with a picture of peoples and nations streaming to Jerusalem to worship. The passage closest in tone or spirit to 8:20–23 was 9:8–10. Thus 9:1–10 appropriately connects Second Zechariah to First. Zechariah 14 closed with the picture of the surviving nations coming to Jerusalem and Judah for the Feast of Booths. Zechariah 9:1–10 and 14:1–21 together framed Zechariah 9–14 with similar pictures of God's defeating the enemies and bringing the survivors into the worshipping fellowship.

In the *NT* Zech. 9:9 took on a new life. Matthew 21:5 and John 12:15 quoted the verse and applied it to Jesus in connection with his triumphal entry. They made explicit what was probably implicit in the other two gospel accounts of this event. In their narratives, the evangelists presented Jesus as the one who fulfilled the prophecy of the righteous king who proclaimed peace.

**11–12.** Not only would God send to Jerusalem a new king, he would also restore to the city her exiled inhabitants. They were living in Babylon (and elsewhere) like prisoners in a waterless pit. Addressing the prisoners, God commanded them to return to their fortress, Jerusalem. Addressing Jerusalem, God promised to double her population. Originated before the drafting of inhabitants for Jerusalem (Neh. 11:1–

2), this verse recognized the reduced size of the population in comparison with that before the exile. Moreover, this promise to repopulate the city was grounded in God's covenant with Jerusalem. Any notion of Jerusalem's inviolability had been destroyed once and for all by Nebuchadnezzar in 586, but the tradition that Zion was God's dwelling place remained alive and furnished the basis for this hope.

**13.** Verse 13 culminated God's address to Zion. First, he declared that he would bend (or had bent) Judah as a bow and would fill it (or had filled it) with Ephraim. *NRSV* understands the two perfect verbs in the past tense, resulting in a double switch from future to past and back to the future. It is also possible to take them as prophetic perfects. Either way God declared victory over his enemies. The image also conveyed the essential unity of Ephraim and Judah, north and south. As bow and arrow, one was useless without the other (Baldwin, 168). Second, God declared that he would wield the sons of Zion as a sword against the sons of Greece, clearly a claim parallel to the first. (See the Introduction to Zechariah 9–14, pp. 91–105, 'especially' pp. 96–97, on the fallacy of treating this verse as evidence that this chapter is concerned with the campaign of Alexander the Great and its aftermath.) One is left to guess what prompted this threat. As the author looked beyond his borders, perhaps Greece appeared to be the remotest power he knew of, and he affirmed that not even distant powers could again capture Jerusalem. On the other hand, economic and political contact with the Greeks began in the pre-exilic period. It would seem likely that Greece had pressed its advantage in whatever contact it had with tiny Judah during the exilic and post-exilic period, thereby earning the wrath of the author.

**14–17.** The next four verses switched from an address by God to a third person presentation of his actions. These verses included two prophecies of salvation: vv. 14–15 and 16–17. Verse 14 opened as a description of a theophany, but quickly turned into a description of Holy War. God would use lightning for his arrow. The image of the **arrow** also connected the last two sections of the chapter (vv. 9–13, 14–17).

**14–15.** These verses are full of battle language. All the forces of nature were at God's disposal. He will use lightning for his arrow in defeating his enemy. He will **sound the trumpet**, calling his hosts (stars? cf. Jg. 5:20) to battle. He **will march forth in the whirlwinds of the south**. (The term "whirlwind" could designate a milder storm; as an image of God's fury in battle, "whirlwind" is the better translation.)

Verse 15 began with a straightforward statement that Yahweh will protect or shield his people. The next clause, however, presents difficulties, which preclude complete understanding. The unnamed subject apparently was God's people. The verbs employed meant "to eat or devour" and "to subdue or tread down". The object of the second verb was slingstones. *NRSV* emends the text to read **slingers** as the object. It is not clear how that helps. It makes equal sense to say God's people tread down slingers as to say they tread down slingstones. Nor would the term "slingers" provide a better object for eat/devour than the term "slingstones", except perhaps in some very figurative sense of "devour". *NEB* has proposed perhaps the most satisfactory translation of the text as it now stands, based on the Targ.: "they shall prevail, they shall trample on the slingstones". In view of the difficulty of these readings, scholars often assume that the original object for "eat/devour" has dropped out.

Nor is the remainder of v. 15 as violent as *NRSV*, following the LXX, makes it out to be. There is no word in the MT for **blood**. One may translate it simply: "they will drink, they will roar, as with wine; they will be full like the bowl, like the corners of the altar". Nor is there any suggestion here of a victory banquet (contra Baldwin, 170). The whole half-verse seems to signify only that people in the new Jerusalem will have plenty.

**16–17.** The last two verses constituted another prophecy of salvation. His people were described with two similes. They were (1) like a flock of sheep and (2) like jewels in a crown. The first part of v. 17 belonged with and concluded the similes of v. 16. God's **goodness** was his people (*BDB*, 375) or flock; his **beauty** was his jewelled crown. Verse 17b had more in common with v. 15b than with 16–17a. It reflected again upon the bounty God will bring, and said that **grain** would **make the young men flourish, and new wine** would make **the young women** flourish.

### THE REUNION OF THE HOMELAND
### 10:1–12

Chapter 10 constituted a new section in Zechariah 9–14. It is, however, a redactional unity. Saebø (*Sacharja 9–14*, 205) and many commentators call vv. 1–2 an admonition, and note that vv. 3–12 vacillate between first and third person speeches. The theme of the return to and reunion of the homeland, seen already in 9:11–17, resumed first in v. 3b and continued to the end of the chapter. To which verses, then, did v. 3a belong? R. L. Smith (263) argues that v. 3a cannot belong with vv. 1–2, because they ended with the statement that there was no shepherd, while v. 3a said God was angry with the shepherds. This suggestion leaves the tension between the two verses unresolved. It would be better to argue that v. 2b decried the lack of a genuine shepherd, and v. 3a condemned the impostors trying to play the role. If so, one is justified in seeing vv. 1–3a as a redactional creation introducing 10:3b–12 and connecting those verses to 9:1–17. This introduction, of course, was the first of the "shepherd oracles", all of which began with admonitions or imperatives.

**1.** Chapter 10 opened with an admonition to **ask rain from the Lord**. Rain, in turn, would make possible the growth of vegetation. The LXX added a reference to the early or autumn rains, but despite *NEB* there is no reason to adopt that reading. The reminder that God **makes the storm clouds** and **gives showers of rain** drew upon Jer. 14:22 and emphasized the power of God to do things other gods or people cannot. It implied that the people had not been trusting God.

**2a.** This implication became explicit in v. 2a, which condemned **teraphim, diviners**, and **dreamers**. Teraphim are usually understood to have been images of household gods that could vary in size. Teraphim stolen by Rachel from her father were small enough to be concealed under a camel's saddle (Gen. 31:34), but the one used by Michal was large enough to fool observers into thinking David was sick in bed (1 Sam. 19:13). They were sometimes referred to in association with divination (2 Kg. 23:24; Ezek. 21:21) or with the ephod (Jg. 17:5; 18:14, 17, 20). They were condemned in 1 Sam. 15:23, and Josiah attempted to eliminate them in his reform (2 Kg. 23:24). Since they were mentioned in no other post-exilic text than Zech. 10:2, scholars often suggest they were no longer in use and think v. 2 has in mind practices of Babylonians of practices exiles might have engaged in while there. It is probably the case, then, that this verse actually condemned the use of some kind of oracular device by calling them teraphim.

Divination had to do with discerning that which was hidden. Thus people like Samuel, who was consulted by Saul while seeking lost donkeys (1 Sam. 9), could be considered diviners (or seers). On the other hand, divination was often prohibited (see Lev. 19:26, 31; 20:27; Deut. 18:9–14). Like false prophecy (Zech. 13:3–6), it needed replacing. The practice of divination could take many forms, one of which was the interpretation of dreams. When practised by Joseph and Daniel, it was treated as laudatory. At other times – as here – it was condemned.

**2b–3a.** It was not the case that the people had no leaders at all; rather, they had only false guides to lead them. Hence, they wandered as aimlessly as sheep and suffered accordingly. What they lacked was a real shepherd. God would punish the false shepherds, those who led through divination.

**3b–12.** The remainder of chapter 10 offered another prophecy of salvation. Taken in and of itself, it predicted the restitution of Judah (vv. 3b–6) and Ephraim (vv. 7–12). It opened by speaking of Yahweh in the third person, announcing his presence among the army of Judah (vv. 3b–5). In v. 6 Yahweh himself proclaimed his compassion for Judah and also for the house of Joseph, thus providing the transition to Ephraim in v. 7. That verse promised the return of Ephraim and spoke

of Yahweh in the third person again, but in vv. 8–12 Yahweh
whistled for the people of Ephraim, calling them home. This
restitution of north and south echoed 9:10 and 13, but contained no reference to a messiah; instead, Yahweh would lead
their armies.

**3b–5.** The connection between 3a and 3b was so smooth
that *NEB* and *NRSV* treat the verse as one sentence drawing
a contrast. In v. 3a the verb *pqd* was used in the positive sense
to "visit with punishment", but in v. 3b it was used in the
sense of "visit with grace". The translation of the *NRSV* that
God **cares for** his flock does not reflect the twofold use of the
same verb, but does catch the sense that God would punish
the shepherds because of his compassion for his flock. Unlike
the hireling shepherds, God was the good shepherd who would
rescue his sheep from danger. He would also **make them like
his proud war horse**. The contrast between hapless sheep
and proud war horses could hardly be more stark, depicting
the change that God's positive visitation would mean to
Judah.

Verse 4 divided into two parts. The first half gave three
titles for the commanders who would emerge from Judah to
lead her: **cornerstone**, **tent-peg**, and **battle bow**. A corner-
stone was a stone laid at the intersection of two walls to bind
them together, and the term was used in the *OT* as a symbol
of strength. Commentators often point out that the *OT* used
it for rulers (see, for example, Jg. 20:2 and especially Ps.
118:22). The peg could refer to a tent peg or to a peg used to
fasten a thing in place, as in Isa. 22:23, where it is used
figuratively in connection with a future ruler. Further, the
battle bow symbolized power. Verse 4 closed by making the
point that the commanders would emerge once again from
the people of Judah rather than from foreign peoples. The
word **together** in v. 5 actually stood at the end of v. 4 in the
MT and could go with either verse. The point of the verse
was that God would once again lead the warriors of Judah in
holy war.

**6.** This verse provided the transition between the future of
Judah and that of Ephraim. On the one hand, it repeated the

thought of vv. 3b–5, that God would strengthen Judah. On the other hand, it introduced the new motif of the return of exiles to Ephraim. Had the verse spoken of the return of Israel, one might argue that the name designated the southern kingdom of Judah, as it did often in the *OT*. The explicit use of the names Joseph in v. 6 and Ephraim in v. 7 made it clear that the author thought that God would bring home northern Israelites exiled to Assyria (v. 11). God would restore them because he had compassion on them. He would restore them to the status they held before he rejected them, sending them into exile (2 Kg. 17:1–6). His action was expressed also in terms of his answering them.

**7.** As would be the case with Judah, so also Ephraim would become strong. Her men would become warriors, making all her people happy. Even the children would perceive the change and become glad.

**8–9.** The MT reads: I will whistle for them. Mitchell (*Haggai, Zechariah*, 291) describes the word as the sharp, clear signal the shepherd used in calling his sheep. God had scattered Ephraim by means of the Assyrian Empire. Even so they would remember him (while they were in exile), rear their children (properly), and return home. Their return would be God's work alone, a result of his grace. He had **redeemed them** (cf. Jer. 31:11). The word was used of the redemption of the firstborn by means of a sacrifice (Num. 3:45) and of God's acting redemptively toward his people in the exodus (Deut. 7:8). It carried this latter meaning here as well.

**10–11.** God promised to bring them home from **Egypt** and from **Assyria**. The language was probably traditional, taken from Hos. 8:13 and 11:5, where the prophet spoke metaphorically of the exile to Assyria as a return to bondage in Egypt (see James Limburg, *Hosea–Micah*, Interpretation [Atlanta, Knox, 1988] 39; Henry McKeating, *Amos, Hosea, Micah*, Cambridge Bible Commentary [Cambridge; Cambridge University, 1971], 124). Verse 11 is full of exodus imagery (cf. Mason, 102; Elliger, 157), drawing the comparison between God's future rescue of the Joseph tribes from Assyria with his past rescue of the Joseph tribes from Egypt.

Verse 10b promised that God would bring them **to the land of Gilead and to Lebanon**. Gilead, of course, was the land allocated to the tribes of Gad and Reuben by Moses in Transjordan (Num. 32:33). Lebanon, by contrast, remained outside the territory of Israel, but bordered on it. The point of v. 10b was, therefore, that when God returned the people of the northern kingdom, their old homeland would not hold them; its boundaries would be broadened. In 9:3 Tyre and Sidon were included in the lands God would capture; 10:10b saw the land in between as part of the future kingdom.

**12.** This picture of the restoration of northern Israel closed with two interrelated statements: (1) God would strengthen them, (2) so they could follow him.

The picture of the future articulated in 10:3b–12 was placed within a larger context. The picture was introduced by the first shepherd passage in 10:1–3a, which articulated God's anger against the shepherds or leaders of the people. The picture was followed by the second shepherd passage (11:4–17) with its introduction 11:1–3. These verses also spoke of judgment upon the shepherds. This redactional context was written later to explain that God had not carried out these plans for Judah and Ephraim because of the sins of the shepherds, which the next chapter elaborated.

## THE TREACHERY OF THE SHEPHERDS
## 11:1–17

Chapter 11 consisted entirely of shepherd materials. Verses 1–3 constituted a taunt song, introducing vv. 4–17, which gave an extended portrayal of the prophet as a shepherd. The genre of 11:4–17 has been identified as an allegory, a parable, a vision, or a report of a symbolic act. The verses probably do not fit any of those categories precisely, but do contain elements of at least two. On the one hand they resemble a report of a symbolic act (cf. Isa. 20:1–6; Jer. 27:2). However, it clearly would be impossible for the prophet to carry out the command to become the shepherd of the people, so the report was only a literary device and not a report of something the prophet actually did. Beyond that, the sheep certainly represented the people and the shepherds their leaders, so to that extent the passage also reads like an allegory.

**1–3.** Verse 1 began with an appeal to Lebanon to open her doors. It followed the reference to Lebanon in 10:10, which included that area in the land to be settled by Israel in the future. At first glance one might even suppose that 11:1 was repeating that idea in talking about a fire which would burn her cedars. Verse 2 then called upon two other kinds of trees in the forest to bewail the loss of the cedars. The first is usually understood as a **cypress**, as in the *NRSV*. However, since the cypress does not now grow in Lebanon, many scholars have concluded that the reference is to an evergreen, either a fir, a pine, or a juniper. The second type of tree called upon to lament were the oaks of Bashan. The reference is quite surprising since Bashan is better known for its lush pastureland. Mitchell (*Haggai, Zechariah*, 296–7), therefore, argues that the verse is secondary. In any case the name "Bashan" may well be.

Verse 3a spoke, not of the wail of the trees, but of the wail of the shepherds. The parallelism suggests that the trees all represent shepherds (or rulers). Verse 3b then spoke of the roar of the lions, apparently displeased over the destruction of the **thickets of the Jordan**. The imagery is difficult to understand in particular details, but the overall impact is one of destruction. It would appear, then, that this taunt was aimed against the shepherds or rulers, who had been or were about to be destroyed. If so, it formed a fitting introduction to the allegory or report of a(n imaginary) symbolic act which followed in vv. 4–17.

**4–17.** This allegory/report opened (vv. 4–6) with God's calling or commissioning the prophet to assume the role of shepherd. The prophet then assumed the role for the first time, taking and naming two staffs. Verses 7, 10, and 14 described the disposition of the staffs, while vv. 8–9 and 11–13 described the action of the shepherd/prophet and the reaction of other shepherds and some merchants. Finally, in vv.

15–17 the prophet again resumed the role of the shepherd, who this time was identified as worthless. However, a reader should resist the temptation to understand the prophet's first role as good. He quickly became impatient with the people and abandoned them to destruction, clearly not the behaviour of a good shepherd. The overall point of the entire allegory/report was that the shepherds, whom the prophet represented, have sold out the people, rather than protecting them. The passage also depicted their struggles against each other. These behaviours had destroyed the possibility for favour and union, Davidic king and Davidic kingdom.

**4–6.** God's commissioning of the prophet to the role of shepherd was reported tersely: **Be a shepherd of the flock doomed to slaughter**. God appointed the prophet to the role of shepherd, hired by a group called buyers and sellers (v. 5). These people invoked the name of God and constituted the rich and powerful members behind the ruling class. The charge that the buyers killed the sheep, yet went unpunished, implied that they had less than full rights over the sheep. Likewise, the sellers exceeded their rights, but praised God for their wealth. One might suppose that the buyers and sellers would recognize their moral failure, but they did not. This was primarily because the shepherds were in collusion with them and did not spare (*yaḥmôl*) the people. So God said: "I will still not spare (*'eḥmôl*) the inhabitants of the land" (v. 6). What the leaders of the community had sown, the people would reap. Lawlessness would prevail, as people fell into the hand of their neighbours or their king. The mention of a king does not necessitate a date during the pre-exilic period. All through the post-exilic period Judah was under the control of one king or another, into any of whose hands a hapless Judaean might fall. Kings of the future, like conquerors of the past, would wreck havoc on the leaderless, hence defence-less, **land**. (*NRSV* translates the word *'ereṣ* by the word "earth", but there is no reason to assume a broad meaning for the word here. The land in question was Palestine or just Judah.)

**7.** Having been commissioned by God, the prophet began

to shepherd the people. The MT contains a difficult phrase *lākēn 'ăniyê haṣṣon*, which the *KJV* translates "verily the poor of the flock". However, recent scholars have concluded that the first two words should be joined into one, and translate as *NRSV* does: **for the sheep merchants**. The same emendation occurs in v. 11 also.

The prophet/shepherd procured two staffs and gave each a name. The first he called **Favour** (*RSV*, Grace), an appropriate name for an instrument a prophet would use in caring for his people. The other he named **Unity**, taken from a word meaning "bind". Again, this name would be appropriate for an instrument a shepherd would use in holding a flock together. The name alluded to the symbolic act of Ezekiel, who joined two sticks together, symbolizing the reuniting of Judah and Ephraim (Ezek. 37:16–17). Staffs in hand, the shepherd began to tend the sheep.

**8–9.** The prophet/shepherd's next act was to depose **the three shepherds** (or three of the shepherds) in one month. The history of the futile search for the identity of these shepherds was sketched in the Introduction to Zechariah 9–14 (pp. 97–8). Suffice it to repeat here that the act most likely portrayed on-going conflict within the ruling party, behaviour the prophet considered characteristic of those people, so no one single event is likely in view. Then (v. 8b), the prophet/shepherd became impatient with the people, who in turn came to detest him. As a consequence (v. 9) the shepherd resigned his office with a lack of concern typical of a hireling: **What is to die, let it die; what is to be destroyed, let it be destroyed; and let those that are left over devour the flesh of one another**. In other words the prophet/shepherd was abandoning the flock to all external and internal danger, hardly the behaviour of a good shepherd.

**10.** Consequently, the prophet broke his staff named Favour, symbolizing the annulment of the covenant between the shepherd and the people (see 2 Sam. 5:3; 2 Kg. 11:17). The noun *'ammîm* is plural, and could be translated **nations** as *NRSV* does. However, the noun is used in the plural in the phrases "To be gathered to one's people" (i.e. to be buried with one's family or kin) and "To be cut off from one's people" (D. I. Block, "People," *ISBE* 3.760), and in 1 Kg. 22:28 and Job 36:20, among others. In the context of the shepherd materials, it probably designated the prophet's people themselves. The passage makes so much more sense if seen as concerned with the prophet's people that *BHS* and Elliger (162) emend the plural to a singular.

**11–13.** Mason (108–9) argues that these verses are intrusive (1) since they disturb the connection between the verses describing the staffs (10, 14), and (2) because no preparation had been laid for the mention of wages. While the verses are problematic, Mason's observations do not prove that the verses are secondary. There is some ambiguity in the first half of v. 11, however, with the phrase *NRSV* translates **sheep merchants** (cf. v. 7 above). A translation reflecting the Hebrew word order would run: "the merchants of the flock". Some scholars argue that the flock itself observed the shepherd. That can hardly be correct, however, because in the following verse the prophet continued to address the same people, requesting of them his wages. Thus, it was the merchants who had been watching the prophet. The word for watching was the same as that for tending sheep or holding a captive. The sentence constituted a word-play: the one tending the sheep was held captive by the merchants. He was not a good shepherd; he was their uncaring hireling. By acting as a hireling, the prophet revealed the judgment of God on the merchants.

When in v. 12 the prophet/shepherd requested his wages, the merchants **weighed** them out. Coins were not minted in Judah until 350 BC or later, and did not become common until the Greek period. Before then one weighed out metal on scales. The amount of the shepherd's wages was thirty shekels, the price of a slave (Exod. 21:32). The amount was not insignificant, but its association with the price of slaves elicited the sarcastic comment (v. 13) that it was **lordly**.

The final problem in v. 13 is where or to whom the prophet threw the silver. *NRSV* follows the Pesh. and reads: **Throw it into the treasury** (*'ôṣār*). The MT instead reads: "Throw it to the *yôṣẽr*". The word is a participle from a root meaning to form or fashion. A person who forms or fashions things is a craftsman, often a potter (Isa. 19:26; 41:25; Jer. 18:4, 6), but perhaps also a silversmith. Whether the word designated a treasury or a craftsman, it was associated with the Temple, so the silver went there.

**14.** Breaking the first staff symbolized the annulment of the covenant between the people and the shepherd; breaking the second staff symbolized the annulment of the brotherhood between Judah and Ephraim. Thus, the allegory contradicted the hope for the reunion of north and south. Not only that, the fault lay with the shepherds. Since the term "shepherd" was often a title for a king, the prophet probably meant that no eschatological king would arise out of such a group.

**15–17.** God told the prophet once again to take the implements of the shepherd. This time the shepherd was called **worthless**. What made him worthless was that he would not **care for the perishing, or heal the maimed, or nourish the healthy**. That behaviour was scarcely different from the behaviour of the prophet/shepherd in the first episode. There he abandoned the flock and let the weak die, the enemy attack, and the survivors devour each other (v. 9). Here the prophet/shepherd, like the merchants, devoured the sheep. The concluding phrase in v.16, **tearing off even their hoofs**, is enigmatic. The MT employed a subject and a verb with the same two initial consonants in their roots. Clearly, the clause represented a word play. *NEB* translates as follows: "throw away their broken bones". Mitchell (*Haggai, Zechariah*, 316) follows the Pesh. and translates: "their legs he will gnaw" Whatever the precise translation of the phrase, the context requires the meaning that the shepherd would devour every possible bite.

The passage concluded with a woe-oracle against the worthless shepherd. God pronounced a curse against him; his right arm and right eye would be smitten so that he could neither draw nor aim a bow. No such person could function as a shepherd.

Zechariah 11:4–17 reversed the hopes of the post-exilic

community for reunion under a Davidic king. The failures of the shepherds precluded the dawning of God's new day. In the last half of Zechariah 9–14, the redactor examined a third element of the post-exilic hope, the role of Jerusalem in the future time.

### THE WAR AGAINST JERUSALEM, VERSION I
## 12:1–9

In Zechariah 9–11, the redactor used traditional materials as he received them, but connected them with shepherd materials that reinterpreted them. In chapters 12–14, he employed two accounts of the future of Jerusalem. Fundamental to the two accounts was the motif of the nations versus Jerusalem. Hanns-Martin Lutz (*Jahwe, Jerusalem und die Völker*, 208–12) argues that the motif was used differently in each chapter, indicating that they derived from different authors. The second of those accounts (chapter 14) was employed with few modifications, but the first underwent considerable correction. In that account one finds two different views of a future attack on Jerusalem. In what was probably the original scenario (vv. 1–2a or 2, 3–4a, 5, 8–9) other nations attacked Jerusalem, but God protected and elevated her inhabitants to kingly status and her king to divine status. In the other verses (4b, 6–7), God gave victory to Judah first, and Jerusalem was not exalted above the surrounding territory. Presumably the redactor himself was responsible for this pro-Judahite recension. Verse 2b is short and awkward and might have been a scribal gloss intended to smooth out some of the tension, between the two views (see comments below). The genre of 12:1–9 is neither a prophecy of disaster nor a prophecy of salvation, but something of both. The basic thrust of the verses was the future victory of Jerusalem (and Judah) over the surrounding peoples. Obviously that eventuality would involve both disaster and salvation, and both were described.

**1.** The opening of the verse was very similar to 9:1; see the commentary on that verse. The reference to Israel is rather surprising in light of the chapter's total concentration on Judah and Jerusalem. It is likely that the term was used here not in a political sense but in a genetic sense, as it was in Isa. 8:18 and Jer. 10:1, where it clearly referred to people in Jerusalem and Judah.

The messenger formula **Thus says the Lord** opened the oracle itself. The formula was expanded by a hymn-like praise of God. God was celebrated both for his creation of the heavens and the earth and for his creation of human beings. The choice of words for the physical creation derived from Ps. 104: (1) **stretched out** is *nṭh* (cf. 104:2; you stretch out the heavens like a tent; see also Isa. 42:5), and (2) **founded** is *ysr* (cf. 104:5; you founded the earth on its fixed place). The statement that God **formed the human spirit within** drew upon Gen. 2:7: "and Yahweh Elohim formed the man [out of] dust from the ground, and breathed in his nostrils the breath of life". The verse evidenced no reliance on the priestly account of creation in Genesis 1.

**2.** According to v.2a God will use Jerusalem as a cup of strong drink to make the peoples around it reel. As Baldwin (188–9) points out, Jerusalem herself had had to drink the cup of the Lord's wrath; now it was the nations' turn. How v.2b fits with that thought, however, is not clear. Some scholars drop the preposition before the name Judah (cf. *NEB*) and understand it to participate in the battle against Jerusalem. *NRSV* retains the proposition and offers a fairly literal translation: **it will be against Judah also in the siege against Jerusalem**. That would apparently mean that Judah as well as Jerusalem would suffer in a siege. One could treat that statement as part of the original scenario: any siege of Jerusalem would inevitably affect Judah. Other ways to understand v. 2b should be considered, however. The entire passage subsequently underwent a pro-Judahite recension, in which the perquisites of Jerusalem were specifically guaranteed to Judah. It is doubtful, though, that the revisionist responsible for that addition would have included Judah in the siege too. On the other hand, v. 2b might have been added by a scribe. Only v. 2b mentioned a siege, while v. 4a spoke of horses and riders, clearly not needed in a siege. Indeed, nowhere else did 12:1–9 mention a siege.

**3.** The next verse opened with the adverbial phrase **On that day** (cf. vv. 4, 6, 8, and 9), which often served as a technical term that set what followed in an eschatological context, as it did here. It also could connect independent oracles to each other. God promised to make Jerusalem a heavy stone, a thought parallel to making her a cup of reeling to the nations in v. 2. One might expect the idea to continue that the nations would suffer hernias trying to lift such a stone, and the *NRSV* translation **grievously hurt themselves** might allow that interpretation. The MT, however, used the verb *śrṭ*, to cut or scratch. So here the meaning was to gash or lacerate deeply. Verse 3b set the stage for God's intervention by highlighting the threat against Jerusalem: **all the nations of the earth shall come together against it**.

**4.** The account continued in v. 4a where God threatened to **strike every horse with panic and every rider with madness**. Verse 4b was an addition, promising to exempt the house of Judah from that disaster. It was the first pro-Judahite addition to the depiction of Jerusalem's future elevation. This addition could well have caused a later scribe to add v. 2b.

**5.** *NRSV* emends the text of v. 5 slightly to read **clans** instead of chief. It treats the word the same in 9:7, where the context seems to require the meaning "clan". The clans will say to themselves concerning God's defence of Jerusalem: "**The inhabitants of Jerusalem have strength through the Lord of hosts, their God**." Such a statement is best understood as part of the original scenario, proclaiming divine favour upon Jerusalem, a proclamation strongly contested in vv. 6–7 and 12:10–13:9. The theme of the superiority of the Jerusalemites over the clans of Judah resumed in v. 8.

**6–7.** Verse 6 made essentially the same claim for Judah that vv. 2–3 made for Jerusalem. Whereas those verses had depicted Jerusalem as a cup of reeling against the surrounding peoples and a stone on which they gashed themselves, v. 6 depicted Judah as a blazing pot and a flaming torch among the same peoples. The images of a cooking pot set on a wooden fire and torches burning a field of sheaves depicted sheer destruction, symbolizing judgment. Behind the judgment stood God himself.

The implication of the last phrase of the verse was probably that Jerusalem could only be repopulated with the assistance of Judah (reading with the *NRSV*) or perhaps that she would remain secure from any harm from Judah (reading with the *NIV*). Once again it is not certain that a siege was in view; v. 7 spoke of victory coming to the tents of Judah rather than to people trapped in cities. In any case the point of these two verses, stated at the end of v. 7, was that Jerusalem would in no way supersede Judah.

**8–9.** Verses 8 and 9 brought to a close the first account of the attack upon Jerusalem. God himself would shield the inhabitants of the city from harm when the nations assembled to do battle with Jerusalem, and he would defeat those nations. If the point of vv. 6–7 was that Jerusalem was in no way superior to Judah, the point of vv. 8–9 was that Jerusalem was above all the nations. Verse 8 portrayed even the weakest citizen of the city as a veritable David in battle and the Davidides as divine warriors. Verse 7, by contrast, denied that either the Davidides or the inhabitants of Jerusalem would rise above the Judahites. It is difficult to avoid the conclusion that vv. 6–7 were written to claim for Judah the same status vv. 8–9 reserved for Jerusalem.

It is also difficult to avoid the conclusion that the sympathies of the author of vv. 6–7 (and v. 4b) lay with the Judaeans rather than with the Jerusalemite élite. Further, the following verses (12:10–13:6) shared the same perspective that Jerusalem was not superior; indeed those verses contended that sinful Jerusalem, particularly her leading families (12:12–14), badly needed cleansing. That evaluation of Jerusalem was followed in turn by the last of the shepherd materials (13:7–9).

### THE CLEANSING OF JERUSALEM
### 12:10–13:9

These verses constituted a supplement to 12:1–9 from the perspective of the author of 12:4b, 6–7. They appear also to have been a literary composite made up of diverse materials, articulating condemnations of the leading families in Jerusalem (12:10–13:1), false prophets (13:2–6), and a shepherd (13:7–9). The first of these components (12:10–13:1) opened and closed like a prophecy of salvation, depicting God's gracious intervention. The result of his intervention, however, would not be rejoicing, but mourning and cleansing! The second component (13:2–6) sounds more like a prophecy of disaster. It continued the theme of ridding the land of sin. The third component (13:7–9) opened with an admonition in which God addressed his sword, commanding it to strike his shepherd, a thought that follows nicely upon the woe oracle at the end of the shepherd allegory (11:17). Following a description of the destruction of two-thirds of the population of the land (13:8–9a), the passage concluded on a note of salvation (v. 9b).

**10.** God announced that he **will pour out a spirit of compassion and supplication** on the Davidides and the Jerusalemites. As a result, they will mourn. The reason given for their mourning constitutes another difficulty in Zechariah 9–14. The *NRSV* reads: **when they look upon the one whom they have pierced**, **they shall mourn for him**, . . . Where the *NRSV* translates "one", however, the MT points the preposition and pronominal suffix 'ēlai as a first person singular ("to me"). While some scholars and both the *NEB* and *NIV* translate the suffix in the first person, *BHS* suggests either dropping the final vowel or (better) repointing the word as the rarer form of the proposition: 'ēlê. Adopting this suggestion would result in agreement with the *NRSV*.

Also unclear is the identity of the "pierced one". If one retains the first person singular suffix in 'ēlai, the "pierced one" would seem to be the speaker, God. In that case the word obviously would not connote death from the wound, but would represent striking, metaphorical language. On the more likely reading of *ʾēlê* as a preposition, the "pierced one" could be an individual or a group. Scholars have offered a number of candidates ranging from the Messiah to the prophet/ shepherd of 11:4–17 to Onias III or Simon Maccabeus, from Jewish martyrs to a group of priests who had fallen out of power. It is obviously not possible to recover his identity, but one can say that the author of 12:10 held the population of Jerusalem responsible for a past deed, perhaps an execution. A spirit of compassion from God would cause them to repent and mourn for him. The depth of the mourning was compared to the sorrow one would feel over the death of one's only child or one's firstborn. Behaviours associated with mourning included putting on sackcloth and ashes or tearing one's garments, lamenting, and praying. Sometimes other manifestations of grief included such measures as cutting oneself. Those mourning rites typically lasted a week.

**11.** The description of the mourning in Jerusalem continued by means of a comparison with a mourning rite in the plain of Megiddo. **Hadad-rimmon** could be a place name, but was more likely the name of a divinity. Ezek. 8:14 spoke of women weeping over the vegetation god Tammuz, whose annual death and resurrection caused the variations in the seasons. Their weeping was probably part of a ritual in which laments were sung for the divinity like laments at funerals for real people (Walther Zimmerli, *Ezekiel 1* [Hermeneia, Philadelphia, Fortress, 1979], 242). Zech. 12:11 presumably had in mind the same kind of ritual. Other interpretations focus on the Aramaic text. For example, M. Delcor (*VT* 3 [1953], 67–73) emends even the Aramaic text to read "son of Amon" (i.e. Josiah). Such extreme measures are not convincing.

**12–14.** The opening clause in v. 12 said that even **the land shall mourn** over the "pierced one". More importantly the principal families would also mourn, each one by itself; both husbands and wives. No one would be influenced by the others (Baldwin, 194). The families mentioned by name include the houses of David, Nathan, Levi, and Shimei. The family of **David** would be the descendants of the royal family. The descendants of **Nathan** might have been descendants of David's illustrious prophet, but are more likely descendants of one of the sons of David (2 Sam. 5:14). Besides, the prophets receive special condemnation in 13:2–6. The family of Levi may well have included all the priests, the distinction between Aaronites (or Zadokites) and Levites apparently being of no importance to this author. (See the comments on Mal. 2:4.) One priestly family, that of Shimei (Num. 3:18), was specifically mentioned, unless the reference was to the Shimei of the house of Saul, who cursed David when he retreated from Jerusalem before Absalom (2 Sam. 16:5–8) and begged David's forgiveness on the king's return to his throne (2 Sam. 19:18–20). The mention of one royal and one priestly family may well have been intended as representative of all the families rather than indicative of their especial sinfulness. In addition to these families, all the other inhabitants of Jerusalem would mourn also.

**13:1.** Not only would God make the inhabitants of Jerusalem compassionate and contrite (the opposite of the shepherds), he would also open a fountain for them to cleanse themselves from **sin** (general human misconduct) and **impurity** (ritual violations, particularly idolatry). An ever-flowing fountain would guarantee continuous cleansing. The closest parallel to this thought appeared in Ezek. 36:25, where God promised to sprinkle the repatriated exiles to cleanse them of the filth of life in the Diaspora. Here it was the life lived in Jerusalem from which they must be cleansed.

**2a.** Ezekiel's use of the term **impurity** to mean idolatry (36:17, 25) suggested the next target of God's purge: **the idols of the land**. Given the experience of the exile, the inhabitants of Jerusalem were not likely using images of foreign gods, or even of Yahweh. This verse, like 10:2, probably condemned the use of some kind of device its author chose to associate with idolatry, even though the people using them would surely have denied the charge. To **cut off the names** was to cut off the idols themselves, for a name symbolizes and represents the thing named. The polemical nature of the charge precludes a more precise understanding of the practice in question.

**2b.** The word **unclean** referred to all kinds of sins, both ethical and ritual. Here the charge against the prophets was that they uttered that which was ethically and/or ritually unclean, so false. This half verse introduced the following four, which delivered a scathing condemnation against prophets.

**3.** The premise for vv. 3b–6 was stated in 3a: "if a man prophesies again . . ." The father and mother who bore such a person were to condemn him to death: **You shall not live, for you speak lies in the name of the Lord.** Deut. 13:1–5 gave two tests for genuine prophecy: (1) it must be spoken in the name of Yahweh, and (2) it must come true. The parents were to charge their son with failure to meet the second test. What is more, they were to **pierce** him through. The same word was used here as in 12:10. There Jerusalem was to mourn over someone they pierced; here the parents were to pierce a son who prophesied. The relationship between the two sentences is so striking that one wonders if prophets in Jerusalem led its inhabitants to commit their crime.

**4.** Obviously, not all parents would carry out such a requirement. So, prophecy had not yet died out, if it ever did. T. W. Overholt (*JSOT* 42 [1988], 110) argues that official prophecy would come to an end "when prophets lost their base of support within society". Nevertheless, prophets would have continued intermittently under appropriate stimuli (p. 113). Zechariah 12:10–13:6 is one piece of evidence indicating that prophecy was losing its support. Its author belonged to a group that had no use for contemporary prophets, and foresaw the day when no one would wear the mantle of the prophet. Further, he engaged himself in applying older, written prophecy to his day. If the redactor of Haggai –Zechariah 1–8 looked toward the post-exilic continuation of the offices of king and prophet, the redactor of Zechariah 9–14 thought those hopes were dead. For him a person would assume the role of prophet only to deceive others.

**5–6.** Rather than prophesy, every prophet would say: **I am no prophet.** The phrase is a shortened version of Amos's denial to Amaziah that he was a (professional) prophet (Amos 7:14). Whereas Amos had claimed to be a shepherd and a dresser of sycamore trees, the prophet in the future would say he was only a **tiller of the soil**, that he had owned his land since his youth. Verse 6 returned to the piercing by the parents mentioned in v. 3, indicating that it need not necessarily have been fatal. If someone were to see the scars of that wound, the prophet would make up an explanation, claiming he had received them **in the house of my friends**.

**7–9.** As noted above, these verses, which constituted the last of the shepherd passages, would fit nicely at the conclusion of 11:17. Consequently, *NEB* and a number of commentaries move them there (e.g. Mason, 110; Mitchell, *Haggai, Zechariah*, 316–17; Rudolph, 213). There is no compelling reason to rearrange the text, however; it is sufficient to recognize behind 11:4–17 and 13:7–9 a common author, who also was the redactor of Zechariah 9–14 and placed these verses at the end of this long supplement to 12:1–9.

**7.** The transition to v. 7 was abrupt, with God suddenly addressing his sword. If 11:17 expressed God's wish that a sword would destroy the arm and eye of his shepherd, 13:7 commanded his own sword to strike his shepherd. The shepherd was also called a *geber*, a man of strength. If he was strong, his sheep were **little ones**, who would be scattered when the shepherd was struck. Because of the sins of God's shepherd, the flock would suffer too; God himself would turn his hand against them.

**8–9.** Two-thirds of the inhabitants of the land would be scattered and perish, and only one-third would survive. The fractions certainly were not precise. Assuming, however, that the redactor thought he and his group would be among the survivors, the fractions do reveal a minority perspective on the part of the redactor. Unlike Zechariah 1–8 and the inherited traditions the redactor worked with, which seem to have been plans for unity, the redactor saw a purging on top of the cleansing discussed in 12:10–13:6. The survivors themselves would be refined by the coming disaster. Then they would call on God's name. He, in turn, would say in words reminiscent of Hos. 2:23: **They are my people**; and they would respond in words reminiscent of the people in the same verse: **The Lord**

**is our God**. The dialogue would reconstitute the covenant, the breaking of which had been portrayed by the breaking of the second staff in the shepherd allegory (11:10).

### THE WAR AGAINST JERUSALEM, VERSION II
### 14:1–21

On the one hand Hanson (*Dawn*, 369) argues that 14:1–21 is full-blown apocalyptic (cf. for at least chs. 12–14, Hartmut Gese, *ZTK* 70 [1973], 41–9), while others (Plöger, *Theocracy and Eschatology* 78–96; and R. North, "Prophecy to Apocalyptic via Zechariah", 70–71) prefer to see the chapter as what one might call "proto-apocalyptic", in that the chapter resembles full-blown apocalypses, but lacks some essential characteristics. The conclusion a scholar reaches is based partly on a determination of the essential characteristics of apocalyptic literature and thinking, an issue too broad to discuss here. It must suffice to say, however, that 14:1–21 had much in common with 12:1–9. In addition, it employed and extended motifs from earlier prophets and the Psalms. Hence, it seems best to consider this chapter eschatological, even proto-apocalyptic, like Isaiah 24–7 and the last half of Joel, but not fully apocalyptic.

Like other sections of Zechariah 9–14, chapter 14 was a composite, consisting primarily of prophecies of salvation (vv. 6–11, 16, 20–21) typically introduced by the phrase "on that day", but also displaying that mix of salvation and disaster encountered in 12:1–9. Furthermore, the chapter contained at least one addition. Verse 14a, with its reference to Judah, was a scribal gloss.

Chapter 14 offered a second version of the future battle of the nations against Jerusalem. It opened (vv. 1–5) with God's gathering the nations to despoil Jerusalem and punish half of her inhabitants. Then he will turn to attack the attackers and bring weal to the city. He will employ the forces of nature in his holy warfare on Jerusalem's behalf, a theme that continued in a series of short oracles in vv. 6–7, 8, 9, 10–11. Verse 12 returned to the original focus of the chapter, the nations gathered against Jerusalem. A plague will fall upon their soldiers (v. 12), who will fight against each other (v. 13). Their wealth then will pour into Jerusalem (v. 14), and a plague will fall on their animals (v. 15). The survivors among those nations will worship in Jerusalem or be punished (vv. 16–19), and the sacred precincts of Jerusalem will extend throughout the territory of Judah (vv. 20–21).

Several differences between 14:1–21 and 12:1–9 may be noted here. (1) According to 14:2, God himself will gather the nations against Jerusalem, while 12:1–9 made no such statement. This gathering is reminiscent of the one by the nations against Jerusalem under Gog of Magog in Ezekiel 38–9. (2) Also according to 14:2, half of the population of the city will perish, while 12:8 clearly said that God will protect the inhabitants. (3) According to 14:3–4, 6–10, geological and climatic changes will accompany God's victory over the nations, while 12:(6–7) 8–9 envisioned his use of the people of (Judah and) Jerusalem themselves.

**1–2.** The basic expectations of post-exilic, eschatological prophecy included a return from the exile (Jer. 30:10; 31:8; Ezek. 36:8; 37:14; Isa. 48:20–22; 55:12–13), the rebuilding of Jerusalem (Jer. 31:38–40; 33:9; Isa. 49:14–23; Zech. 8), a new Davidic king (Jer. 30:21; 33:15, 17, 19–26; Ezek. 34:23–4; 37:24–5; Isa. 55:3–4; Hag. 2:23), a new temple (Ezek. 37:27–8; chs. 40–48; Zech. 4:6b–10a), a new covenant (Jer. 31:31–4; Ezek. 34:25; 37:26; Isa. 55:3), the reunion of Israel and Judah (Ezek. 37:15–23), a renewed environment (paradise-like conditions, Isa. 65:25), renewed fertility (Ezek. 36:8–9), and increased population (Ezek. 36:10–11). Such renewal would require first the demise of Babylon (Isa. 47:1–15), after which the other nations would become jealous (Ezek. 38–9). God would reveal his holiness through the revival of his people, even at the cost of bringing the nations against them (Ezek. 38:16, 23) in battle, where he would protect them. Zech. 12:1–9 fit well within this context. Zech. 14:1–2, on the other hand, went beyond this typical thinking by depicting a future battle against Jerusalem that – like the battles waged by Nebuchadnezzar – would result in widespread destruction within Jerusalem itself.

The fate of Jerusalem was described in some detail. It would be defeated and plundered, with the spoils divided in its very midst. The houses would be looted and the women raped. Both ideas were taken from Isa. 13:16, which announced the same fate upon Babylon. The verb *šgl* (rape, ravage) was considered obscene by the Masoretes, who offered *škb* (shall be bedded) as the *Qere* in both verses. Half of the city would be taken into exile. This last detail might suggest that Jerusalem would be punished less than the land as a whole, where two-thirds of the population would die. Several factors militate against such a conclusion, however. (1) These are images of destruction, rather than precise predictions; the details should not be pressed. (2) Those to be sent into exile in 14:2 probably should be understood as the guilty parties who deserve punishment, whereas the deaths in 13:8 seem to be the result of sin by the shepherds and not necessarily punishment for sin. (3) Perhaps also 14:2 was inherited by the redactor, who did not change the percentage of those who would be killed.

**3.** With no explanation, v.3 suddenly announced Yahweh's gracious turn toward his people. One might infer that when the guilty parties have been exiled from Jerusalem God could be gracious to those who remained. Regardless of the cause for the turn, God was portrayed as waging war on behalf of his people. The **day of battle** is equivalent to the day of Yahweh, when he would punish his enemies.

**4–5.** Verse 4 opened with the redactional phrase **On that day**, and described a geological wonder. It portrayed God standing on the Mount of Olives, which lay to the east of Jerusalem across the Kidron Valley. Ezekiel had seen God depart to that same locale when he abandoned the city to its sin (11:22–3). In Zech. 14:4 it split from east to west. While the word "earthquake" was not used until the next verse, that was what v. 4 envisioned.

Verse 5 contains many difficulties (and for that reason has sometimes been considered an addition). The opening verb *nastem* was used twice. One should probably read the word as a second masculine plural perfect from *nûs* ("you shall flee" as *NRSV*) rather than repointing it as a Niphal from *stm* ("it shall be blocked" as in *NEB*). In that case the following phrase would read "(via) the valley of my mountains", which probably should be understood as the new valley dividing the Mount of Olives over which God would stand like a colossus. Alternatively, the valley could be the Kidron, between Zion and the Mount of Olives (Dentan, "Zechariah 9–14," *IB*, 6.1111), or the Valley of Hinnom (*BHS*), except that it lies south of Jerusalem. This new valley would reach to **Azal**. Unfortunately, the meaning of the term is unknown. F.-M. Abel (*RB* 45 [1936], 385–400) argues that the term is a proper noun designating Wadi Yasoul, a tributary of the Kidron. Even this reading, however, supposes an alteration in the spelling. *BHS* suggests another emendation, namely *'el-'eṣlô* (to its sides). Clearly, the correct meaning is unrecoverable at the present.

The valley would provide an escape to those trapped within Jerusalem. Through it the inhabitants of the city would flee just as they **fled from the earthquake in the days of King Uzziah of Jerusalem**. (Alternatively, if the word *nastem* is taken as a Niphal from the root *stm*, the sentence should be translated as the *NEB* does: blocked it shall be as it was blocked by the earthquake . . . ) Uzziah had reigned approximately 790 to 740 (depending on whose dating scheme one follows). Serious earthquakes in Palestine occur every fifty years or so and minor ones more frequently (Denis Baly, *The Geography of the Bible* [New York, Harper & Brothers, 1957], 22). The earthquake in Uzziah's time must have been especially violent; Amos 1:1 dated the career of that prophet two years before it struck.

Once the Mount of Olives has split and the inhabitants of Jerusalem have escaped, Yahweh will come. He will bring **all the holy ones with him**. The identity of the "holy ones" is unclear, but they may have been his heavenly host (Baldwin, 203; Elliger, 181).

**6–7.** Verses 6–7 continued the theme of cosmic change seen already in v. 3. Verse 6 is as obscure as v. 5. The *NRSV*

follows the LXX, the Pesh., the Vulg., and the Targ. in reading the words **cold or frost**. Literally v. 6 reads: "There shall
be no light; the splendid [things] shall thicken (or congeal)".
Baldwin suggests (203) that the phrase meant the stars will
lose their brightness, and she may well be correct. In v. 7 the
world was conceived as returning to the condition of the first
day of creation in Genesis 1. The first phrase may be translated: "And it shall be [as] day one". The end of the verse
may be translated: "there shall not be day and night, but at
the time of evening there shall be light". In the middle of the
verse stands a phrase taken as parenthetic by the *NRSV*: **it is
known to the Lord**. Perhaps the parenthesis meant that God
knows when that day will come.

**8.** Verse 8 depicted Jerusalem as the navel of the earth
from which the blessings of God, depicted here in the form of
water, will flow out. This verse calls to mind Ezekiel 47, where
the prophet saw water flowing from the east side of the Temple
to the Dead Sea, which would be revitalized by the fresh
water. This verse seems to push the image farther. The reference to the eastern and western seas suggests that the blessings
would be worldwide, a new motif in this chapter. This picture
continued the idea of cosmic change as well as that of end-time
reversal. The weak point of Jerusalem's defence had always
been its dependence on an external water supply for part of
the year. With the new Jerusalem, that would no longer be
so. It would itself be the source of ever-flowing water.

**9.** The God who created the world in the first place and
who was in the process of remaking it in the second place
would become king over all the world, an idea familiar from
Pss. 47 and 97. Zech. 9:9–10 envisioned a new king, but 14:9
did not. In light of the shepherd materials and the materials
about the purging of Jerusalem and the Davidides in 12:10–
13:1, one can see that this element of 14:1–21 would have
been very palatable to the final redactor. The last half of v.
9 calls to mind Deut. 6:4. The oneness of God would stand
at the heart of Israel's faith and the faith of any others under
his reign.

**10–11.** The land around Jerusalem would be turned into

a plain. **Geba** was a Levitical town (Josh. 21:17) in Benjamin (Josh. 18:24), which has been identified with modern Jeba, five and one half miles or nine kilometres north of Jerusalem (A. van Selms, "Geba," *ISBE*, 2.420). **Rimmon** was apparently situated at Khirbet Umm er-Ramamin about nine miles or 14 kilometres north-northeast of Beer-sheba (A. van Selms, "Rimmon," *ISBE*, 4.196). Jerusalem, by contrast, would **remain aloft on its site**, from the **Gate of Benjamin** on the east to the **Corner Gate** on the west, from the **Tower of Hananel** on the north to the **king's wine presses** to the south. The parameters describe pretty much the large eighth/seventh century city (see map, W. S. LaSor, "Jerusalem," *ISBE*, 2.1101). A city on such a hill would be impregnable against its foes and visible to all pilgrims. Verse 11 emphasized that it would never (again) be destroyed, but would dwell in security. Verse 16 spoke of all the nations coming to Jerusalem to worship. The city would also be repopulated, but not even the draft during the days of Nehemiah (Neh. 11:1–2) restored the city to the size or population suggested by v. 10.

**12–15** Mason (130) argues that these verses interrupt the connection between v. 11 and v. 16. Actually, v. 16 continued the basic account of the battle against Jerusalem found in vv. 1–5, 9, and 10–11. Moreover, vv. 16–21 added a new motif, namely the observance of the Festival of Booths by foreign peoples who will come to Jerusalem. Interspersed in the basic account were other details: climatic and geographical changes (vv. 6–8) and the fate of the nations (vv. 12–15). While a number of hands may have contributed to the chapter, vv. 12–15 fit the overall plan so well they were probably written for their present context. The mention of the plague (vv. 12 and 15) anticipated the mention of the plague in vv. 17–19, and the description of the battle against the nations elaborated upon the battle description in v. 3.

**12,15.** These verses described a plague that would fall upon the soldiers and animals in the camps of the opposing nations. The plague would cause their flesh, eyes, and tongues to rot away. Verse 18 also mentioned a plague, but it was not further described. The mention of Egypt in v. 18 calls to mind the plagues upon Egypt, but the rottenness here seems to go beyond the boils or other diseases upon the livestock of the fifth and sixth plagues (Exod. 9:1–12).

**13–14.** In addition to a plague, vv. 13–14 predicted that a panic would fall upon the nations and their wealth would pour into Jerusalem. The mention of the **panic** was a clear allusion to the conduct of holy war, in which God would throw the enemy into a great panic and enable Israel to defeat them (Deut. 7:23). In this case the foreign nations would defeat each other. Verse 14a constitutes a special case. It appears to be a gloss based on the pro-Judahite additions in 12:1–9, but 14:14a is not pro-Judahite. The idea (v. 14b) that the wealth of the nations would flow into Jerusalem agrees with Hag. 2:7–9, where Haggai foresaw their wealth beautifying the new Temple.

**16–19.** Zechariah 9–14 concluded with a scene similar to 8:20–23, in which the nations of the world go to Jerusalem to worship. According to 14:16 the survivors of the nations that assembled against God will be required to go to Jerusalem yearly at the Festival of Booths to worship God. (This idea is comparable to Isa. 56:3–8, but is not as far sweeping as the thought in 19:19–25, which envisioned Assyrians and Egyptians worshipping God in their own land.) Any of the survivors that failed to worship would suffer from drought (v. 17). Harrelson ("The Celebration of the Feast of Booths," 92–3, 5) argues that the nations are not simply converted to Judaism and made to observe Jewish rituals. Rather, they will worship with no conditions imposed upon them. It is not surprising that Egypt was singled out (vv. 18–19) for mention; it was the nation in the past that had suffered the most from plagues at God's hands. If it did not participate in the future, it would suffer again.

**20–21.** The thrust of the final two verses was that the holiness traditionally associated with Jerusalem would be shared with Judah. War-horses, which were usually viewed with suspicion by Israelites (Harrelson, 93), would wear bells inscribed with the phrase **Holy to the Lord**, which was engraved on the plate of gold on the turban of Aaron

(Exod. 28:36). The **cooking pots** in the Temple would be as holy as the vessels used in worship, because the distinction between sacred and profane would be eliminated. Indeed, the pots in Judah also would become sacred, a note compatible with the pro-Judahite sentiment of the redactor of Zechariah 9–14 (and from his hand?). The press of worshippers (vv. 16–19) would require the use of every available bowl for preparing sacrificial meals.

The final sentence proclaimed that there will be no **traders** in the Temple. The word used is "Canaanites", which meant "traders". It is possible that the verse denied access to Canaanites (or even Samaritans), but that seems out of place in the context of worship by the survivors of the nations. Hence, *NRSV* is probably correct in translating the term "traders". Harrelson argues (94) that since the distinction between the secular and the sacred will have disappeared, worshippers may make whatever gift they wish to God; there will be no need to exchange them for more appropriate ones.

## SUMMARY

Zechariah 9–14 transmitted three basic hopes of the post-exilic community: (1) that the old Davidic kingdom, north and south, would be reunited, (2) that the Davidic monarchy would be restored, and (3) that the king would rule from Jerusalem. The redactor of these chapters considered the reunion of Israel and Judah a dead issue and the restitution of the monarchy problematic. Both of these hopes had been vitiated by the sins of the shepherds, the ruling élite in Jerusalem, including the Davidides. God himself would rule in the future. Jerusalem still had a role in the future, but as a purged city in no way superior to the Judaean countryside.

The redactor very likely lived in the tiny state of Judah outside of Jerusalem. He did not share the self-perception and hopes held by the élite in Jerusalem. His doubts concerning the reunion of Israel and Judah were probably based on a sober view of the political realities of his day (see Redditt, *CBQ* 51 [1989], 639–40).

Cognitive dissonance theory (see Leon Festinger, *A Theory of Cognitive Dissonance* [Standford, Stanford University, 1957]) suggests that if the future turns out differently than people or their prophets imagined, it becomes necessary for them ". . . to construct a system of explanation showing how failed predictions can be rescued by reinterpretation and reapplication" (R. P. Carroll, *ZAW* 92 [1980], 141). Zechariah 9–14 seems to be a textbook case of that behaviour. The failure to experience the promises in the received tradition was explained in terms of the behaviour of the shepherds. The prophets were renounced in favour of the biblical prophets as interpreted by the redactor and his community. The redactor's view of the future was more realistic about the institutions of his day, but no less idealistic about what God would do when he intervened to set the world aright.

Recent scholarship has demonstrated the factionalism of the post-exilic community. The Jerusalemite élite would have wielded most power, but various groups emerged as the tiny Judahite community struggled with the conditions of post-exilic life, and each splinter group defined itself over against the Jerusalemite élite. Zechariah's hope for a new Temple with peace and harmony between priest and king had faded before the reality of a Temple securely in the control of one faction of the priesthood and no Davidide on the throne.

This division within the post-exilic community raised a basic question: who was Israel? Was the real Israel the Jerusalemite elite? Was it all those who returned from Babylon? Was it this or that peripheral group? Each group claimed that it belonged to Israel, but no one group (not even the élite) could speak for all groups. In pressing their own cases, each group inevitably slighted or excluded others. No one of them saw the full truth. Therein lies perhaps the most important lesson of Zechariah 9–14 for today (Redditt, *CBQ* 51 [1989], 641).

# INTRODUCTION

## to

## Malachi

The book of Malachi concluded the so-called Minor Prophets. Indeed, it concluded the Christian Old Testament, and did so with a glance (4:5–6) at the coming Elijah, whom the Synoptic Gospels (Mt. 11:10–14; Mk. 9:13; Lk. 7:24) identified with John the Baptist. The Hebrew Bible, of course, concluded with the Writings, but Malachi closed the Book of the Twelve (Hosea to Malachi), the prophetic corpus (Isaiah to Malachi), and the "Law and the Prophets" (Genesis to Malachi). It is possible that the author of 4:4–6 had that whole corpus in view when he enjoined remembering the teaching of Moses and promised the coming of the prophet Elijah.

Likewise, the book of Malachi itself looked forward to the day when God would act to set aright the conditions of his day, and it looked back to an earlier, purer time when Levites performed their duties properly. The time in which the book emerged, however, was marked by priestly cynicism and professional boredom and by marital discord and failure to support the Temple on the part of the laity. The book of Malachi spoke out of and to this spiritual strife.

## A. DATE AND HISTORICAL BACKGROUND

Scholars have reached a general consensus about the date of the book of Malachi. The reference to a "governor" (1:8) instead of a king as the chief secular officer eliminates the pre-exilic period. The existence of a functioning Temple (1:6–2:9; 2:11; 3:1, 4, 10) precludes a date during the exile or before the completion of Zerubbabel's Temple in 515 BC (contra Julia O'Brien, *Priest and Levite*, 113–33). On the other hand scholars usually argue that the conditions of divorce and remarriage addressed in 2:13–16 resemble the state of affairs addressed and corrected by the reforms of Ezra (9:14; 10:1–15) and

Nehemiah (13:23–31). They conclude that "The book of Malachi fits the situation amid which Nehemiah worked as snugly as a bone fits its socket" (J. M. P. Smith, *Malachi*, 7). Those who try to date the chapters more precisely often disagree as to the exact time between 515 and Ezra/Nehemiah that the book arose. For example, Joel Drinkard (*RevExp* 84 [1987], 389) suggests 500; Jerome Kodell (93) offers 460–450; while R. C. Dentan ("Malachi," *IB* 6.1118) says the date is "unmistakably 450"; and Pieter Verhoef (*Haggai and Malachi*, 160) argues for a time just after Nehemiah's return to Jerusalem for a second term in 433. Actually, the *terminus ad quem* for the redaction of the book should probably remain open, but a date between 515 and 456 (or 445, if one dates Ezra later than Nehemiah) seems warranted for the career of the prophet.

Those years, however, are quite obscure, since the book of Ezra skips from 515 to Ezra's career. The best one can do is to reconstruct conditions from the glimpses of post-exilic life provided by Ezra 1–6, Haggai, and Zechariah 1–8 (see the Introduction to Haggai, pp. 4–10). The population of the tiny province of Judah would have grown from about 20,000 to about 50,000 by the time of Nehemiah. Political power would have been held in Persia, which granted Samaria general oversight for Judah; hence Samaria's continued interest in the affairs of Jerusalem (Ezr. 4:6–23). The governor (Mal. 1:8) would have exercised local control, perhaps arbitrarily.

The Temple of Jerusalem would have served as the focus of religious life of the province. The promises of Second Isaiah and Ezekiel for a new day in the land, along with the promises of Haggai that God would crown the Temple with splendour, remained unfulfilled. The hope that Zerubbabel would restore the Davidic monarchy had proved futile as well. In the place of the monarchy were a priesthood and a governor (whether Judaean, Samaritan, or Persian) committed to Persian policy. The author of the book of Malachi charged the priests with professional contempt for the altar and sacrifices (1:13) and false teaching (2:8). While nothing in the book of Malachi approaches the pessimism of the author of Zech. 11:1–17, 13:7–9 on these issues, people in the land were openly asking (2:17): "Where is the God of justice?" and complaining (3:14): "It is useless to serve God". The book attempted to address these problems and to encourage the faithful.

## B. AUTHORSHIP

The superscription to the book (1:1) attributed it to someone called *mal'ākî*. Strictly speaking the word was a title meaning "my messenger", and it is so translated in both the LXX and the Targ. Baldwin (212) argues that the word is comparable to other names in the *OT* ending with the first person possessive pronoun "î", such as Ethni (my gift) and Beeri (my well). Many other commentators argue that the name "my messenger" would be inappropriate for parents to give a child. They sometimes suggest *mal'ākî* was a shorter form of a supposed name like malkijah, which should be translated either as the blasphemous "God is my messenger" or "Messenger of God". The difficulty of the proposed form, however, argues against its acceptance. Probably, then, the word *mal'ākî* is a title, most likely taken from 3:1, where the word occurs again and where it almost certainly means "my messenger". Even if *mal'ākî* were understood as a proper noun, however, the superscription provided no further information about the prophet. It reveals neither the genealogy nor the hometown of the prophet.

What can be known about the prophet must be deduced from the book itself. Even a cursory reading reveals that he addressed both priests (whom he called Levites) and laypeople. He was quite interested in the altar and proper ritual (1:6–2:9); he was also concerned that the laity pay the full tithe (3:8–12). Consequently, he is often considered a priest. The difficulty is that in the post-exilic period, starting even with the repatriates who returned from Babylon in the sixth century (Rudolph, 267), the Levites were divided into two groups: Zadokites (called "priests") and non-Zadokites (called simply "Levites"). When the prophet designated temple priests as "Levites", he was implicitly denying the distinction so important to the Zadokites. One should also remember that in the post-exilic period the Levites were the officials responsible for the collection of the tithes (H. Jagersma, "The Tithes in the Old Testament", 124). So, when the prophet demanded that farmers pay the full tithe, he once again sounded like a Levite. Thus, he was probably a non-Zadokite Levite and promoted reforms in the interest of a purer cult and a unified priesthood. His followers very likely came from the ranks of the Levites as well, though they may have included a few sympathetic Zadokites and some dedicated laypeople as well. It is clear that his reformation of the priesthood was not successful, so it is likely that his followers found themselves on the periphery of the Jerusalem cult. Since they appear to be addressed in 3:16–4:3 in particular, and since the book evidences considerable redactional shaping, the next topic to be discussed is the growth of the book.

## C. LITERARY HISTORY AND STRUCTURE

The place to begin a literary history of Malachi is with the observation that the book as it now stands consists of six disputes between God or the prophet and members of the community, priests and laity alike (E. Pfeiffer, *EvT* 19 [1959], 546–68). These disputes share a basic structure: (1) the prophet makes a claim through an affirmation or a rhetorical question, which (2) his audience disputes, so (3) the prophet offers evidence in support of his claim. Beyond this structure, the disputes exhibit considerable diversity in their development. Scholars debate whether the structure rests upon and reflects genuine debates between the prophet and his opponents (e.g. Wallis, "Wesen und Struktur der Botschaft Maleachis", 232), reproduces the essence of such a debate (Rudolph, 250), or represents only a literary device (so Dentan, "Malachi", *IB*, 6.1119). The results of this investigation will favour the last of these possibilities. There is widespread agreement about the limits of these disputes: 1:2–5, 1:6–2:9, 2:10–16, 2:17–3:5, 3:6–12, and 3:13–4:3. The book opened with a superscription (1:1) and closed with verses (4:4–6) that concluded the Book of the Twelve (see above). The structure was redactional, and the disputes themselves at times included different types of literature and showed other signs of being composite.

The main dispute with the priests (1:6–2:9) exhibited this composite nature. Commentators, in fact, sometimes consider 1:11–14 and 2:2, 7 secondary (e.g. Elliger, 2.189, 195), though that conclusion has also been attacked (Rudolph, 250, 262, 265–7). It seems better to see the passage as a composite in view of (1) its relative length in comparison with others in the book, and (2) the fact that the question-and-answer format gives way in 2:1–9 to a warning and a prophecy of disaster. It seems to have been constructed from three, perhaps originally separate, sayings of the prophet (1:6–10, 1:11–14, 2:1–9) around the general theme of the "name of the Lord". Of the nine times the phrase was used in Malachi, seven appear here. The passage charged that the priests despise and refuse to honour God's name (1:6, 2:2), while it was honoured (or will be honoured) among the nations (1:11, 14), and Levi stood in awe of it (2:5). It is quite possible, though beyond proof, that the prophet himself was responsible for this composition.

The next dispute (2:10–16) also appears to be a composite, this one built around the theme of faithlessness. It opens with a series of rhetorical questions: "Have we not all one father? Has not one God created us? Why then are we faithless to one another, profaning the covenant of our ancestors?"? (*NRSV*) It is the third question that presents a problem. Who was meant by "we"? Was someone other than the prophet speaking here? If so, the text gave no indication of a change in speaker. Was the prophet identifying himself with the sinners he was condemning? If so, he did not do that anywhere else in the book. The solution of the LXX to this problem was to treat all three verbs as second person plurals. The key is the verb *nibgad* (to act faithlessly). The MT pointed it as a Qal, imperfect, stative, or as a Niphal, perfect, third masculine singular. Both *BHK* and *BHS* suggest repointing the verb as a Qal, imperfect, active, but Rudolph (268), though not adopting the

reading, notes that the Masoretes intended to exclude the
prophet from the sinners by pointing the verb as a Niphal.
Alternatively, one might delete the *nun* as a gloss, the purpose
of which was to bring the third verb into agreement with
the first two. Either way, then, the third question would be
translated: "Why does a man deal treacherously with his
brother to profane the covenant of our fathers?"

The thought of v. 10 continued in v. 12: "May Yahweh cut
off the man who does this!" Such behaviour would disqualify
one from bringing a gift to the altar. The intervening verse
(11) introduced the subject of vv. 13–16. Of course, in the
newly constructed sequence of 10–12, the offence under discussion in v. 12 has become marriage to a foreign woman.
Verse 11 also grounded the charge against divorce in vv 13–
16. Divorce per se had never before been prohibited in the
*OT*, but divorcing a Jewish wife to marry a foreign (and thus
idolatrous) woman had become another matter to the prophet.
While vv. 10, 12 apparently were aimed at the laity (those
who brought gifts to the altar), vv. 13–16 perhaps originally
were addressed to the priests, those who cared for the altar
(v. 13). If so, v. 11 may have originally belonged with vv. 13–
16 and named the priests, and it may have been revised to
name Judah in its new context.

The next dispute (2:17–3:5) was composite as well. B. V.
Malchow (*JBL* 103 [1984], 252–5) argues that 3:1b–4 was an
addition, with 2:17–3:1a+5 constituting the original dispute.
This suggestion makes sense of several anomalies. (1) The
question in 2:17 was not really addressed until 3:5. (2) Verse
1 seems repetitious, and 1b suddenly addressed an audience
that sought the Lord of the Temple and his messenger or
covenant. That audience can hardly be the audience the
prophet had been condemning. Rather, it is more likely a later
audience, the audience for whom the redactor prepared the
book. It is addressed again in 3:13–4:3, another dispute that
is composite as well. The first three verses (13–15) charged
the people with speaking harsh words against Yahweh, but
in 3:16 the disputation speech turned into narrative, then in
v. 17 into a prophecy of salvation for those who revered the

Lord. The original conclusion to 3:13–15 has apparently been lost in the reshaping of the dispute, but v. 18 in some form may have belonged to it.

The dispute in 3:6–12 shows signs of revision also. Its basic subject was tithing, and it asked (v. 8) if anyone would rob God. Within 3:6–12, vv. 8–12 seem self-contained. Nor do vv. 6–7 seem to conclude the previous dispute, which ended (3:5) with the threat of God's punishment. Rather, vv. 6–7 focused on the issue of God's immutability despite Israel's infidelity from the days of the ancestors. In addition, the word *kî* with which v. 6 opened, usually functioned as a transition word within a thought rather than as an opening word. In the whole book of Malachi, the place that most emphasized God's abiding love was the opening dispute (1:2–5). So, 3:6–7 (as opposed to 3:6–12, suggested by Sellin, 591) formed its conclusion. The redactor of the book wished to begin on the note of God's abiding love of Israel, and separated 1:2–5 from its original conclusion. If so, the redactor was clearly working from written materials.

The book of Malachi gives evidence, therefore, of extensive editorial shaping. The redactor probably inherited two separate written collections. One (1:6–2:9; 2:[11?], 13–16) castigated the priesthood, while the other (2:17–3:1a+5; 1:2–5+3:6–7; 3:8–12; 3:13–15 and 2:10, 12) addressed the laity. He tied the two collections together by placing the section about God's love first (1:2–5), then including the materials against the priests (1:6–2:9), and then the rest of the collection against the laity (2:10, 12; 2:17–3:1a+5; 3:6–7; 3:8–12; 3:13–15). The glue that held together the collections was the piece about divorce (2:11, 13–16). He added the superscription (1:1), drawing the title *mal'ākî* from 3:1, and his own words to his audience in 3:1b–4 and 3:16–4:3. A later redactor added 4:4–6.

## D. MESSAGE

The heart of the theology of the book of Malachi was expressed in the lengthy dispute with the priests in 1:6–2:9, where God identified himself as the father of Israel (1:6; cf. 2:10). D. M.

Bossman ("Kinship and Religious System", 130–6) has shown that much of the language in Malachi can be understood from the perspective of family kinship between God and Israel. The details of this argument will be presented in the commentary. God also presented himself as king (1:14), whose power over the borders of Israel is to be recognized (1:5), and who will judge and refine the people (3:2–3, 5). He is God of his people both through creation (2:10) and covenant (2:4–5; 2:10; 3:1). He is immutable (3:6–7), so his love for his people abides (1:2), and the community of the redactor could count on future blessing (3:16–4:3).

To such a God Israel owed honour (1:6) expressed through sincere worship and proper sacrifices (1:7–14), interpersonal integrity (2:10, 12), godly family life (2:13–16), tithes (3:8–12), and reverence (3:16–4:3). The priests were primarily responsible for worship, but they had treated the sacrifice with professional contempt (1:13) and failed to instruct the laity in proper worship (2:8). Further, the laity were apparently quite willing to offer substandard animals (1:8, 13). As children of the same father (2:10), Israelites were brothers. Further, they were bound to God by the same covenant. However, they violated that covenant in faithless behaviour toward one another (2:10) and by divorcing Israelite women to marry pagan wives (2:11, 13–16). Nor were they paying the full tithe necessary to support the sanctuary and priesthood (3:8–12). Instead of trusting in God, they questioned either his ability or his will to protect his people (2:17; 3:14–15).

The obligations of Israel to God included cultic obligations, but went far beyond to include both faith and moral conduct. The redactor of the Book of the Twelve actually summarized the contents of Malachi fairly well in 4:4–6: remember the law of Moses in daily life, and look forward to the coming Day of Yahweh, when God would reward the faithful and punish the sinful.

# E. CONTENTS

1:1–5 God's Love for Israel
1:6–2:9 Pollution by the Priesthood
2:10–16 Unfaithfulness within the Community
2:17–3:5 Cleansing of the Community
3:6–12 Paying for Cultic Worship
3:13–4:3 Hope for the Community
4:4–6 Living in the Community

# COMMENTARY

## on

## Malachi

The opening dispute focused on the crucial question for the post-exilic community: did God still love them? The exile had forced the question upon all Judaeans, and Second Isaiah especially had responded affirmatively. His high hopes and those of Ezekiel, Haggai, and Zechariah had not materialized. To be sure some exiles had returned home, and the Temple had been rebuilt, but it remained a plain little building in a ruined city. Hence, the prophet sounded the note anew that God loved his people, but it brought a negative retort. Next, the prophet looked for evidence of God's continued love and found it not in the present or future glory of Judah, but in the destruction of the Edomites (1:3–4). Try to rebuild though Edom might, God himself would prevent it. The people would then have to admit that God was great beyond the borders of Israel.

It is not immediately clear that even such a confession would prove the prophet's point that God "loved" Jacob, though it clearly showed that he "hated" Esau. The original dispute, however, continued in 3:6–7, which did show God's abiding love for Judah. In contrast with the experience of Edom, Judah had not perished, even though she had sinned and did not even know how to repent (3:6–7). By severing these last two verses from the opening dispute, the redactor concluded it on the positive note: the Jews themselves would confess God's greatness. The redactor looked to the future (3:lb; 3:16–4:3) to a glorious Day of Yahweh.

**1.** The similarities between 1:1 and Zech. 9:1, 12:1 were discussed in connection with Zech. 9:1. Like Zech. 12:1, Mal. 1:1 named Israel as the object/recipient of the message. The new note here was the phrase **by Malachi**, lit. "by the hand of my messenger". The term *mal'ākî* appeared again in 3:1. In 3:1a God spoke of "my messenger" who was already preparing or was about to prepare the way of the Lord. "My messenger" in 3:1a could have been the prophet himself or the angel of the Lord (see Wallis, "Wesen und Struktur der

Botschaft Maleachis", 230). In 3:1b, however, the redactor repeated the noun *mal'ākî*, calling him the **messenger of the covenant** and looking forward to his coming. The redactor thus did not understand the prophet as that messenger. Since 1:1 derived from the redactor also, *mal'ākî* there presumably had the same meaning as in 3:1b. It would appear, then, that the redactor was claiming that God had revealed the whole book through an intermediary, that same (angelic?) messenger whose coming 3:1b predicted. If so, he was claiming divine inspiration for the book of Malachi, since the distinction between God and his angel is often very thin, as it is in 3:1b.

**2–4.** The premise of the first dispute was that God had **loved** Israel. The prophet's audience, however, challenged that premise by asking how God had loved them. God responded: **I have loved Jacob, but I have hated Esau**. The allusion, of course, was to the election of Jacob, the younger son of Isaac, in place of Esau his older brother. In the Genesis narratives (25:29–34; 27:1–46) Jacob was chosen as the one through whom the promise to Abraham and Isaac would pass, but Esau was not hated. Indeed, he seems to have fared quite well while Jacob was in Mesopotamia (32:9). The course of subsequent relations between the nations of Israel and Edom, however, was marked with animosity. Edom's participation in the sack of Jerusalem by Nebuchadnezzar (Ob. 9–14; cf. Jer. 49:14–16) appears to have been the ultimate betrayal so far as Israel was concerned. Thus throughout the exilic and post-exilic period, Edom was condemned for her deeds (e.g., Ezek. 25:12–14; Isa. 63:1; 34:9–17; Jl 3:19).

The terms "love" and "hate" are relative to each other. Some scholars argue, therefore, that they really amount to "choose" and "not choose", or even "elect" and "reject". They find it inappropriate to speak of God's hating anyone. Sometimes they argue that Edom had earned God's abiding wrath (v. 4). Others simply appeal to the power of God to elect or love whom he wishes (Deut. 7:7–8). Another way to deal with the problem is to see the contrast as an expression of Judah's feelings, given their experiences with Esau, rather than an expression of God's judgment.

Bossman ("Kinship and Religious Systems", 132) thinks the relationship reflects an absolute but inegalitarian family structure, in which one son remains in union with the father, while the second is granted a lower rank. Hence, the prophet was expressing his thinking metaphorically, in terms of human families. In this metaphor Western sentiments may well be offended, but in ancient Israel the metaphor would have worked well. Bossman's view also makes sense in the earlier version of this dispute (1:2–5+3:6–7). In 3:6–7 the abiding union with the father is articulated.

Sometimes vv. 2–4 are used in an attempt to date the rise of the book of Malachi. They most likely presupposed the destruction of Edom (see O'Brien, *Priest and Levite*, 115), whether by the Nabataeans in the fifth century (see Cresson, "The Condemnation of Judah in Post-Exilic Judaism", 138) or the Babylonians in the sixth century (see O'Brien, 116–8). However, the information provided by Mal. 1:2–4 is too slim and current knowledge of the post-exilic period is too spotty to form a basis for dating the book.

**5.** Israel would see with its own eyes that God would prevent Edom from ever rebuilding. That insight would lead Israel to confess: **Great is the Lord beyond the borders of Israel**. The word translated "beyond" can be translated "above" (Elliger, 2.190), but the context, which deals with God's work in Edom, demands the meaning "beyond" the borders. Unlike that of tiny Judah, God's power knows no limits and recognizes no political boundaries. The redactor ended the first dispute on this high note for the future.

### POLLUTION BY THE PRIESTHOOD
### 1:6–2:9

The second dispute was between God and the priesthood. It was comprised of three sections, perhaps originally independent. The first (1:6–9) chided the priests for accepting improper sacrifices. The second (1:10–14) blamed both them and the laity for the impure sacrifices. They treated their duties at the altar with contempt and ignored their obligation to teach the laity. In the third (2:1–9) God invoked an earlier covenant with Levi, contrasting the priests' behaviour with that of their founder. He concluded by condemning them for not fulfilling their teaching role.

**6.** The dispute opened with twin statements: **A son honours his father, and servants their master**. The priests would have agreed. Next came two rhetorical questions: **If then I am a father, where is the honour due me? And if I am a master, where is the respect due me?** The word translated "master" was *'ădônai*, which also functioned as a name for God. God was called "father" in Deut. 32:6; Jer. 3:19, 31:9; Isa. 63:16, 64:8 and in Mal. 2:10; and his parenthood was clearly implied elsewhere (e.g. Exod. 4:22; Deut. 18:1; Hos. 11:1; and Isa. 1:2). The priests would no doubt accept the further premise that God was both **father** and **master**. The problem was that they did not behave in accordance with God's status; they showed him neither **honour** nor **respect**. The word for honour (*kābôd*) derived from a root that means "heavy" or "burdensome". That which is "weighty" is also "honourable". The word for respect (*môrā'*) derived from a root meaning "to fear". "Fear" of God carried with it the idea of holding him in such high esteem that one obeys. So in 1:6 God contended that instead of showing him proper deference, the priests **despise his name**, that is treat God himself in a contemptuous manner. The priests again denied the contention.

**7.** The first piece of evidence that the priests despised God was that they offered **polluted food** on the altar. Offering polluted food constituted despising the **Lord's table** or altar. Pollution here meant "unacceptable" or "unfit for use as a sacrifice" not "spoiled". To be sure the food would have been brought by a layperson, but it was the priests' responsibility to guarantee that nothing polluted touched the altar. They had failed in that responsibility.

**8.** The pollution consisted of offering animals that were **blind, lame,** or **sick**. Lame and blind animals were forbidden in Deut. 15:21. Typically, laws required sacrifices to be without any defect or blemish (Exod. 12:5; 29:1; Num. 6:14, 19:2;

Ezek. 45:23), and Lev. 22:18–25 added a long list of disqual-
ifying blemishes. It is clear, then, that v. 8 accorded well with
the prevalent theory about sacrifices held by the Zadokites,
who were, thus, condemned by their own words. God himself
supplied the clinching argument: if they were to say such an
offering showed no disrespect, they should try giving it to their
Persian-appointed **governor**.

God was more than a governor or a master; he was the
father of the people. The function of the priests was understood in terms of the duties of a son to a father. According to
Bossman ("Kinship and Religious Systems", 133), the priests'
cultic obligations were comparable to the sons' obligations to
their father and the altar was comparable to the household
table at which God was served food. Their failures were an
affront to God's parenthood.

**9–10.** The prophet's voice broke through in v. 9. He commanded the priests to intercede with God on behalf of all the
people, himself included. Since disrespectful sacrifices would
not be accepted by God, the sins of the people had not been
forgiven. The fault lay with the priests, and the prophet asked
whether God would forgive them. Verse 10 expressed a wish
of God himself that one of the priests would **shut the temple
doors**. These doors apparently stood at the entrance to the
court of the priests, where tables for sacrifice were located
(Baldwin, 226). The priests were offering polluted sacrifices
in vain and might as well cease.

**11.** Verse 11 is one of the most widely discussed in the
book of Malachi because it spoke of the recognition of God's
name and of sacrifices beyond the borders of Israel: **from the
rising of the sun to its setting**. In what sense did the author
mean that God's name was **great among the nations**? What
did he mean when he claimed **in every place incense is
offered to my name, and a pure offering**?

Numerous suggestions have been offered to account for the
language, the most important of which will be reviewed. (1)
The author might have had in view Jews in the Diaspora.
Scholars holding this view (e.g. D. R. Jones, *Haggai–Malachi*,
187; Kodell, 100) point to exiles in Babylon and Assyria and

to the temple at Elephantine or even to the prayers of pious
Jews in the synagogues (Swetnam, *CBQ* 31 [1969], 206). The
suggestion is frequently rejected on the basis that the verse
has in mind wider boundaries than the places where exiles
dwelled.

(2) The author had in view gentile worship, but not of just
any sort. Rather, he had in mind people who worshipped "the
god of heaven" (see Sellin, 596; cf. Dentan, "Malachi", *IB*
6.1128; Mason, 144). The problem with this suggestion is that
elsewhere (1:5, 2:13–16) the author spoke negatively about
foreigners and foreign gods. Consequently, scholars adopting
this view sometimes conclude that the verse (or even vv. 11–
14) is secondary (see Elliger, 2.9, 189, 195; Horst, 261).

(3) The author had in mind proselytes or gentiles who worshipped Yahweh (see Rudolph, 263). The typical objection is
that the number of such people would be very small.

(4) The author was speaking of the eschaton or the messianic age. Scholars holding to this view (e.g. Glazier-
McDonald, *Malachi*, 60–1; Rehm, "Das Opfer der Völker
nach Mal 1:11", 205) think the author was drawing a contrast
between present Jewish worship and future gentile worship.
The typical objection is that the first clause has no verb at
all, the second clause employs one participle, and the context
discusses conditions in the present; hence, the sentences
should be construed in the present.

None of these suggestions is totally satisfactory, but the
general sense of the verse comes through anyway. In contrast
with the present worship in Jerusalem, almost anything else
(present or future) is preferable. Beyond this conclusion one
should be reluctant to speak of the "universalism" of the book
of Malachi.

**12–13a.** Verses 12–13a returned to the topic of the pollution of the Lord's table. Not only did the priests offer
improper sacrifices, they also complained that the rites had
become wearisome, their boredom causing them to **sniff** (literally "snort") at God.

**13b–14a.** Verse 13b might have continued the address to
the priests, or it might have begun the address to the laity. If

the first alternative is correct, v. 13b largely repeated v. 8. If, as seems more likely, the second alternative is correct, v. 13b condemned the laity for bringing maimed, lame, or sick animals to the priests. Verse 14a certainly condemned them by pronouncing a curse upon one who owns an acceptable animal but substitutes an unacceptable victim. A curse was more than simply an angry utterance or a wish for bad luck. People in ancient Israel believed that curses possessed the inherent power of putting themselves into effect (R. K. Harrison, "Curse", *ISBE*, 1.838).

**14b.** Verse 14b returned to the motif of the reverence for or fear of God's name among the nations. Hence, it formed an inclusion device with v. 11. These two verses, in turn, provided the glue to hold together 1:6–2:9. They were editorial, but derived from the hand of the prophet (or whoever arranged his two original collections) rather than the hand of the redactor. Verse 14b (and thus vv. 11–14) offered a different motivation for ritual purity than filial obligation (v. 6): God is such a great king that his name is **revered among the nations**. Hence, priests and laity alike would do well to obey.

**2:1.** The third section of this dispute included 2:1–9, which formed a prophecy of disaster. Verse 1 itself may be redactional; if the message was originally delivered orally, it might not have been necessary to name the audience. As the text stands, the prophet's attention returned to the priests. The verse spoke of a **command**, but the only command in 1:6–2:9 is the command to intercede in 1:9. The context (especially 2:6–8) suggests that the command in question was a command to teach the people.

**2.** The heart of the threat was that God would **curse your blessings**. The blessings could either be those the priests announced upon the worshippers or the blessings the priests themselves received. The context makes clear that the second alternative is correct. Nor would the curse take effect at some future date. God had already cursed their blessings because they did not **lay to heart** (take seriously) their responsibilities.

**3.** The curse was twofold. First, God would **rebuke their offspring**. The participle *nō'ēr*, translated "rebuke" was used to speak of God's rebuking the forces of nature (e.g. the sea, the watery chaos). In Mal. 3:11 it was used of driving back locusts. Thus it was a powerful term. The word *zera'* ("offspring") literally meant "seed". If it referred to the children of the priests, God would be correcting their children. If it referred to the seed for planting crops, God would be damaging their crops. Second, God would spread **dung** on the faces of the priests. The word *pereš* actually designated the offal ripped out in preparing the sacrificial victim. These parts were considered unclean and were taken out and burned (Exod. 29:14; Lev. 4:11, 8:17, 16:27; Num. 19:5). The picture of God rubbing offal onto the faces of the priests is shocking. The effect of such contact would be to render them ritually unclean and, hence, unable to offer the sacrifices.

**4.** In v. 4 God appealed to a **covenant with Levi**. No such covenant was described in the *OT*, though it was mentioned in Jer. 33:21 (cf. Neh. 13:29). Scholars have found in the name an allusion to the covenant between Yahweh and Phinehas (the grandson of Aaron) in Num. 25:10–13 (see E. M. Meyers, *HAR* 10 (1986), 232), but if so this is another case of the prophet's deliberate refusal to make distinctions within the post-exilic priesthood. Although it is not presented as a covenant, the blessing of Moses (Deut. 33:8–11) seems closer to the themes of Mal. 2:4–6 since it praised Levi for fidelity to Yahweh, for keeping God's covenant, for teaching God's ordinances, and for offering sacrifices.

**5–6.** The covenant was described as one of **life and well-being**. It called for **reverence**. The root *yr'*, translated "reverence", meant "to fear", and reverence involved not merely standing in awe of God but also obeying his commandments (see also the comments on 1:6). Levi was the model of compliance. He gave **true instruction** by deed and word. He taught without error, and he walked with God in **integrity and uprightness**. The word *šālōm*, translated "integrity", indicated completeness, soundness, welfare, and peace. The word *mîšôr*, translated "uprightness", derived from a root meaning smooth, straight, right or even level. By his words and actions Levi **turned many from iniquity**.

**7.** In light of the covenant with Levi, the prophet could say that it was the priests' responsibility to **guard** knowledge. The root *śmr*, translated "guard", also meant "to keep" and "to preserve". The translation "guard" catches both nuances of obeying and preserving. The people should seek out the priest for instruction, because he was the **messenger** of God. The irony of this word would become clear in v. 8: God had to send his word by *mal'ākî* to the priest, who should have been the *mal'āk*.

**8.** Instead, the priests had **turned aside** from God's **way** or path. That path was smooth or level (v. 6), but the false instructions of the priests constituted obstacles that caused many of the people **to stumble**. The false teaching presumably included wrong or incomplete instructions about sacrifices, resulting in the offering of polluted sacrifices. The material against the priests in 2:13–16 shows that the prophet viewed their moral instruction as flawed too. So by giving false teaching, the priests were breaking the covenant with Levi.

**9.** Consequently, the priests who had despised the Lord's table (1: 6) would themselves be despised. God levelled one last charge against them: **you ... have shown partiality in your instruction**. Literally, the whole clause could be translated: "you are neither following my ways nor lifting up faces by the law". "To lift up a face" was to grant a request or show favour (BDB, 670). They were not scrupulous about the condition of the animals they accepted for sacrifice; nor were they gracious to the worshippers. Perhaps they demeaned those who came to them. Or perhaps they refused to be gracious where their self-interest was at stake.

## UNFAITHFULNESS WITHIN THE COMMUNITY
## 2:10–16

The third dispute included two separate charges. The first (vv. 10, 12) condemned the faithlessness of one to another; the second (vv. 11, 13–16) condemned divorce carried out for the purpose of marrying a foreign woman. The second charge was probably originally addressed to the priests who would have been in a position to "cover the Lord's altar with tears" (v. 13). However, Ezr. 9: 1–2, 10: 1–15 and Neh. 23–30 show that laypeople as well as priests intermarried with non-Jews. Hence, a charge the prophet levelled against the priests was applied to the laity as well by the redactor.

**10.** The dispute opened with three rhetorical questions. The first reads: **Have we not all one father**? While some scholars suggest that the word "father" refers to Abraham or Jacob, the use of the word in reference to God in 1: 6 and the parallel term "creator" in the next question make it clear that the father in question was God. Even so, the "we" in the verse was the nation Israel; there was no reference here to humanity as a whole. The prophet thus opened the dispute by establishing that the people were the children and creation of God. In the third question the verb *nibgad* should be read as a Niphal perfect, third masculine singular, or else the *nun* should be dropped, resulting in a Qal perfect, third masculine singular verb (see the Introduction to Malachi, pp. 153–4). Either way the question should be translated: "why does a man deal faithlessly with his brother?" It is unclear what the prophet had found objectionable, but it set brother against brother. In the *OT* the term "brother" applied not just to other male siblings, but to more distant relatives and even to one's fellow countrymen. The term was used in its broad sense here. Their mutual faithlessness had led to a profanation of the covenant, presumably the covenant at Sinai. The word *ḥll* (profane) here meant "to violate" in the sense of breaking the covenant.

**11.** The condemnation of this faithlessness is found in v. 12. Verse 11 introduced the subject of divorce, which would be explored further in vv. 13–16. In v. 11 the charge of faithlessness was explored under two headings. First, Judah and Jerusalem had **profaned** the temple. The word *ḥll* was used again in v. 11, this time in the sense of "defile". Another word used to describe the offence was **abomination**, a word encountered frequently in Deuteronomy. It designated that which was repugnant or caused revulsion. Thus something had happened to defile the Temple and make it repugnant. The Temple was called **the sanctuary of the Lord, which he loves**. If his contemporaries questioned God's commitment to his Temple, the prophet did not.

Second, the nature of the defilement was articulated: Judah had **married the daughter of a foreign God**. Scholars have held two basic opinions about this verse: the offence was either idolatry or divorce. In favour of the former alternative are the use of the singular (Judah, the daughter), the general lack of prohibitions against divorce in the *OT*, and the reference (in v. 13) to weeping at the altar, perhaps suggestive of a ritual act. In favour of the second alternative is the plain sense of the words. Besides that, if the charge is idolatry, then the wife of Judah's youth (v. 15) would have to be God. Elsewhere in the Bible God is called the father (as twice in Malachi) or the husband, but never the wife (Smith, 323). It would seem then that divorce was really the issue here (see comments on v. 16). The divorce in question was for the purpose of marrying a foreign woman. Such a women would have worshipped foreign gods, so marriage to her would have amounted to rejecting God's exclusive claim on Judah (Glazier-MacDonald, *JBL* 106 [1987], 604). Bossman argues that God is conceived here as "a particular, extended family deity whose household is with the family of Israel" ("Kinship and Religious Systems", 134). Exogamy, marrying outside the family (Judah), was forbidden.

**12.** In its present context v. 12 implored God to prevent anyone who divorced his wife from bringing an offering to the altar. Two words in the text are troublesome: *ʿēr wĕʿōneh*, literally translated "being aroused and answering". Glazier-MacDonald attempts to read the MT, arriving at the translation "the aroused and the lover" (*JBL* 105 [1986], 298). *NRSV* emends *ʿēr* to *ʿēd* and translates **any to witness or to answer**. R. Fuller (*JBL* 110 [1991], 51) finds the proposed term *ʿd* in the Qumran scroll 4QXII, concludes that it was original, and follows a suggestion by J. Wellhausen that the two words prohibited even a representative from bringing an offering for the excommunicated person. While certainty is impossible, *NRSV* and Fuller seem to offer an acceptable reading.

**13.** Verse 13 spoke of covering the Lord's table with tears. Traditional Jewish commentators thought that those weeping were the divorced wives (A. Cohen, *The Twelve Prophets*, 346). The verb, however, was second masculine plural, and the guilty parties had access to the altar. Most likely v. 13 originally had in view the priests, but in the new context it accused all men who were guilty of divorce. One more piece of evidence that v. 13 originated independently of v. 12 appears here; they were already crying over what v. 12 looked ahead toward, namely that God no longer accepted their sacrifices. It is not clear how they would know he rejected them, but one would assume they had drawn that conclusion on the basis of personal, probably economic, setbacks. If so, 3:11 might provide one clue. There God promised to call off the locusts and end barrenness if the people would again pay their full tithes.

**14.** That God had ceased accepting their sacrifices they knew, but they did not know why. The prophet, on the other hand, had the answer. God was a **witness** (the same word supplied by *NRSV* in v. 12) against each man on behalf of the wife of his youth, to whom each had been faithless. The mistreated wife was called **your companion**. The noun *ḥăberet* is the feminine form of a noun designating people united in a group. She was also called *'ēset bĕrîtĕkā*, "your covenant-wife". The precise meaning of the phrase is unclear. Did the prophet mean that the marriage relationship was a covenant? Or did he mean that the wife too belonged to the covenant with God? The overarching concept of family with God as father and the requirement for endogamous marriage suggests the latter.

**15.** The first half of v. 15 is extremely choppy. The word *'ĕḥād* (one) appears twice in the verse, and *NRSV* takes it as a reference to the one God, while *NIV* sees in it an allusion to Gen. 2:24, which reads "the two shall become one flesh". Most translators also assume that the opening phrase should be treated as a question, implicitly or explicitly reading a *he* interrogative for the opening *waw*. Many commentators also repoint the word *śĕʾār* ("rest", "remnant") as *śĕʾēr* (flesh). So construed, the sentence can be translated as follows: **Did not one God make her? Both spirit and flesh are his** (*NRSV*), or "Has not the Lord made them one? In flesh and spirit they are his" (*NIV*).

Such measures are not necessary, however. Glazier-McDonald (*Malachi*, 82) proposes the following translation of the MT: "And not one does it and has a remnant of spirit". She understands the phrase "remnant of spirit" as a reference to sexual capacity (pp. 105–8), and that could be correct, especially in view of the following reference to godly seed. Or the term might simply indicate the life force, as it often did. In that case, the prophet might be warning the husbands that they were in mortal danger. One other explanation comes to mind. Ezek. 11:19 employs the phrase "new spirit" in parallelism with "undivided heart". Further, this new heart of flesh, which would respond to God, was contrasted with an old heart of stone, which could not. It would appear, then, that Ezekiel was using the terms "spirit" and "heart" to designate one's spiritual capacity (cf. 18:31, 36:26). Perhaps the word "spirit" carried the same meaning in Mal. 2:15. If so, what the prophet would have meant was that anyone who mistreated his covenant-wife thereby diminished his spirituality.

The next phrase is scarcely clearer. Continuing the train of thought indicated in the previous passage, Glazier-McDonald translates it (p. 82): "And what is that one seeking – a seed of God?" In the context of marriage, the word "seed" appears to refer to children as opposed to crops. The prophet warned the men that their wish for children given by God (Glazier-McDonald, 108; *NRSV* **godly children**) was doomed.

The last half of the verse is somewhat easier to understand. The prophet admonished the men to guard their life-spirit or spirituality by not treating their original wives faithlessly. The wife was once again, as in v. 14, called **the wife of his youth**. The repetition of the phrase certainly suggests that older men were taking new wives. Two possibilities suggest themselves.

In light of the reference to "seed", one might imagine older men marrying younger women in order to have children. Alternatively, some commentators have thought that the men might have been taking new, foreign wives for economic reasons, i.e. they were marrying women well-connected to Persian or other wealthy foreigners. One wonders, though, how many such women might be available. If the suggestion offered above that this passage originally indicted the priests, the offending parties may have been more conspicuous than numerous.

**16.** Only in v. 16 does one find spelled out the full offence against which the people should guard themselves. The key word is *šalaḥ*, usually translated **divorce**. Literally, the word is "sending away", and A. S. van der Woude ("Malachi's Struggle for a Pure Community", 66) argues that the word did not mean divorce, but indicated the wives' being relegated to a lower status when their husbands took a second wife. In defence of van der Woude's view, one should note that polygamy did occur in ancient Israel, particularly among the upper classes in cases of a barren wife. However, the root *šlḥ* was used with such meanings as "send away", "dismiss", and "cast out", and it meant "divorce" in Deut. 22:19, 29; 24:1, 3; and Jer. 3:1. A less bold suggestion, based on the preference for monogamy throughout the *OT*, was offered by S. Schreiner (*ZAW* 91 [1979], 207–28), namely that the prophet did not oppose divorce, only remarriage. A response to Schreiner depends on how one understands the whole of v. 16a.

The opening phrase of v. 16 (**for I hate divorce**) is itself difficult to construe grammatically. The verb *śānē'* is a Qal perfect, third masculine singular: literally, "he hates". The following word *šalaḥ* is a Piel infinitive construct: literally "sending away". Both *BHK* and *BHS* recommend emending the first verb to a first person singular, resulting in the translation of *NRSV*. Probably the majority of scholars hold to this understanding of the text, namely that God hates divorce. Other scholars (e.g. D. C. Jones, *Presbyterion*, 15 [1989], 17) follow the suggestion of Albin van Hoonacker to repoint that verb as a Piel perfect, agreeing with the verb *kissāh* (covers) in the last half of the verse. They arrive at the following:

> *If [anyone] hating [his wife] divorces [her],*
> *Says the Lord God of Israel,*
> *Then violence covers his garment,*
> *Says the Lord of Hosts.*

This second suggestion requires only repointing and not emending the text, but the result is the same, if less forceful: they have divorced their wives, and God disapproves.

## CLEANSING OF THE COMMUNITY
### 2:17–3:5

If 1:12 portrayed a high level of professional contempt on the part of the priests toward their duties, 2:17 evidenced a high level of cynicism on the part of the people about the justice of God. They appeared to believe in God's existence and power, but to question his goodness. In a world where the faithful grew poorer and the wicked grew richer, they asked: "Where is the God of justice?" and claimed that God actively favoured evil people (2:17). The prophet answered that God was about to come to his people and his Temple in power and judgment (3:1a) and that social sins would be punished (3:5). The intervening verses derived from the redactor (Malchow, *JBL* 103 [1984], 253; cf. Mason, 136). The redactor dwelled on the need for purifying the priests (3:1b–4) and added that afterward the sacrifices of Judah and Jerusalem would again be acceptable (3:4).

**17.** The prophet made a new charge against the people, this one concerning their faith. They had wearied the Lord by their words, in particular by saying **All who do evil are good in the sight of God**. The people seemed to make allusion to Isa. 5:20, where the prophet denounced sinful people: "Ah, you who call evil good and good evil" (*NRSV*). The difference is that in Mal. 2:17 the sceptics were accusing God of calling evil good. Confronted with the question of theodicy, they asked: **Where is the God of justice**? Priests and others who considered themselves moral thought they should be rewarded for their proper conduct. Since some of these people, at least, were well placed in Judaean society, but were not wealthy, they probably were complaining about the success of certain members of the élite and of people who collaborated with the Persians for gain. The thought seemed to be that only cheats and collaborators could succeed in their society.

**3:1a.** God himself responded to the cynics: **See, I will send my messenger** (*mal'ākî*). As shown in connection with 1:1, it is impossible to determine whether the prophet had himself or an angel of the Lord in mind as *mal'ākî*. Either way, his function was clear: to prepare for the coming of God. The work of God was spelled out in v. 5, the original continuation of v. 1a, but in essence it consisted of bringing justice.

**1b.** The redactor added the second half of v. 1, switching from the first person to the third person and repeating the thought of v. 1a. In v. 1a the messenger and the Lord seem distinct, but in 1b the distinction is blurred. It was not unusual in the *OT* for the functions of God and his angel to merge so that telling them apart was difficult (cf. Gen. 18–19; 32; Zech. 3). Further, v. 1b addressed a new audience identified as those **in whom you** [God] **delight**. It seems inconceivable that the cynics would be so designated. Rather, it was the audience of the redactor who delighted in the **Lord**. Some scholars (e.g. Dumbrell, *RTR* 35 [1976], 49; and van der Woude, "Der Engel des Bundes", 298) contend that the "Lord" was the messenger, but in view of the further comment that he will **come to his temple**, it is difficult to see the Lord as anyone but God.

**2a.** In words reminiscent of Amos's warning about the coming Day of the Lord (5:18–20), the redactor asked:

> **But who can endure the day of his coming,**
> **and who can stand when he appears?**

The answer, of course, is that no sinner could endure or stand on the day in view here, the day of the Lord. That day was the day God would punish his enemies. The prophet Amos had introduced to Israel the idea that she herself would be numbered among those enemies (5:18–20). Here in 3:2a, the redactor reiterated Amos's warning, and he developed that thought further in vv. 2b–3a.

**2b–4.** The redactor used two symbols of the justice of God, those of a refining fire and a cleansing soap. The image was one of punishment reminiscent of the messages of earlier prophets that God would send fire, storms, enemies, or other catastrophes upon his people because of their disobedience. The redactor argued that the polluted people needed stringent measures of purification. Verse 3 focused on the priests (called Levites, of course) as those in need of purification. God was pictured now as the refiner, i.e. the agent, rather than as the fire, i.e. the means, of that purification. Elliger (2.208) argues that v. 3 was an addition because of the change in images, but they were so close that a transition from one to the other is not unlikely for an author. The result of the purification would be that they would again bring pure offerings. Once they were cleansed and functioning properly, the offerings of Judah and Jerusalem would be acceptable again. According to the prophet the people brought unfit offerings (1:8, 14) and incomplete tithes (3:8–12), thus sharing the blame. The redactor, however, seemed to say that when God purified the priesthood the offerings of the people of Judah and Jerusalem (presumably he included his own group) would be acceptable.

**5.** Verse 5, which formed the conclusion to the original dispute, answered the question raised in 2:17: where is the God of justice? God promised to draw near for judgment, but the judgment would fall on people guilty of social sins. **Sorcerers** were concerned primarily with influencing people or events for personal gain or that of their clients (D. E. Aune, "Magic", *ISBE*, 3.215). **Adulterers** violated their marriage vows, and **those who swear falsely** were guilty of perjury. Both types of behaviour threatened the social fabric of their society. People who defrauded hired workers violated the social legislation of Deut. 24:14–15. The **widow, orphan, and alien** (along with the poor) constituted types of people with little or no economic or political clout. The possibility of their

getting fair treatment often served as a kind of litmus test to
gauge the justice of Israelite society (e.g. Isa. 1:17; Jer. 7:6,
22:3; Ezek. 22:7; Zech. 7:10). Judah was God's extended
family, so the power of the father extended to the maintenance
of justice and the avoidance of evil (Bossman, "Kinship and
Religious System", 137). People who mistreated fellow
Israelites by that conduct also failed to **fear** Yahweh. On the
meaning of "fear" see comments on 1:5, 2:5.

### PAYING FOR CULTIC WORSHIP
### 3:6–12

If the priests were guilty of taking the sacrificial system for
granted (1:13) and of failing to teach the people how to worship (2:8), the people were guilty of bringing polluted sacrifices (1:8, 13–4) and insufficient tithes (3:8–10). Hence, the
prophet called them not only cheats (1:14) but robbers (3:8).
In both places (1:14, 3:9) he pronounced a curse upon them
for their failures. If they were to bring the "full tithe", God
would revoke the curse and they would be happy (3:10–12).
As the book of Malachi now stands, the dispute over the tithe
is introduced by 3:6–7, verses that contain a statement of
God's immutability and the people's inability to repent, which
originally concluded 1:2–5 (see above, Introduction to
Malachi, p. 155).

**6–7.** As the conclusion to 1:2–5, 3:6–7 grounded God's
abiding love for Jacob in his immutability. Jacob, like Edom,
had suffered, but Jacob, unlike Edom, had not perished. God
would frustrate Edom's every attempt to rebuild (1:4) and
Israel would praise him for it (1:5). Since God never changes,
however, his love for Israel would abide. Sin though the people
had from the days of their ancestors, God continued to call
them to repentance. Unfortunately, they did not know how
to repent. In their present context, however, vv. 6–7 form a
vague introduction to the dispute over tithes in that they
charge the people with violating God's **statutes** of old.

**8.** The prophet asked if anyone would **rob** God. The meaning of the Hebrew root *qbʿ* is uncertain; it might mean "deceive" or here even "circumvent" (*BDB*, 867). Regardless, people in the audience would respond in the negative; no one could rob or deceive God. Yet, the prophet continued, that was exactly what they were attempting to do by withholding some of their **tithes** and **offerings**. The word *maʿaśēr* (tithe) came from the word for ten. Tithes were to be taken to the sanctuary. Part was to be shared with the priests, and the rest consumed by the worshippers. Perhaps they were not bringing all they should or sharing what they brought. Or perhaps the dispute reveals a difference between the Levitical prophet and the people about what had to be tithed. The word *tĕrūmâ* (offering) could designate both cereal and animal offerings, and in particular the portions for Levites and priests.

**9.** Once again the prophet pronounced a curse on behalf of God (cf. 1:14a). The first time he cursed cheats who possessed acceptable sacrificial victims but brought flawed animals to the altar. Here the prophet cursed people who failed to pay their full tithe. To be sure the priests had to be paid, but there was another matter at issue as well. The sacrificial system was a means given by God whereby the people could express their gratitude and their contrition. If their hearts were right with God, they would want to bring him their best and in sufficient quantity for themselves and others the system was designed to support.

**10.** The term **full tithe** (cf. Deut. 14:28) suggests that the people claimed to be tithing, but the prophet disagreed. Since he further stipulated that the tithes were to be brought to and left at the **storehouse**, one may surmise that the dispute dealt at least partly with the portion to be given to the priests and Levites at the Temple. Deut. 26:12–15 required that the tithe of the third year be given to the Levites, aliens, orphans, and widows in one's own town. Would they also tithe at the Temple? Presumably not (E. E. Carpenter, "Tithe", *ISBE*, 4, p. 862), but the prophet might have wanted them to. J. M. P. Smith observes (*Malachi*, 71) that the prophet's views here seem to fit the laws of the Priestly Code (Lev. 27:30–33; Num. 18:21–31), which require that all the tithes be given to the

priests and Levites and imply that they should be brought to
the storehouse. Other passages (e.g. Neh. 10:35–39 [MT 36–
40], 12:44, 13:4–5) indicate that a number of chambers for
storage and other priestly use were located on the Temple
site. Those passages also speak of lagging support for the
Temple. The phrase **food in my house** interprets the tithe
and offering in terms of household duties and, thus, loyalty to
the father (Bossman, "Kinship and Religious Systems", 135).

God challenged the people: **put me to the test**. Such a test
is rare, but not unique in the *OT*. Smith (334) points also to
God's inviting Ahaz to ask for a sign (Isa. 7:11–12), of
Gideon's fleece (Jg. 6:36–40), signs to Moses to bolster his
faith (Ex. 4:1–9), and fire from heaven in response to Elijah's
prayer on Mount Carmel (1 Kg. 18:22–39). The task of the
people addressed in Malachi would involve giving more and
better offerings at a time when they were not sure religion
was worth the effort. If, however, but only if, they would bring
their "full" tithe, God would **open the windows of heaven**.
Gen. 7:11 and 8:2a (both P; cf. Isa. 24:18) used the same
phrase in connection with the flood in the days of Noah. The
firmament held the waters above the earth separate from those
below the earth. There were windows in the firmament that
only God could open, allowing the heavenly ocean to **pour
down**. In Mal. 3:10, however, the image is symbolic; God
would release **an overflowing blessing**. Moreover, the blessing was contingent upon Israel's bringing the tithes and
offerings.

**11.** Verse 11 promised a reversal of the curse pronounced
in v. 9 in light of the conditional blessing articulated in v. 10.
In particular, God promised to **rebuke the locust**. The word
translated locust is *bā'ōkēl*, literally "devourer" (*NRSV*
note).
Because the verbal form is used explicitly of locusts (in Jl.
1:4, 2:25; 1 Chr. 7:13), and because the "devourer" had been
eating the crops, many versions translate the word "locust",
though *NIV* and *NEB* translate it with the more generic term
"pest". Nor would the grape vine **be barren**. The root *škl*
denoted being bereaved or childless, and it could even be used
of a miscarrying womb (Hos. 9:14). Apparently the prophet's

message was that God would also prevent all other causes of crop failure.

**12.** In v. 12 God made a promise to the people: the nations would count them happy. As the recipients of God's blessing instead of his curse, their joy would be obvious to all who saw them. The reason for this happiness would be the restoration of their territory, which then would be a delightful land.

## HOPE FOR THE COMMUNITY
### 3:13–4:3

The sixth and last dispute opened with a charge by the prophet that the people had spoken against Yahweh by saying that it did not profit one to serve him. The charge was similar to that in 2:17, where the people questioned God's justice. If 3:10 challenged the people to put God to the test, 3:15 registered their complaint that when evil people put God to the test they escaped punishment. The original dispute broke off at this point, though v. 18 may have originally belonged to it. Verse 16 constitutes a narrative by the redactor about a rendezvous by people who revered the Lord and his affirmation of them (v. 17). Then the faithful would again see God's justice (v. 18, cf. 3:1b-4, also from the hand of the redactor). The following verses (4:1–3, MT 3:19–21) depicted the future victory of the righteous (the redactor's community) over the wicked. Bossman ("Kinship and Religious Systems," 135) sees in their redemption the father's compassion on his loyal children and the punishment of the wicked as the punishment appropriate to the children who fail in their service to their father.

**13–14.** The dispute opened with a typical charge and denial: God charged the people with speaking harshly against him, and the people denied their guilt. God next quoted the people (v. 14): **It is vain to serve God**. The word *šāwē'* (vain) was used in the Decalogue to prohibit taking the Lord's name in vain. Its use in v. 14 was reminiscent of that earlier use. It was also used repeatedly in Ecclesiastes in the phrase "Vanity of vanities". It denoted that which was empty, worthless, or transitory. In v. 14 (as in Ec. 1:1) it carried the basic meaning of "not profitable", as the next clause made clear. **What do we profit?** they ask.

Implicit in the question was the assumption that religion ought to "pay". If God is just, he ought to take care of the people who worship him. This same thought appeared in wisdom literature in the form of proverbs that promise the righteous good fortune (e.g. Prov. 10:3, 22; 11:8), long life (10:27; 11:19), and the Lord's favour (12:2). Where there was no belief in rewards and punishments beyond the grave, the traditional wisdom held that

> "*If the righteous are repaid on earth,*
>   *how much more the wicked and the sinner!*" (Prov. 11:31)

To be sure the wise were aware that one might have to choose between righteousness and ill-gotten gain and advocated choosing the former (10:2; 16:8, 19). Even so traditional wisdom taught that a righteous lifestyle should result in material benefits, and the people of post-exilic Judah expected God to keep his promises given through Second Isaiah, Ezekiel, Haggai, and Zechariah. To many it was clear that he had not. The prophet laid the blame on the people and the priests for their moral and ritual failures; the people blamed God and concluded that he would not deliver (v. 15). Neither keeping his command nor mourning for their sins had produced tangible results.

**15.** If the prophet promised in 3:12 that the people would be happy if they tithed, their response in v. 15 was that for now only the **arrogant** were happy. In this context, the arrogant were people who refused to tithe or serve God. It was easy for the people and the priests to blame them, since they were likely quite conspicuous. From the prophet's perspective, many religious people (priests and laity) also had sinned and their sin was now compounded: not only were they robbing God, but also they denied their sins, accused others, and blamed God for not rewarding them.

**16.** The redactor interrupted the dispute in v. 16 with a short narrative, which described a conversation among those who **revered** the Lord. (The word *yr'* meant "to fear", and it was used earlier in Mal. 1:6, 2:5, 3:5; see comments.) The result of the conversation was that **the Lord took note and listened**. The names of those who revered him were inscribed in a **book of remembrance**. A book by this name appeared only here in the *OT*, but God himself recorded the names of people in a book elsewhere in the *OT* in Exod. 32:32–3; Ps. 69:29 [MT 29]; 87:6; and (later) Dan. 12:1. Smith (338) suggests that the practice of Persian kings of recording events in a book may have stood behind this idea.

**17.** God promised that those whose names were recorded in the book would be his **special possession**. The term was used five times in the *OT* in connection with God (Exod. 19:5; Deut. 7:6, 14:2, 26:18, and here), each time with reference to Israel. The other four texts made explicit that out of all the nations Israel was God's special people. That promise was now applied by the redactor to his group. The sceptics, priests though they might be, did not represent the true Israel. The day when God acts would be, of course, the Day of Yahweh (see comments on 3:2a). The second half of the verse made this thought clearer. The redactor employed the image of the family again. Just as a man spares (i.e. does not punish, disinherit) a son who serves him, so God would spare the righteous who revered him.

**18.** As v. 18 now stands, it continued God's promise to the "righteous". In the context of vv. 16–17, these people were not the sceptics that God addressed in vv. 13–15, but the redactor's community. When God spared them and punished the wicked, they would again be able to see a difference in the way he treated righteous and sinful people. It is possible, however, that something like this verse originally stood at the conclusion of the prophet's dispute with the sceptics (vv. 13–15). If so, we should probably assume that the prophet announced some kind of punishment against the "arrogant" that would teach the sceptics that God does punish sinners and reward the righteous.

**4:1.** The redactor continued his discussion of the coming day, the Day of Yahweh, with an image reminiscent of God as fire and a refiner of silver in 3:2–3 (also from the redactor). Here he was depicted as a hot, burning **oven** (literally a fire pot or portable stove). The arrogant and the wicked were compared to stubble which the fire pot would **burn up** on the coming day. *NRSV* and others (e.g. Glazier-MacDonald, *Malachi*, 233) think that the phrase *hayōm habbā'* (the coming day) is the subject of the verb "burn up", but that is an unlikely image. It is also possible to construe the noun "oven" or "fire pot" as the subject and treat the phrase "(on) the coming day" as a temporal adverb. So complete would be the destruction of the arrogant and the wicked that neither **root nor branch** would survive.

**2–3.** The last two verses of the dispute depicted the future punishment of the wicked in terms of the victory of the redactor's community (those who revere God's name) over them. On the Day of Yahweh **the sun of righteousness shall rise**. Glazier-McDonald (*Malachi*, 234) notes that God was elsewhere called "light" (e.g. Ps. 27:1; Isa. 10:17; 60:1; Mic. 7:8), and he "shines forth when he comes" (Deut. 33:2; Ps. 50:2; 80:1 [MT 80:2]; 94:1). Verses 2–3 envisioned God's epiphany in the form of the sun with one wing on either side, a symbol which was used in the ancient world from Egypt to Persia, and which was used in Syro-Palestine as early as the close of the second millennium (Glazier-McDonald, 236–40). The sun would come **with healing in its wings**. God himself would heal the hurt his people had suffered.

The effect of God's coming was expressed in two additional images. The first depicted the righteous as calves freed from their stall in the spring and allowed for the first time to leap about and exercise their legs. The second depicted a vanquished people, used to being trampled down by their oppressors, turning the table on them. The former oppressors would be no more than ashes under the feet of the righteous after God came as a searing fire (4:1).

## LIVING IN THE COMMUNITY
### 4:4-6

It is likely the redactor closed his edition of the book of Malachi on the high note of victory sounded in 4:1–3. Some scholars, recently Glazier-McDonald (243–52), argue that the content of 4:4–6 fits the book well enough to consider them authentic also. However, the last three verses of Malachi did not utilize the dispute format. Nor did the verses continue the thought of 3:13–4:3. Verse 4 called the reader's attention to the Mosaic legislation (Genesis to Deuteronomy), while vv. 5–6 promised a new Elijah. Verses 5–6 did not explicitly identify Elijah with *mal'ākî* and may not have intended any such identification. It is better to see vv. 4–6 as two additions from the hand of a later redactor, which additions made an appropriate end to the Law and the Prophets. At the same time, these verses were written as a new conclusion to the book of Malachi.

**4.** The final redactor commanded the reader to remember (not only recall but live by) the teaching of Moses, specified as the **statutes** and **ordinances**. The words *ḥuqqîm* (statutes) and *mišpaṭim* (ordinances) were not exact synonyms, but here were used to refer to the same laws. The language of the verse sounds Deuteronomic, including the use of the name Horeb for the mountain where Moses received the law. Since there is a little evidence (e.g. the laws about tithing) that the prophet already knew the Priestly Code, it seems fairly clear that this verse had in view the whole Pentateuch. Moreover, the book of Malachi repeatedly faulted the priests and the laity for disobeying various laws; hence, it is appropriate at the close of the book.

**5–6.** The last two verses had in view either the Book of the Twelve in its entirety or the whole prophetic corpus. Elijah was known from the Former Prophets. Tradition saw him as the coming prophet, and the reference to a prophet like Moses in Deut. 18:15 probably accounts for pairing the two. In their persons they represented "the law and the prophets". Elijah's function would be to turn the hearts of **parents and children**

(literally fathers and sons) to each other. It is impossible to judge from such general terms the specific conflict the author had in mind, assuming he had one. Suggestions to the effect that he was speaking of conflicts between generations during the Greek period remain unproven. It is not definite that the final redactor meant to say that Elijah was the coming messenger, but if he did it is an example of an editorial interpretation of 3:1.

## SUMMARY

The book of Malachi spoke generally to conditions in the post-exilic community between the completion of the second Temple in 515 and the coming of Ezra and Nehemiah, though its final redaction probably came later. The prophet responsible for most of the messages in the book was a non-Zadokite Levite, interested in reforming the post-exilic cult and unifying the priesthood. He thought that the priests' professional cynicism (1:6–14) and marriage to foreign women (2:13–16) had led the laity to bring unfit animals to sacrifice (2:8, 13) and to act unfaithfully toward one another (2:10, 12). Most of the prophet's followers would have been Levites, but perhaps included a few sympathetic Zadokites and some lay people as well. Eventually one among them edited the book of Malachi, updating the original messages and applying them to new conditions, before or perhaps after the careers of Ezra and Nehemiah.

The teachings of the prophet consisted of two series of disputes. The first, directed against the priests, encompassed 1:6–2:9, 2:(11?)13–16. The second, directed toward the laity, included 2:17–3:1a+5, 1:2–5+3:6–7, 3:8–12, 3:13–15 (and v. 18 in some form?), and 2:10, 12. The prophet (or an early follower) reduced them to writing. The redactor added the superscription (1:1), moved part of the passage about God's love to the front (1:2–5), and supplemented the prophet's message with his own in 3:1b–4 and 3:16–4:3. He used the composite passage 2:10–16 to unite the two earlier series. A later redactor added the final three verses.

The book depicted God as the father of Israel (1:6; 2:10), the king (1:14), the judge of sinners (3:2–3), and the creator of the world (2:10). Moreover, God entered into a covenant with his people (2:4–5, 10; 3–1), and his love for them was unshakable. In return, Israel owed God honour (1:6), to be expressed through sincere worship and proper sacrifice (1:7–14), faithfulness toward other Israelites (2:10, 12), including one's spouse (2:13–16), godly family life (2:13–16), tithes (3:8–12), and reverence (3:16–4:3).

# CONCLUSION

The books of Haggai and Zechariah 1–8 depict those two prophets as successors of the pre-exilic prophets, advocates of the reconstruction of the Temple, and supporters of Joshua and Zerubbabel. Further, the traditions transmitted in Zechariah 9–10 expressed hopes for the reunion of Israel and Judah under the Davidic monarchy in Jerusalem. Likewise, 12:1–4a, 5, 8–9 expressed positive hopes for Jerusalem. Chapter 14, however, tempered its optimism with a picture of the future Jerusalem suffering in war before the new day. The final redactor of Zechariah 9–14 abandoned most of the traditional hopes he inherited and looked toward the necessary punishment of the élite in Jerusalem. Both the prophet and the redactor of the book of Malachi opposed the Zadokite priesthood. Thus while Haggai and Zechariah supported the claims and efforts of the leaders of the post-exilic community, the redactors of Zechariah 9–14 and Malachi voiced the perspectives of peripheral groups.

When their protests were incorporated with Haggai and Zechariah 1–8, however, their recriminations lost their peripheral flavour and became part of the "official line" about Jerusalem, its Temple, and its priesthood. This transformation of their messages was accentuated further by the inclusion of Haggai, Zechariah, and Malachi in the Book of the Twelve. To see this transformation, it will be useful to reread briefly the books of Haggai, Zechariah, and Malachi as a single document. That reading will trace a continuous concern with the Temple in Jerusalem, the rise in the importance of the priesthood, and the growing significance of written text over oral prophecy. At the same time it will trace the diminution of the importance of the monarchy.

# REREADING HAGGAI, ZECHARIAH, AND MALACHI

*Context.* The book that precedes Haggai in the Book of the Twelve is Zephaniah. It opened with an announcement of worldwide destruction brought about by sin. A later reader might well have seen the destruction of Jerusalem and the widespread turmoil of the Babylonian and early Persian periods as the fulfilment of Zephaniah's expressions of doom. The book of Zephaniah closed on a positive note, promising a new day for Zion, a day when Yahweh would again dwell in her midst. The edict of Cyrus in 539 seemed to make possible the realization of that hope. Almost twenty years later, however, it was nowhere near realization.

*Haggai.* The book of Haggai addressed that discrepancy between hope and realization. For God to dwell in Zion, his people must rebuild the Temple. Hence, the prophet Haggai urged the completion of that project (1:1–15a). The day of its founding should have marked the beginning of the new day (2:1–9, 10–19). Another part of the Zion tradition was God's covenant with the Davidic dynasty, so it seemed clear to Haggai that God would install Zerubbabel as the new king (2:20–23). Likewise, the high priest Joshua appeared in the book as one addressed by Haggai. In light of the increasing influence of the priesthood, a later reader would have been surprised if the role of the priest Joshua had not been mentioned.

*Zechariah.* When a reader turned to the book of Zechariah, he found himself in familiar territory. The visions portrayed God's turning toward Jerusalem and punishing her captors. The task of rebuilding the Temple was still primary. Zerubbabel and Joshua were still at the forefront of the action. The book clearly identified Zerubbabel as the one responsible for rebuilding the Temple (4:6b–10a), and it described the heavenly installation of Joshua as high priest (3:1–10). That second scene came first in the book, however, and the importance of Zerubbabel lessened in the later chapters. Indeed, in

3:8 and 6:12-13 Joshua could have been understood as the "Branch", even though neither text made that identification explicit. Chapter 7 looked back to the "former prophets", i.e. the pre-exilic prophets, and warned the post-exilic community to avoid the sins of the pre-exilic community. Chapter 8 combined that warning with a new picture of the future Jerusalem, where people from various nations came to worship.

Chapters 9-14 continued to develop the programme for the future of Jerusalem. Chapters 9 and 10 depicted God's work to restore the Davidic kingdom and reestablish the Davidic ruler. That ruler's kingdom would include both Israel and Judah; his subjects would include repatriates from the exile, as well as people already in the Holy Land. Those hopes, however, remained unfulfilled too, a development requiring explanation. The answer was that the leading families of Jerusalem became selfish and uncaring. They became sheep merchants or (what was worse) hirelings instead of shepherds, people who bought, sold, and slaughtered sheep instead of tending them (11:4-17).

Hence, the future of the city had to be rethought. For one thing, foreigners would again attack it (12:1-9; 14:1-21). For another, its leaders (Davidides and Levites alike) would have to be cleansed (12:10-13:1). False prophets would have to be silenced, by their own parents if necessary (13:2-6). God himself would have to assume kingship (14:9). Naturally, one would read nothing more about an earthly king in Zechariah or Malachi. Rather, God would restore, renew, and repopulate Jerusalem and Judah. Jerusalem would become the centre of worship for all peoples (14:16-19). So numerous would be the pilgrims that every pot and pan in Jerusalem and also in Judah would be sacred to God for use in worship (14:20-1). In the new Jerusalem there would be no more traders or merchants (14:21).

*Malachi.* The new day of the cleansed Jerusalem did not dawn either, and that circumstance required explanation one more time. It certainly was not the case that God did not love his people, for love them he did (1:2). Nor was it the case that he could not care for his people; they would see his power beyond the borders of Israel to carry out his purpose (1:5; cf. Zech. 9:1–8). Rather, the fault lay with the priests and with the people. The priests despised the name of God (1:6) and did not teach God's law properly (2:8). The people offered blemished animals in sacrifice (1:8, 13), denied the justice of God (2:17), failed to pay the tithes (3:8–9), and saw no benefit in the worship of God (3:13–15). Some of the men even divorced their Jewish wives and married foreign, idolatrous women.

The task of God's people was to revere him until the Day of Yahweh (3:16, 4:2), not to build an earthly kingdom. Those who did so would be God's special possession (3:17). The knowledge of how to do so was contained in the law of Moses (4:4). The voice of prophecy, now understood as warnings to follow the law and as explications of what would happen if one did not (Zech. 1:4–6, 7:8–14), had fallen silent officially. It had been preserved in writing for God's people to remember and obey. Only the future Elijah would break that silence (4:5–6); meanwhile the people had Moses and the Prophets. The people of Judah were well on the way to becoming the people of the book.

## CLOSING THE LAW AND THE PROPHETS

Malachi 4:4–6 closed the book of Malachi. The verses commanded Israel to obey the law of Moses and to look forward to the coming of Elijah prior to the terrible Day of Yahweh. Moses and Elijah embodied the Law and the Prophets. The redactor who added those verses very likely had in view the whole Book of the Twelve, not just the book of Malachi; indeed, he may have intended to close the entire corpus of the Law and the Prophets. Regardless of his intention, that was what his words ultimately came to do. The mention of Elijah as the coming prophet doubtless reflected a growing tradition about Elijah. Since he dominated the second half of 1 Kings, his name carried the reader back to the "former prophets" of the Hebrew Bible: Joshua, Judges, Samuel, and Kings. As pointed out in comments on various texts, allusions to the "latter prophets" abounded in Haggai, Zechariah, and Malachi. For example, Zechariah 1–8 had already summarized the teachings of the pre-exilic prophets (1:4–6) and utilized Jeremiah's description of the exile as seventy years in duration. Likewise, Zechariah 9–14 employed the shepherd materials from Jeremiah and Ezekiel and the servant motif of Second Isaiah, as well as reworking the denial by Amos that he was a prophet. The book of Malachi, by contrast, appealed overtly to the law, particularly to D but at times to P also, indicating an acquaintance with all levels of the Pentateuch, perhaps in something like its final form.

These last three books in the Book of the Twelve constituted a block of traditions that opened and closed with disputes between the prophets and the people over the Temple, combined with narratives about the results of those disputes. In Hag. 1:1–15a the prophet and the people debated whether the time had come to rebuild the Temple, and in Mal. 3:13–4:3 the prophet and the people debated whether it was worthwhile to worship God. In both cases the narratives showed that the prophets' positions were correct and described the outcome of the situations. Zech. 7:1–7 narrated the coming of an envoy to ask Zechariah a question. The author of Mal. 4:4–6 surely considered the three the last authentic prophets before Elijah, a conviction not far removed, perhaps, from that of the redactor of Zechariah 9–14, who was responsible for the condemnation of false prophets in 13:2–6.

# INDEX OF AUTHORS

Abel, F.-M., 140
Ackroyd, P. R., 6, 12, 20, 28, 32, 76, 81
Albright, W. F., 5–6
Alt, A., 5–6, 8
Amsler, S., 44–5
Andersen, F. I., 19
Aune, D. E., 177

Baldwin, J., 12, 37, 44, 53, 62, 69, 96, 112, 116–17, 129, 133, 140–1, 151, 165
Baly, D., 40
Beukin, W. A. M., 12, 27, 64, 82
Beyse, K.-N., 4, 11, 33
Bič, M., 52
Blocher, H., 63
Block, D. I., 126
Bossman, D. M., 156, 163, 165, 171, 178, 180–1
Brockington, L. H., 7
Broshi, M., 5, 19, 86

Carpenter, E. E., 179
Carroll, R. P., 145
Childs, B., 93
Clark, D. J., 30, 38, 52
Clements, R. E., 28
Cody, A., 28
Cohen, A., 172
Cresson, B., 163

Delcor, M., 95, 99, 133
Dentan, R. C., 96, 140, 150, 152, 166
Drinkard, J., 150
Dumbrell, W. J., 176

Eichrodt, W., 63, 76
Eissfeldt, O., 37

Elliger, K., 17, 23, 25, 27, 40, 43–4, 61, 68–9, 75, 81, 95, 114, 121, 126, 140, 153, 163, 166, 177
Ellul, D., 103

Festinger, L., 145
Fuller, R., 171–2

Galling, K., 4, 42, 57, 69, 75
Gese, H., 44, 137
Glazier-McDonald, B., 110, 166, 171, 173, 184–5
Good, R. M., 57
Gowan, D., 20

Hanson, P. D., 95–6, 98–9, 101, 105, 109–10, 137
Harrelson, W., 66, 143–4
Harrison, R. K., 94, 167
Henry, M.-L., 18
Hermann, S., 5
Hill, A., 98–9
Horst, F., 27, 63–4, 95, 166
Hyatt, J. P., 80

Jagersma, H., 152
Jones, D. R., 95, 165–6, 174
Josephus, 97
Jouguet, P., 96

Kloos, C. J. L., 60
Koch, K., 27
Kodell, J., 150, 165–5

Lamarche, P., 95
LaSor, W. S., 111, 142

Limburg, J., 121
Lipinski, E., 55, 69, 81
Long, B. O., 39, 51
Lutz, M., 128

Malamat, A., 94
Malchow, B. V., 154, 175
Mason, R. A., 25, 38, 52–3, 76, 93, 99, 121, 126, 136, 142, 166, 175
May, H. G., 26–8, 51–2
McEvenue, S. E., 6
McHardy, W. D., 52
McKeating, H., 121
Meyers, C. L. and E. M., 5, 9, 26, 52, 57, 69, 71, 168
Mitchell, H. G., 53–4, 58, 95, 97, 103, 114–15, 121, 123, 127, 136

North, R., 44–5, 67, 137
North, F. S., 80, 87

O'Brien, J., 149, 163
Otzen, B., 37, 94–5, 98
Overholt, T. W., 135

Petersen, D., 28–9, 31, 59–60, 64, 69, 73, 83, 85
Petitjean, A., 63, 69
Pfeiffer, E., 152
Plöger, O., 101, 137
Press, R., 38–9

Radday, Y. T., 37, 98–9
Redditt, P. L., 104, 144–5
Rehm, M., 166

Rothstein, J. W., 27–8
Rudolph, W., 11, 27,
    94–7, 109, 136, 138,
    151–3, 166

Saebø, M., 94, 110, 118
Sauer, G., 32
Schreiner, S., 174
Sellin, E., 25, 27, 76,
    95–6, 98, 155, 166
Seybold, K., 33, 40, 42
Siebeneck, R. T., 44
Sinclair, L., 42
Smith, J. M. P., 150,
    179

Smith, R. L., 23, 44, 72,
    75, 98, 118, 171, 180,
    183
Smith, G. A., 142
Steck, O. H., 21
Stern, E., 6

Thomas, D. W., 81

van Selms, A., 142
van Der Woude, A. S.,
    53, 69, 97, 174, 176
Vanderkam, J. C., 65
Verhoef, P., 150
Vos, H. F., 112

Wallis, G., 152, 161
Westermann, C., 23
Whedbee, J. W., 17,
    19
Whitley, C. F., 54–5
Wickman. D., 37
Widengren, G., 4, 7
Willi-Plein, I., 104
Wilson, R. R., 38
Wolff, H. W., 27
Wright, G. E., 19

Young, E. J., 94

Zimmerli, W., 133

# INDEX OF SUBJECTS

Aaronites, 134
admonition, 17, 24, 30,
    41, 49–50, 80, 82,
    86–7, 118, 132
Alexander the Great,
    95–7, 100, 110, 116
allegory, 97–9, 104,
    122–4, 127, 132, 137
altar, 8, 10, 28, 57, 117,
    150–1, 154, 164–5,
    170–2, 179
apocalypse, 137
apocalyptic, 39, 44–5,
    59, 101, 137
Artaxerxes, 6–7
Ashdod, 112–13
Ashkelon, 112–13
Assyria, 97, 121, 165–6
Assyrian(s), 55, 83,
    111–12, 143
Assyrian Empire, 98,
    112, 121

Babylonia, 4, 84
Babylonian(s), 7, 9, 17,
    29, 57, 68, 83–4,
    88–9, 98, 113, 119,
    163, 190
Babylonian Empire, 55

Benjamin Gate, 99, 142
blessing, 12, 20–1, 56,
    66, 68, 84, 86, 141,
    156, 167–8, 180–1
Book of the Twelve, 149,
    153, 156, 185,
    189–90, 192–3
Branch, 44, 62–3, 66,
    78–9, 191
bullae, 5

Cambyses, 4–5, 9–10
Canaanites, 144
Corner Gate, 99, 142
curse, 21, 72, 86, 93,
    127, 134, 167,
    178–81
Cyrus, 4–5, 7–10, 54,
    190

Darius, 4–5, 7–11, 18,
    23, 29, 32, 39, 42,
    49, 54, 80
David, 10, 12, 31–3, 44,
    66, 88, 98, 104, 112,
    119, 131, 133–4
Davidic, 9, 13, 32–4, 42,
    44, 49, 102, 104–5,
    109, 115, 124, 128,

138, 144, 150,
    189–91
Davidide(s), 79, 103–4,
    131–2, 141, 144–5,
    191
Day of Yahweh, 139,
    155–6, 161, 183–4,
    190, 192
Deuteronomy (D), 64,
    83, 170, 185, 193
disputation speech,
    17–18, 20, 23, 154
divination, 119
divine warrior hymn,
    109
divorce, 149, 154–5,
    169–72, 174–5, 192

Edom, 161–3, 178
Egypt, 4, 9, 61, 86,
    96–7, 110, 121,
    142–3, 184
Egyptian(s), 60, 143
Ekron, 112–13
Elijah, 149, 180, 185–6,
    192–3
Ephraim, 102, 109,
    115–16, 119–22,
    125

Esau, 161–2
eschatological, 20, 25, 33, 44, 51, 99, 101, 103, 127, 130, 137
eschatology, 12, 44
exogamy, 171
Ezra, 3, 100, 149–50, 186
Ezra (book of), 3, 5–7, 9–10, 70, 100, 149, 150

false prophecy, 119
Feast of Passover/Unleavened Bread, 10, 17, 82
Feast of Tabernacles/Booths, 17, 53, 82, 115, 142–3
Feast of Weeks, 17, 82

Gaza, 112–13
Geba, 142
Gilead, 122
God, characteristics of immutability, 155, 178
  justice, 51, 175–8, 181, 192
  oneness, 141, 153, 170, 172–3
God, fear of, 22, 164, 167–8, 178, 183
God, titles of
  Father, 153, 155–6, 163–5, 170–2, 178, 180–1, 187
  King, 23, 32, 141, 156, 167, 187, 190
  Lord of Hosts, 12, 18, 20, 50, 61, 70, 78, 82, 84, 130, 175
  Master, 164–5
  Sun of Righteousness, 184
  Witness, 172
governor, 5–8, 17–18, 32, 69, 100, 149–50, 165

Greece, 37, 96–7, 116
Greek(s), 96–9, 114, 116, 126, 186
Greek Empire, 96

Hadrach, 111, 114
Hamath, 96, 111–12
Heroldsruf, 114
holy war, 103, 109, 114, 116, 120, 137, 143

Joseph, 119, 121
Joshua, 8, 12–13, 17–18, 22, 24–31, 33, 38, 40, 42, 44–5, 62–6, 69, 77–9, 88, 93, 189–91
justice, 49, 54, 182

kalu, 29
king (human), 17, 23–4, 32, 44, 57, 77, 102, 104, 112–5, 124, 127–8, 135, 140, 144–5, 149, 190

laity, 149, 151–2, 154–6, 163–4, 167, 170, 182, 185–6
Lebanon, 10, 122–3
Levi, 133–4, 153, 164, 168–9
Levite(s), 134, 149, 151–2, 177, 179–80, 186, 191
Levitical, 142, 179

marriage, 154, 171–3, 177, 186
Masoretes, 139, 154
messiah, 44, 120, 133
messianic, 44, 63, 65–6, 78, 166
messianism, 44, 53
monarchy, 18, 33, 88–9, 144, 150, 189
Moses, 26, 98, 122, 149, 156, 168, 180, 185, 192

Nathan, 133–4
Nebuchadnezzar, 8, 17, 32, 116, 162
Nehemiah, 3, 5–7, 17, 19, 35–7, 59, 85, 89–100, 103, 142, 150, 188
Nehemiah (book of), 3, 5, 100

oracle, 12, 23, 37, 39, 43, 49, 51–2, 55–6, 58, 68, 70, 77, 84, 86–7, 110, 118, 129–30, 132, 137
oracle of salvation, 22, 86

parable, 122
Persia, 9, 32, 112, 150, 184
Persian(s), 6–8, 32–3, 57, 79, 98–100, 103, 112, 150, 165, 174, 176, 183, 190
Persian Empire, 4–6, 53–4, 69
Philistine(s), 112–13, 115
population, 4–5, 18, 22, 54, 86, 100, 113, 115–16, 133, 138–9, 142
pre-exilic prophets, 43, 50, 82–3, 89, 189, 193
priest(s), priesthood, priestly, 10, 18, 26, 28, 33–4, 38, 44, 64, 65–6, 78, 80–2, 88, 101, 103–5, 129, 133–4, 145, 149–57, 163–70, 172, 174–5, 177–80, 182–3, 185–7, 189–90, 192
priest, high, 8, 13, 17, 40, 42, 44, 62–4, 66, 78–9, 88, 190
priest-king, 44

Priestly Source (P), 3,
    179, 185
prophecy of disaster,
    128, 132, 153
prophecy of salvation,
    23, 27, 29, 56, 58,
    60, 84–6, 114, 117,
    119, 128, 132, 154
proto-apocalyptic, 137

remarriage, 149, 167,
    174
remnant, 22, 85, 173
Rimmon, 142
ritual, 26, 29, 44, 65, 89,
    133–5, 143, 149,
    151, 167–8, 171,
    173, 182

sacrifice(s), 20, 26, 29,
    109, 121, 150, 156,
    163–6, 168–9, 172,
    175, 186–7, 192
Samaria, 5–8, 58,
    100–1, 150
Samaritan(s), 6–8, 10,
    27–8, 69, 98, 100,
    144, 150

Satan, 63
Sebaoth, 18
shepherd, 94, 98–9,
    102–5, 118–28,
    131–7, 139, 141,
    144–5, 191, 193
Sheshbazzar, 4–10, 18,
    33
Shimei, 133–4
Sidon, 96, 11, 122
spirit, 23, 25, 44, 69,
    75–6, 83, 110, 115,
    129, 132–3, 149,
    173
superscription, 17, 37,
    49, 51, 80, 110–11,
    151, 153, 155, 186
symbolic act, 122–3,
    125
Syria, 97, 111

Tattenai, 6–8, 18, 69–70
temple, 11, 13, 18, 23,
    25–6, 28–31, 33–4,
    38, 40–4, 50, 54, 56,
    58–9, 61, 63, 65–6,
    68–74, 76, 78–81,
    85–9, 93, 100, 102,

105, 109, 113, 127,
    138, 141, 143–5,
    149–51, 154, 161,
    165–6, 170–2,
    175–6, 179–80, 186,
    189–90, 193
tithes, 68, 152, 156, 172,
    177–80, 187, 192
Tyre, 96–7, 110–12,
    122

vision(s), 10, 12–13, 20,
    32, 39, 41–3,
    50–60, 62–3, 65,
    67–8, 71–7, 79–81,
    84, 86–9

woe oracle, 127, 132

Zadokite(s), 101, 103,
    134, 151–2, 165,
    186, 189
Zerubbabel, 4–9, 11–13,
    17–18, 20, 22,
    24–5, 31–4, 38–40,
    42–4, 63, 65–71,
    78–9, 88, 93,
    149–50, 189–90